ARCHITECTURE
TODAY AND
TOMORROW

CRANSTON JONES

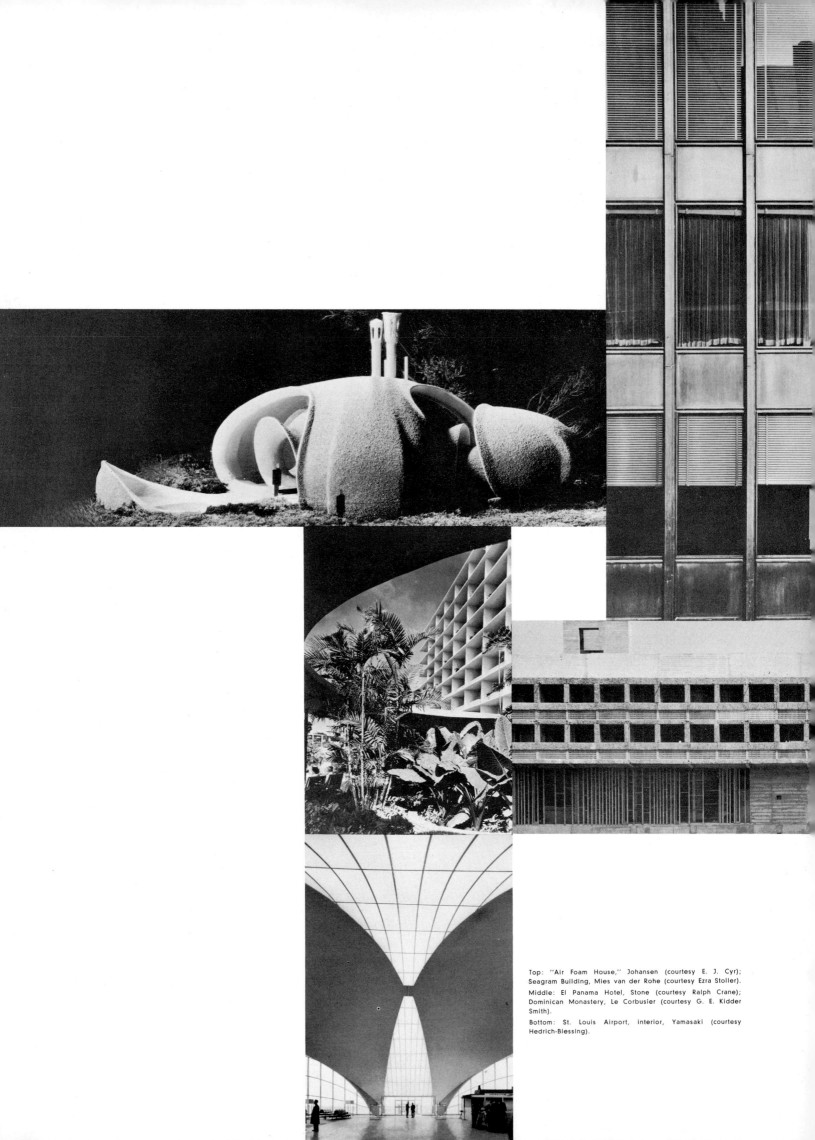

Top: "Air Foam House," Johansen (courtesy E. J. Cyr); Seagram Building, Mies van der Rohe (courtesy Ezra Stoller).

Middle: El Panama Hotel, Stone (courtesy Ralph Crane); Dominican Monastery, Le Corbusier (courtesy G. E. Kidder Smith).

Bottom: St. Louis Airport, interior, Yamasaki (courtesy Hedrich-Blessing).

ARCHITECTURE
TODAY AND
TOMORROW
CRANSTON JONES

McGRAW-HILL BOOK COMPANY, INC.

New York   Toronto   London

Picture Credits

To Jean, Abigail, and Baird

Preface

The building is forever the touchstone of architecture. Photographs, even great photographs, can only remain vivid visual synopses to recall or entice. *What* the architect has done, and *how* he has done it, require study of the structure. Why the architect created as he did, and his plans for a future still years distant, only the architect himself can illumine. For this reason the present analysis of twentieth-century architecture views each building against the totality of the man's work, both past and future, and relies on the architect's own words whenever possible; these words can also serve to introduce the reader to the great creative architectural personalities of our own time.

I am overwhelmingly grateful for the hours spent in conversation with the men discussed in this book, including time passed with the late Frank Lloyd Wright at Taliesin North and Taliesin West. My debt is nearly as great to many whose work is barely touched upon in these pages. My hope is that, in telling in some detail of the few, I may have illuminated the achievements of the many.

Appreciation is also gratefully acknowledged to my many colleagues on *Time,* in particular to the late Edward O. Cerf, as well as to *Time*'s staff of correspondents who assist so wholeheartedly in discovering and reporting world-wide excellence in architecture. To the publisher of *Time* I wish to express my appreciation for his permission to use the color plates that have accompanied my weekly articles. I would also like to thank the publishers of *Life* and *Architectural Forum* for permissions granted for the use of color plates.

While the pleasure in architecture can be shared, much of the task of writing cannot. Therefore, most of all, I extend my deep and abiding gratitude to my wife, whose forbearance has been sorely taxed but whose support and assistance have been boundless.

Cranston Jones

Contents

At no time and in no instance has architecture been other than an index of the flow of the thought of a people—an emanation from the innermost life of the people LOUIS SULLIVAN

PART ONE The Form Givers

Architecture, in the largest sense, is the total of all those spaces man has created for his own use. It is also his greatest public art, and today his liveliest as well. It is the one art form in which we are all involved, if for no other reason than that we all need and use it. Isolated from society, man will almost immediately begin to recapitulate architectural history, whether he seeks shelter in the cave, stretches a tent, fells a tree, or even burrows into the earth. But architecture is something beyond the necessity for elementary shelter. Man also requires an order of spaces which meet his inner needs both as a complex psychological animal and as a creature whose ultimate values are of the spirit.

The great initial stimulus for the architecture of our time has come, as it will continue to come, from the revolutionary advances in our technology. And yet the bewildering array of new forms is perhaps less strange than they at first seem. The multistory skyscraper and apartment house have their prototype in the pueblo cliff house; the principles of the tent are used in cable suspension bridges and roofs and even in concrete shells; Frank Lloyd Wright incorporated the basic earth-hugging shelter and broad eaves in his early prairie houses. What makes the new forms uniquely our own are the materials—the alloys, metals, and synthetics with which they are constructed—and the novel way in which we use the spaces within our structures.

Drawing on the structural inventiveness of the engineer and the artistic imagination of the modern artist, the first radical formulation of a new architecture had been made by the mid-1920s. It was not the final one, although the image of flat-topped cubes on stilts, illuminated by a vast expanse of glass and austerely furnished with chromed metal furniture captured the public imagination.

"Modern" is a concept in constant evolution, as has been proved by the continuously developing forms created by the three polarizing personalities of this century, Frank Lloyd Wright, Le Corbusier, and Ludwig Mies van der Rohe.

At the same time that these principal form givers were prodigal in new solutions, a vigorous second generation came to power, at times challenging the founders, at times elaborating and refining their insights. Today modern architecture has become a universal phenomenon, achieving unity by the acceptance of a common discipline. But it is far from static. Already a new world of shell structures is emerging to take its place along with the forms already evolved, creating space enclosures which may soon allow man to live in a constant environment anywhere on earth, from the equator to the arctic, perhaps even to sustain life on the moon and in outer space.

Architecture has thus become the great adventure of our time. To share its excitement there is no substitute for the actual knowledge and experience of the forms themselves. Participation cannot be passive. The approach to Le Corbusier's Chapel at Ronchamp, on foot, up a winding mountain path, is as much a part of the experience of the church as the dark, cavelike interior that awaits the visitor at the summit. The full mystery and delight of Frank Lloyd Wright's buildings can be known only by traversing the spaces themselves, whether through the dramatic sequence of rooms within Taliesin or up the mighty spiral of the Guggenheim Museum. The classical calm and probity of Mies van der Rohe's structures impose an order that at the same time enhances nature by its clearly stated division between what is man and what is nature; but the full appreciation of Mies's achievements requires our involvement with the structures themselves.

1 : **LOUIS SULLIVAN :**

SKYSCRAPER POET

Beauty is the promise of Function

HORATIO GREENOUGH

It was a dramatic moment in the history of modern architecture, late one afternoon in the year 1890 when Louis Sullivan strode into the Chicago office of his chief draftsman, Frank Lloyd Wright, and proudly tossed on the table the manila stretch on which he had drawn the elevation of St. Louis's Wainwright Building. "Look at it," Sullivan commanded. "It's *tall!*" [1]

Tall it was, every line of it. This was the building in which Louis Sullivan first gave logic and form to the skyscraper, that structure which announced the beginning of modern architecture. It was Sullivan's genius that he was able to conceive of the tall office building as a great unity, infused "with a single germinal idea, which shall permeate the mass and its every detail with the same spirit." As Frank Lloyd Wright was later to put it, "Until Louis Sullivan showed the way, the high buildings lacked unity. They were built up in layers like a great wedding cake. All were fighting height instead of gracefully and honestly accepting it." [2]

American and European architecture at the time was in the heyday of Victorian revivalism. In France there was a preference for an ornate and florid neoclassicism. In the United States high fashion was represented by the more historically correct eclecticism of the powerful firm of McKim, Mead & White, a firm adept at applying Renaissance forms to such large structures as Boston's Public Library and New York's University Club. Meanwhile, abroad, a revolt against machine vulgarity was taking the form of a return to the crafts in a stillborn movement called *art nouveau*, labeled *fin de siècle* almost before the century had in fact ended.

But behind Sullivan's emergence as the first great form giver of modern architecture there was also an intense half century of engineering discovery. The highly inventive James Bogardus as early as 1848 had worked out a system of prefabricated iron façades and columns that had spread the vogue for iron store fronts across the United States. These cast-iron pillars and structures proved highly vulnerable to fire, as one disaster after another demonstrated. But they did make iron and glass familiar construction materials for a whole generation of American architects.

A multitude of other innovations and improvements coalesced to make the skyscraper possible. Fireproofing had just been developed. Elisha Graves Otis had, in 1853, demonstrated a safe steam elevator, an absolute necessity if buildings were to rise much above six stories. Major William Le-Baron Jenney, a highly creative engineer and one of Sullivan's teachers, took a daring step in 1885 and finished off his Home Insurance Building in Chicago with the new bessemer-steel beams and columns just developed for the railroads. When Jenney proved that steel could hold up buildings, and the walls as well, the skyscraper was born.

Height—witness the towers of Bologna—is often equated with arrogance. But the pressures behind the cliffs of Chicago skyscrapers were basically mercantile in origin. In the decade 1880–1890 Chicago's population had doubled to reach 1 million and was still growing. Land in the business district was at a premium, and the only way to expand was up. So pressing was this need that Chicago architects had been attempting the seemingly impossible, mounting higher and higher with masonry walls whose immense weights caused some buildings to sink as much as 18 inches into the ground. In Burnham & Root's seventeen-story Monadnock Building (the tallest masonry building ever erected) the walls were 12 feet thick at the base.

Sullivan and his immensely talented engineering partner Dankmar Adler also tried their hand at masonry construction. Their Auditorium Building,

1·2 Buffalo's Guaranty (now Prudential) Building
(1894–1895) is the finest of Sullivan's eight skyscrapers.
Terra-cotta ornament sheathes mullions and spandrels.

1·3 Auditorium Building (1886–1889), Chicago, showing the entrance on Michigan Avenue. The grandest masonry structure of its day, its powerful facade enclosed the opera house, while the massive tower for years housed the offices of Adler & Sullivan.

1·4 Arches of the Chicago Auditorium (above) provide superb acoustics, unexcelled even in contemporary structures.

with its handsome opera house, was one of the wonders of architecture when it was completed in 1889. But it was Gustave Eiffel's great tower in Paris, finished in the same year, that pointed to the future. Sullivan, who had long felt that ". . . the engineers were the only men who could face a problem squarely,"[3] was quick to capitalize on their discoveries.

Since the Wainwright Building is considered one of Sullivan's two skyscraper masterpieces (the other is the Guaranty Building in Buffalo, New York), we are fortunate that Sullivan recorded his thoughts in "the Tall Office Building Artistically Considered" for *Lippincott's Magazine* in March, 1896.[4] It is one of Sullivan's most lucid prose writings, made doubly interesting because it is here that he first articulated his famous dictum "form follows function," one of the earliest major postulates of modern architecture.

"It is of the very essence of every problem that it contains and suggests its own solutions," Sullivan wrote in *Lippincott's*. And since form should follow function, he began by analyzing the function of the areas contained in a skyscraper: The ground floor was to be devoted to banks or shops. A second floor was to function as a mezzanine, accessible by stairway; this space Sullivan set behind a series of piers. From the third floor upward Sullivan designed ". . . an indefinite number of stories of offices, piled tier upon tier, one office just like all the other offices." For, as Sullivan reasoned, "Where the function does not change, the form is not to change." At the top, Sullivan placed ". . . a broad expanse of wall, its dominating weight and character announcing that the series of office tiers has come definitely to an end." This topmost area, in the form of an expansive cornice, was used, as it is today in all recent skyscrapers, to house mechanical equipment and water towers.

It was a brilliant analysis, but Sullivan was not yet finished. "We must now heed the imperative voice of emotion," he continued. "It demands of us, what is the chief characteristic of the tall office building? And at once we answer, it is lofty. This loftiness is to the artist-nature its thrilling aspect. It is the very open organ-tone of its appeal. . . . It must be tall, every inch of it tall. The force and power of altitude must be in it, the glory and pride of exaltation must be in it. It must be every inch a proud and soaring thing, rising in sheer exultation that from bottom to top it is a unit without a single dissenting line."

1·5 Guaranty Building in Buffalo (below) programed the skyscraper form repeated by architects for the next half century.

1·6–8 Chicago's Schlesinger & Mayer Department Store (1899–1904; now Carson Pirie Scott) combined Sullivan's geometry and his love of graceful ornamentation.

For Sullivan "loftiness" was expressed in the sheer, rising verticals of piers and mullions. But Sullivan also insisted that the building have its grace notes of ornament. It is on this last point that modern architects have most often parted company with Sullivan. A puritan mood was about to sweep over architecture, with a stern emphasis on utility and the clear expression of structure. As a sensitive artist, Sullivan was aware of this. "A building quite devoid of ornament may convey a noble and dignified sentiment by virtue of mass and proportion," he admitted. "I should say that it would be greatly for our esthetic good if we would refrain entirely from the use of ornament for a period of years, in order that our thoughts might concentrate acutely upon the production of buildings well formed and comely in the nude."[5]

What such buildings would actually look like Sullivan himself demonstrated in the last of his great buildings, the Schlesinger & Mayer Department Store (now Carson Pirie Scott) in Chicago. On the ground floor, where Sullivan was faced with the problem of embellishing the setting for elegant window displays, he gave full vent to his love of rich ornament (Figure 1·6). But on the upper stories, Sullivan left the façade a pure statement of structure (Figure 1·7), revealing the horizontal and vertical grid with a purity and rhythm later architects were to refine but rarely surpass.

The panic of 1893 brought to an end the fruitful partnership of Dankmar Adler and Sullivan. For nearly a decade afterward Sullivan continued in his office atop the Auditorium Building, but success gradually eluded him. His final thirty years were spent in the shadow of failure and neglect. In his bitterness, Sullivan blamed the large Eastern architectural firms who had turned Chicago's Columbian Exposition of 1893 into a showcase for classic-revival structures. The effect was to identify classic forms with pomp and dignity, and significantly nearly every state capitol designed after this date employs the classic dome and portico. "Architecture, be it known, is dead," Sullivan wrote bitterly.[6] It was a complaint Frank Lloyd Wright was in turn to utter in his uphill battle to win recognition for his own native genius. "They buried Sullivan and they almost buried me," Wright said in later years.[7]

But if Sullivan in 1924 died obscurely, he left behind him an enduring monument, the skyscraper. Under his hand it had found its place along with the other great architectural types of the past.

2 : FRANK LLOYD WRIGHT :

It is no more possible to consider the work of Frank Lloyd Wright as something apart from his striking personality than it is possible to consider the work of Pablo Picasso without becoming aware of the commanding presence of Picasso himself. The two share much in common: One is the greatest artist of the twentieth century; the other, the greatest architect of his time. Both refused to accept any limitation on the scope of their domain; each felt an overriding compulsion to remake the whole gamut of the form world according to his own vision.

It would have been interesting had these two met. Picasso was one of the very few men to whom Wright attributed genius,[1] despite the fact that he showed no apparent comprehension or even sympathy for Picasso's work. One can even go farther and imagine that Picasso, for his part, would have found little in Wright's work that was to his taste. Neither could have been assimilated by the other, for the reason that the integrity of each man's form world is complete. And yet one senses that Wright's own blindness to Picasso's painting and sculpture hides a tragic fault on the part of Wright. Specifically it points up the fact that Wright's own very personal forms crystallized in a period antedating the emergence of modern art. His major antipathy to later abstract art, indeed, was so marked as to distort Wright's whole intention in his greatest and last work, the Solomon R. Guggenheim Museum, and to allow some critics to proclaim that as a structure it was purposely anti-art.

Perhaps this is only to say that a man may tower above his contemporaries but he is nonetheless rooted in his own time. And the crucial time in Wright's development was his first forty years leading up to 1909. "Had Frank Lloyd Wright created nothing afterwards, he would still have had a permanent place in the history of architecture," the architectural historian Siegfried Giedion has said.[2] Architecture has drawn deeply from this first golden age in the life of Frank Lloyd Wright—a period when Wright was developing his prairie houses, the vocabulary for the office building, and the protocubist perfection of Unity Temple. The work of the later Wright became a fulfillment of his own spatial vision, one which is a rich legacy to the future but which in its own time has been contained within, rather than inspiring afresh, the main currents of modern architecture.

"The most important thing for an architect is to pick the right parents."[3] So Wright was fond of telling his followers. It was advice that many an apprentice found chilling, but it was a keystone to the architect's own private mythology. For Wright had no doubt that he was born under the beneficent sign of a specially preordained constellation, arranged in some mysterious way by both the Muses and the Fates. In fact, Wright was born far from the twentieth century—in the small farming settlement of Richland Center, Wisconsin, on June 8, 1869. His father was William Russel Cary Wright, a minister's son from Hartford, Connecticut, an Amherst graduate whose real en-

THE AMERICAN ARCHITECT

thusiasm was music. He was artistic and moody— a visionary and a drifter.

Far more dominant in the family was Wright's mother, Anna Lloyd-Jones, a determined daughter of a farmer from a Welsh community of pioneers who had settled in the fertile Wisconsin valley near Spring Green. The Lloyd-Joneses were a devout, hymn-singing clan that still retained their Druid motto "truth against the world" and worshiped simply in their own family chapel, adorned with greenery and bright berries. It was altogether in character that Anna Lloyd-Jones should have decorated the nursery with nine wood engravings of great English cathedrals by Timothy Cole, ensuring, she hoped, that her first-born would benefit from his early postnatal influence.

In the 1880s, when machine-made ornament was piled on with reckless exuberance, the Spartan quality of the Wright home taught Wright the virtue of simplicity. (At the same time poverty built up in Wright a love of luxury that in later years made him live vastly beyond his means.) What became Wright's great lesson book was the common heritage of rural America, the endlessly changing seasons, the rhythm of sowing and harvesting. His was a profound immersion in nature, and he was to draw from it lessons to apply to architecture for the rest of his life.

"Architecture is the triumph of human imagination over materials, methods and men, to put man into possession of his own earth," Wright later wrote.[4] From time immemorial, the chosen instru-

2·1–2 Frank Lloyd Wright lived the life of master artist and grand seigneur at Taliesin, Wisconsin (left). For Wright, the rolling countryside inspired the architecture, as the architecture inspired the way of life. "Romeo and Juliet" windmill (left) was designed by Wright as a young man. In the center are Taliesin's farm buildings with pigpens Wright called "Pork Avenue."

ments of the architect have been the triangle, T square, and scale. The key that unlocked this world of abstract geometry for Wright was the Friedrich Froebel kindergarten system of building blocks. Anna Lloyd-Jones had discovered them at the Philadelphia Centennial Exposition of 1876 and seized on the blocks as the perfect supplement to the education available in Weymouth, Massachusetts, where the elder Wright was serving in a brief and unsuccessful pastorate in a small Baptist church.

The Froebel system, first introduced in Germany, was an early attempt at channeling the child's play toward organized, constructive patterns. The toys were called "gifts," each more complicated than the last, and were "awarded" to the child as he progressively mastered each form. Wright was seven at the time he received them, and he repeatedly testified to their germinal importance in developing his own sense of form: "That early kindergarten experience with the straight line; the flat plane; the square; the triangle; the circle! If I wanted more, the square modified by the triangle gave the hexagon—the circle modified by the straight line would give the octagon. Adding thickness, getting 'sculpture' thereby, the square became the cube, the triangle the tetrahedron, the circle the sphere. These primary forms and figures were the secret of all effects . . . which were ever got into the architecture of the world." [5]

This intense experience with geometric forms— "the sense of which was never to leave the fingers" —was indeed as decisive as Wright believed it to be. Grant Carpenter Manson, in his *Frank Lloyd Wright to 1910: The First Golden Age*,[6] has shown the remarkable degree to which the designs of Wright's early work could actually be achieved by using only Froebelian "gifts" of wood blocks, paper plaiting, paper folding, beads, and string. This ability to geometrize structure, which twentieth-century architects owe in large part to the work of Cézanne, thus became Wright's at an early and impressionable age. But for Wright these basic geometric forms were imbued with transcendental meanings: The square stood for integrity, the triangle for inspiration, the circle for infinity.[7]

This symbolism, however quaint it may sound in the mid-twentieth century, remained constant for Wright. His own seal, a red square, was emphatically meant to symbolize integrity; at the same time, its red color echoed the other aspect of Wright's childhood experience, the memory of the red lilies he discovered with such delight as a boy in the haying fields of the Lloyd-Jones farmlands. To a remarkable degree, the symbolism in geometric forms also presents a prophetic program of Wright's own work. The dominant theme of his first decade is the rectangle, just as the middle period focuses on the aspiring triangle. With almost predestined finality the last works came to focus on the mighty circle, the symbol of infinity.

No one who saw Wright in his later years, with his magnificent long white mane, pork-pie hat perched jauntily on his head, and black cloak sweeping majestically from his shoulders, could doubt that Wright was playing the role of Great Master to the hilt. It was a role he assumed early, and it cost him dearly in terms of loneliness and isolation. But it was a manner he could not change, for it was the guardian and guarantee of the wellsprings of his own intensely romantic nature. Wright's endless optimism, that optimism perhaps of the overly indulged child—his assumption that bills could go unpaid and that some day he would create a whole new architecture for the continent—rested on his early acceptance of the role of hero as portrayed by Goethe's destiny-seeking superartist, Wilhelm Meister.

"I not only played at being Wilhelm Meister; I *was* Wilhelm Meister," Wright later remarked of his youth.[8] Apropos of his own theater at Taliesin North, Wright wrote: "I had wanted a theater of my own ever since when, as a boy, I read of Wilhelm Meister's puppet theater in the attic of the house Goethe designed for him. Here it was—far beyond Wilhelm Meister's or any Goethe himself could have designed." [9]

Goethe was the first to point out to Wright that in architecture the classic pilaster is a lie. However, it was in Victor Hugo's great panegyric of fifteenth-century Paris, *The Hunchback of Notre Dame*, which Wright read at sixteen, that Wright found the historical prototype for the city viewed as a homogeneous, organic whole. Hugo's scorn for "the chicories of Louis XV" was later echoed in Wright's statement, "I saw the Renaissance as the setting sun all Europe mistook for dawn." [10] For the Parthenon Wright had nothing but scorn. The "noble and beautiful stone [was] insulted and forced to duty as an imitation enslaved to wood"; [11] Michelangelo's dome of St. Peter's was a great lie held together by chains. Wright set his sights early against classic architecture and, in particular, the Beaux-Arts, with its worship of classic precedents.

2·3 Wright's own house in Oak Park, Illinois, was built in 1889 as a strong triangle set on a low base, echoing the shingle style which was then popular.

It was a romantic orientation that was never entirely absent from Wright's work. The earth-hugging structure, the massive fireplace, the solidity of the Mayan, the light-structured Indian tepee, the clearly articulated Japanese house, even (in the plans for the Baghdad Opera House) the celebration of Haroun-al-Raschid are precedents closest to Wright. Only toward the end of his long life, when his affinity for the form and symbolism of the circle brought him face to face with the great Roman engineering feats, the Pantheon and the villa of Hadrian, did Wright suddenly proliferate Roman arches and domes. In the Guggenheim Museum we are probably correct in seeing him at last throwing aloft his challenge to the Romans by creating a dome that not only needed no supports but actually spiraled outward, achieving as its crown not the keystone but the most fragile and translucent of all man-made materials, glass.

Wright received his first training as an engineer at the University of Wisconsin. At eighteen, just two months short of receiving a degree, he pawned some books and the mink collar his mother had sewn on his overcoat and set out, sporting long hair in the Lloyd-Jones tradition, to seek his fortune in Chicago. His first job was with Joseph Lyman Silsbee, a proficient Eastern practitioner of the eclectic fashion in architecture known somewhat vaguely as "Queen Anne style." After hours Wright read Ruskin, the *Dictionnaire raisonné* of Viollet-le-Duc, and made hundreds of onionskin drawings from Owen Jones's *Grammar of Ornament*. It was homework well done. When Wright, toward the end of his first year in Chicago, presented himself at the doors of Adler & Sullivan,* he was taken on as a draftsman. He soon rose to be Louis Sullivan's top draftsman and, as time went on, his principal confidant as well.

The relationship between these two Celts, Sullivan and Wright, was extraordinarily close. After hours Wright would linger on in the drafting room atop the Auditorium Building and listen to Sullivan discussing his emerging concept of "form follows function," his belief in an "organic design." "Art," Sullivan would say to Wright, "can be no restatement." They were concepts Wright eagerly absorbed and later made his own. The break between the two men came in 1893, when Sullivan discovered that Wright, during his after hours, was "bootlegging" residential designs from his Oak Park studio. When Wright set up shop for himself, he inevitably turned first to the field of residential architecture.

2·4 Charnley house, 1365 Astor Street, Chicago (1891), considered Wright's first masterpiece, was designed while he was employed by Adler & Sullivan. Its severe geometric plan, elegant brickwork, and dressed limestone still remain pleasing.

Describing the state of house design at the time, Wright was later to say, "The aggregation was at the lowest esthetic level in all history, steam heating, plumbing and electric light its only redeeming features." [12] And indeed the picture Wright drew has enough confirmation today in the surviving examples of Victorian eclecticism. "The house walls were be-corniced or bracketed up at the top into the tall, purposely profusely complicated roof, dormers plus. The whole roof was scalloped and ridged and tipped and swanked and gabled to madness before they would allow it to be shingled or slated. The whole exterior was bedeviled—that is to say, mixed to puzzle pieces, with corner boards, panel boards, window frames, corner blocks, plinth blocks, rosettes, fantails, ingenious jigger work in general." Stone and brick were used to give a sense of permanence to communities that still recalled their pioneering days; but as Wright noted, "All material looked pretty much alike in that day." [13]

*See Chap. 1.

2·5–8 Wright's prairie houses, with broad eaves reaching out into space, emphasized the concept of shelter. They evolved between the time of the William Winslow house (1893; top), Heurtley house (1902; above), Ward Willets house (1902; below), and Baker house (1909; bottom). Strong horizontal lines carried out the flatness of the prairies, while spacious porches and carports emphasized indoor-outdoor living.

This being the look of housing, Wright took the first step with his house for William Winslow (Figure 2·5) in 1893. "I had an idea that planes parallel to earth in buildings identify themselves with the ground, make the building belong to the ground," Wright affirmed. "Taking a human being for my scale, I brought the whole house down in height to fit a normal one—ergo, 5 feet 8½ inches tall, say. Believing in no other scale, I broadened the mass out, all I possibly could, as I brought it down, into spaciousness. It has been said that were I three inches taller, all my houses would have been quite different in proportion. Probably." [14]

To get this sense of horizontal line, Wright did away with both cellar (dark, leaking, and unwholesome) and the attic (stifling, warrenlike storage space).* The building now began with a low platform, above which the wall in flat Roman brick was carried up to the second story. Here the texture changed to a richly ornamented terra cotta rising to the eaves. Over all is a wide, sheltering roof. In place of the spindle chimneys, a broad anchoring pivot barely projects above the ridge pole. As Wright noted: "A real fireplace at that time was extraordinary. There were then 'mantels' instead. It refreshed me to see the fire burning deep in the masonry of the house itself." [15]

Wright did not solve all his problems at once. The Winslow house, for instance, has the front door and hall windows set in an independent entablature. Corners are still massive and solid. Orderliness had been reestablished where chaos had reigned, and a beginning made to integrate it to its site. But man and nature still stood in direct confrontation. The great reciprocal give and take of Wright's later buildings was still to come. The form toward which Wright was moving—the famed prairie house—became a full-fledged, broad-winged structure within nine years. The Ward Willets house (Figure 2·4), for instance, threw out its protecting roof to enclose the open porch and *porte cochère* (later to become the "carport"—Wright's term). Set on its own low podium, the Willets house seems to rest lightly on the earth. French windows open from the central living room onto yet another porch (indoors and outdoors becoming one), here decorated with typical Wright urns.

* That the obverse of a good idea can be equally good was proved by Boston architect Carl Koch, whose 1953 Techbuilt houses are made of only the cellar and attic. The effect, oddly enough, is rather Wrightian.

2·9–11 Masterpiece of Wright's prairie houses is Coonley House, Riverside, Illinois (1909), filled with spatial surprises and textures, as well as original ornament.

The bank of second-story windows compensates for the shadow of the deeply overhanging eaves.

What Wright needed to bring his revolution to completion was a client of unlimited means. He found one in Avery Coonley, who, with Mrs. Coonley, searched out all of Wright's buildings before approaching him. To give the Coonley house a setting, Wright had it face a reflecting pool, with a triangular-front terrace bracketed by two of Wright's most monumental urns (Figure 2·11). But the building can be easily misread. Actually the ground floor contains only the playroom in the center; the house itself is on the second floor, a concept Le Corbusier was later to arrive at by placing his buildings on stilts (*pilotis*). The finish up to the main floor is a fine cream-colored sand plaster, the upper story being sheathed in tile work of geometric squares. Elsewhere sheathing of copper is used. A latticework pergola shades both upper and lower stories, creating for the first time that fascinating pattern of light and shadow, changing as the sun moves, that Wright later was to use with such drama in the desert.

The interiors of the Coonley house reveal the revolution Wright brought to the reorganization of interior spaces. Materials are uncovered to reveal their natural finish and treated as flat planes of a single material. Those minute cubicles, closets, have been done away with. Passageways seem to propel the visitor toward the unknown.

2·12 Robie house, Chicago (1909), with soaring eaves and complex play of space, is the second outstanding residence of Frank Lloyd Wright's first golden age.

"Plastic" had always been one of Sullivan's favorite words. Wright preferred "continuity" or "flow." The slight shift in meaning is important. It signifies the change-over for architecture from a design conceived as mass to one of the channeling of space flow. "Let the walls, ceilings, floors become part of each other, flowing into one another, getting continuity out of it all," Wright urged.[16] "Conceive now a new sense of building that could grow forms not only true to function but expressive beyond any architecture known." This led Wright to separate structure into three elements: floor, walls (as transparent, or at least as monolithic, as possible), and the ceiling (which *never* repeats the floor plan).

The second masterpiece of Frank Lloyd Wright's prairie-house period is the Frederick C. Robie house (Figure 2·12), completed in 1909. To gain the wide, soaring wings at each end of the building, Wright encased steel beams; this constituted one of the earliest uses of steel in residential architecture. The geometric pattern of low, floating horizontals —almost an abstract composition and one that all Europe was soon to recognize—heralded the emergence of a new and original genius in architecture. The interior planning was no less inventive. The ground floor was turned over to a children's playroom and billiard room and the second floor contained the living and dining areas. But this living space had now become free-flowing and uncompartmented, a vast open space articulated around the central, pivotal fireplace.

It was widely rumored at the time that Wright's clients had fallen so completely under his sway that they asked Wright to design the clothes to go with their new surroundings. He was, in fact, then designing both his own and his wife's clothing. But if Wright stopped short of becoming his clients' tailor, he showed no hesitation about decorating their houses down to the lamps, tablecloths, napkins, and doorknobs. This perfectionism produced handsome ensembles, of course, but it could become tyranny as well. His clients often endured untold discomfort rather than budge a stick of furniture. With them Wright communed in silent sympathy. "I have been black and blue in some spot, somewhere, almost all my life from too in-

timate contacts with my own furniture," he later confessed.[17] But he insisted that the whole, to be organic, must be Wright.

To give the impression that Wright believed excessively in handicraft would be to warp his achievement considerably. He had, however, embarked at this time on a passionate investigation of the materials he was using. "I learned to see brick as brick, . . . wood as wood . . . concrete or glass or metal for itself. . . . Each required a different handling and each had possibilities of use peculiar to the nature of each."[18] Furthermore, Wright heralded the machine as the great liberating tool for architecture. He warned, however, that "the machine can be nowhere creator except as it may be a good tool in the artist's toolbox."

The essence of the machine, as Wright saw it, was that it not only replaced the power of hand labor, but that it functioned naturally in producing repetitive elements. For the machine thus to fulfill its purpose in Wright's own work, he had need of far larger commissions than the individual residential unit. Such a commission was soon forthcoming in the Larkin Building (Figure 2·14) in Buffalo, New York, a truly great prototype of the huge industrial building that was increasingly absorbing the energies of architects.

The Larkin Building was erected to serve as the clearing house for the large wholesale grocery and soap company. Its space requirements were thus primarily for clerical help. Wright began with this concept of a great workroom lighted from above by a skylight, around which subsidiary offices could be placed in tiers of balconies (Figure 2·14). To keep the space clear, he moved the stairways and fire escapes into separate columns at the corners. Concrete, then a new material, was employed to finish off the interiors. Forced-air ventilation (the first primitive attempts at air conditioning) was included. The interior work spaces were completely insulated from the outside—a highly desirable feature, since across the street trains passed endlessly. Here was an industrial environment that had not only integrity of form but also considerable elements of beauty and delight.

In the rush of creativity so typical of Wright, he tossed off a whole series of other firsts: hung

2·13-14 Wright considered the Larkin Building (below) "the first assertion that the machine in the artist's hands is a great tool," and Unity Temple (right) as proof that a building is not simply "the walls and the roof but is rather the space within."

stall walls in toilets (easier for the cleaning woman), all-metal office furniture, sound-absorbent plastering. It was an impressive performance. The Dutch architect Hendrik Petrus Berlage, one of the early leaders of the modern movement in Europe, saw the building before 1910 and wrote, "I went away with the conviction of having seen a genuinely modern work, and with respect for the master able to create things which have no equal in Europe." [19]

For Wright, the Larkin Building was merely preparation for his Unity Temple in Oak Park, Illinois. Unity Temple was much smaller in scale, but Wright felt that this building first captured the new special concepts which initiated what he called "the destruction of the box" (Figure 2·13). Essentially Unity Temple is two great rooms, one for worship and one for social gatherings, connected by a foyer corridor. Once again Wright took as his beginning concept the major central space. Like the Larkin Building, it was topped by a skylight. Wright lifted up the hall so that the entrance was reached by ramps from below, symbolic of the spiritual uplift. Everything else about the building was subordinated to the central area of a great room fixed in space. "Its significance was emphasis on what is called the third dimension," Wright explained. "It is not thickness but depth, a sense of space. All this adds up to a new dispensation as to what might constitute the life of a building: it could parallel the life of the free individual." [20]

The year 1909 marked Wright's fortieth birthday and became a milestone in his life. By this time the prairie houses had ushered in the free-planned interior. The boxes within boxes of former houses were now open, channeling a continuous flow of space. Connecting doors had been removed, with living and dining areas now one room. The roof was taken as the prime symbol of shelter—a rather Ruskinesque concept—emphasizing a horizontal, earth-hugging line. The use of glass windows in batteries, including the corner window, had done away with heavy corners and let light in where shadow had previously reigned. The house, no longer symmetrically ordered, played a give-and-take game with nature, now projecting out into space, now drawing the gardens within it—the beginnings of indoor-outdoor living. In his industrial and public commissions Wright had reorganized space into clear-cut volumes, expressive of their interior spaces.

If recognition lagged at home, it was coming surely from abroad, where Wright's achievements had entered the blood stream of modern European architecture. Berlin's leading art publisher, Ernst Wasmuth, probably at the instigation of Kuno Francke, visiting German professor at Harvard, was bringing out an elephant edition of Wright's work that was soon to make Wright a hero among advanced European architects. Then, suddenly, in October of 1909, Wright handed over his practice to a nearly total stranger. Selling a good part of his Japanese-print collection for ready cash, Wright departed for Europe with Mrs. Mamah (pronounced "may-mah") Borthwick Cheney, a married woman with two children, for whom Wright had designed a house five years previously. Behind him he left Catharine Tobin,* his wife of nineteen years, and their six children, thus duplicating the action of his own father in abandoning the family some twenty-four years before. It was the beginning of Wright's escapades that kept him in the tabloids for years.

He went first to Berlin to oversee the publication of the Wasmuth monograph of his works, then to Florence, where he and Mamah whiled away time translating a treatise on free love. On his return,

* She died in 1959 in Santa Monica, Calif., at the age of eighty-seven, less than two weeks before Wright.

nearly two years later, he made his way to the seclusion of the ancestral Lloyd-Jones acres. There his mother, Anna, had a site ready for a new house, the first Taliesin (Welsh for "shining brow," named for a Druid poet) set just below the crest of the hill (Figure 2·17).

Taliesin—or Taliesin North, as it came to be called to distinguish it from Wright's later summer headquarters in Arizona—is in itself one of the architect's greatest masterpieces, a rambling sequence of magnificent spaces, galleries, cantilevered balconies, and living rooms that is unique in North America (Figure 2·15). With its Japanese screens, carefully placed Buddhas, and massive fireplaces, it is the incarnation of Wright's romantic agrarianism and an explicit form world encompassing his whole organic philosophy of design. Perhaps only Jefferson's Monticello stands as a comparable dwelling place embodying one man's concept of an aristocratic life. The comparison also highlights the vast distance between Jefferson's classic ideal and Wright's earthy communion with nature.

Taliesin not only snuggles under the brow of the hill; it is *of* the hill. Its masonry elements, handled with such fantasy, are evocative in their stratified layers of the exposed cliff heads atop nearby hills. The great timbers seem to follow nature's own patterns of growth. The low ceilings that suddenly open into high spaces and the ingenious manner in which roof peaks open and clerestories are woven into the structure create the same variety of light shafts, moving as the sun moves, that give the forest its mystery. It projects out into nature with the very assurance with which the courts

2·15–18 Taliesin North, Spring Green, Wisconsin, was Wright's home and workshop from 1911 until his death in 1959. Named for a Druid poet, the rambling complex of buildings snuggled against a hill, curling luxuriously around open sculpture courts. Cantilevered balconies extended into space. The rooms were profusely decorated with Oriental paintings and bronzes of unequal value, but all seemed at home within Wright's organic design.

within its confines welcome nature. In its reciprocal play inward and outward it is one of the most subtle and sophisticated orchestrations of space.

Taliesin North was Wright's refuge from a world that too often proved indifferent and at times openly hostile to Wright's architectural principles and the grandiloquent style he affected in his personal life and pronouncements. The building was also the scene of Wright's greatest tragedy. One day he rushed home to discover it a smoking, charred ruin, and within it Mamah Borthwick Cheney murdered, along with her two children, by a berserk Barbados servant. Later Taliesin was rebuilt, but the blow Wright received that August night of 1914 left him reeling from pain and loneliness. For years his solace lay in his work.

With the commission to build the Imperial Hotel in Tokyo (Figure 2·19), a great opportunity came to Wright. He had long been a Japanophile. So strongly indeed did his prairie houses seem to echo the clearly expressed structure and broad overhangs of the traditional Japanese structure, the Ho-o-den, at the 1893 Chicago Columbian World's Fair that critics have long speculated that it was from this building that many of Wright's forms derived. This Wright consistently denied.* A far more likely source of inspiration was the Japanese prints he had been collecting ever since his first trip to Japan in 1905. He had donned the local Japanese costume and, like a character from *The Mikado*, plunged off on a print hunting expedition

* "I went out to the fair only once, in the morning with my wife and the children. We never even went near the Ho-o-den." (See note 21.)

into the interior.[22] "I saw the native home in Japan as a supreme study in elimination—not only of dirt but the elimination of the insignificant. So the Japanese house naturally fascinated me, and I would spend hours taking it all to pieces and putting it together again," Wright later wrote. "At last I had found one country on earth where simplicity, as nature, is supreme."[23]

The vernacular of Japanese traditional architecture, however, was of little or no help in designing the Tokyo hotel. In fact, it was the failure of Japanese architects to design an earthquake-proof structure that had brought the commission to Wright in the first place. To assist him in the task, Wright invited Paul Mueller, Dankmar Adler's chief engineer, and a small staff of draftsmen including Antonin Rado, later a pioneer in modern architecture in Japan. The problem they faced was erecting a massive masonry pile in land that was marshy and offered no secure footing. The solution is surely one of Wright's most ingenious feats of engineering. A floating foundation made of innumerable piles resting on the mud base was first installed. On these Wright erected columns which branched out at the top to become cantilevers which carried the floors, as Wright so colorfully put it, like a waiter carrying a tray on upraised arm between thumb and fingers. Plumbing was made flexible. As an added provision against fire, Wright inserted into his H plan a pool which incidentally acted as reflecting mirrors but whose real function was to serve as a handy water supply in case of fire.

2·19 Imperial Hotel, Chiyoda-Ku, Tokyo (1916–1922), was a masterful combination of daring engineering and rich architectural forms ornamented with lava sculpture. The building rests on pads of concrete sunk in marshy terrain. Ornamental fountains provided fire protection in case of an earthquake, which the hotel survived.

The ordeal against which Wright had so carefully prepared did not occur until 1923, two years after the hotel was finished. Then in Los Angeles, Wright waited for ten days in agony until at last he received the telegram from Baron Okura: "Hotel stands undamaged as monument of your genius hundreds of homeless provided by perfectly maintained service congratulations."[24] What should have been a professional triumph, however, went largely unnoticed. The American Institute of Architects omitted all reference to the hotel in its report on the Tokyo earthquake; Wright had fallen from favor. With good reason he later referred to the decade that followed as a period when he got "a worm's eye view of society."

Wright's private life, however, continued to be eventful: A second marriage to Miriam Noel, a bemonocled sculptress, proved a failure. His courtship of Olga ("Olgivanna") Lazovitch, a handsome Montenegran some twenty-five years his junior, became another scandal when he was arrested and thrown into Minneapolis's Hennepin County Jail for violating the Mann Act. In 1932, Wright was driven into bankruptcy. He was forced to incorporate himself and convert Taliesin North, along with the buildings he had designed for his aunts' Hillside school, into the Taliesin Fellowship, a school training apprentices for Wright's own projects. However, the more the world seemed to rebuff him, the greater became the messianic force of his preachments. At Taliesin, Wright's organic architecture became a kind of religion, buttressed with readings from Emerson and Walt Whitman, and expanding into the whole spectrum of religious literature. At times Wright's wrath at being shunted aside by society spilled over; democracy became mobocracy. In his own version of America First, he demanded, "How soon will we, the people, awake to the fact that the philosophy of natural and intrinsic building we are here calling organic is at one with our freedom as declared in 1776?"

Such jeremiads soon created a myth around Wright—one he found immensely sympathetic but one which often had little or nothing to do with his development as an architect. His substitution of "Usonian" (a term borrowed from Samuel Butler's *Erewhon*) for "American" did little to advance his cause. His effort to create an ideal community in a rural setting, which he called "Broadacre City," was useful as a poetic landscape in which to situate his own structures, but it ran clearly counter to the whole sociologic and economic trend of the times. It was, in fact, a final effort to revive the vision of a rural utopia in an age which had already left the nineteenth century far behind.

The same cannot be said of Wright's buildings, which maintained a steady evolution. In the 1920s, he began to expand his architectural solutions to areas far from his native Middle West, and the range of his inspiration broadened to encompass historical styles derived from the cultures of all the Americas. The Aline Barnsdall house in Los Angeles, which Wright referred to as "Hollyhock House" (Figure 2·21), clearly owes its form to the Mayan temple, just as the fantasia of resort structures Wright designed for Lake Tahoe echo an Indian wigwam. "La Miniatura," the Pasadena house Wright designed for Mrs. George Madison Millard (Figure 2·20), seems to have had some reference to the grilles of Spanish missions; however it derives far more directly from Wright's effort to find a way to use precast concrete blocks, a material that up until then had been considered fit for cellars and little else. Wright designed a structural system composed of a lattice of reinforcing rods which tied these hollow blocks into a rigid whole. The effect of this textile-block pattern was both striking and highly poetic, and not one to be overlooked for long by Wright's fellow architects. Indeed, "La Miniatura" has today produced a prodigious offspring, not the least of which are the lacy precast grilles which Edward D. Stone more than three decades later wrapped around the United States Embassy in New Delhi (1959).

2·20 Millard house, Pasadena, California (1923)

2·21 Barnsdall house, Hollywood, California (1920)

2·22-23 H. C. Price Tower, Bartlesville, Oklahoma (1956, designed 1929; above), was Wright's first skyscraper, employing the concept of a taproot foundation supporting a central shaft. The David Wright house, Phoenix, Arizona (1957; left), has living area on the second floor. Both buildings show Wright's genius with form.

2·24–27 Taliesin West, Scottsdale, Arizona (1938–1959), a fascinating setting of barbaric exuberance and refined sophistication, was for twenty-one years Wright's winter home. The structure was erected on lava-rock foundations with redwood trusses laid out in 30–60–90–degree triangles, topped with canvas. Included were Wright's dance theater and sumptuous living room (left), a small cabaret theater (above), and a highly ornamental bell tower (right).

In 1927 Wright was offered what seemed like an even more spectacular opportunity to test his precast textile block with a commission to design a very large resort hotel, San Marcos in the Desert, near Chandler, Arizona. This large-scale structure marked the beginning of Wright's great fondness of the 30- and 60-degree right triangle, which he maintained he simply "pulled out of the mountains." [25] The project itself floundered for lack of financing, but it introduced Wright to desert living, which he obviously relished. In the work camp erected on the site he made his first experiments with a batten wall topped with a roofing of canvas.

"The desert is where God is and Man is not," Victor Hugo had written, and Wright was fond of quoting it, [26] if only to prove that, once established in the desert, man is himself "something of a god." [27] It was in a remote spot near Scottsdale, Arizona, that Wright and his band of thirty-five apprentices from the Taliesin Fellowship erected Taliesin West, the most magnificent encampment any desert chieftain could have asked for and one that ranks as Wright's most delightful and extravagant structure, even though it was a temporary one (Figure 2·24–27).

Wright used the local volcanic rock, pouring it into wooden forms and then cementing the rock into place to provide an angular masonry podium and low walls. Above these structures Wright erected the canvas roofs he had used earlier in his temporary work camp. All of Wright's genius seemed here to come into play. Corners were vaporized out of existence; trusses seemed to soar without support. "Taliesin West is a look over the rim of the world," Wright declared. [28] And no one who visited while Wright was there could resist its magic.

Although Taliesin West rose triumphantly in the desert, many of Wright's projects of the 1920s and early 1930s long remained simply paper projects. An outstanding example is Wright's most original skyscraper project, the St. Mark's Tower, which gathered dust from 1929 until it was finally erected as the Price Tower, in Bartlesville, Oklahoma, in 1956 (Figure 2·22). But in the mid-1930s Wright finally made contact with a series of clients as individualistic as himself. Out of their collaboration came Wright's second great period, which kept him in the limelight for the final twenty years of his life.

whole composition becomes an arrangement of these concrete ribbons, strikingly contrasted with the ashlar stone verticals, including the chimneys. The main level within is essentially one vast room, with

2·28–30 "Falling Water," Bear Run, Pennsylvania (1936), is essentially a summer house, with few, if any, equals in architecture. Bold use of the site, whereby Wright cantilevered the balconies out over the waterfall (lower left), the play of horizontals against stone verticals, and the ease with which the forms adapt to nature (below)—including the free acceptance of upthrust rock by the interior fireplace (upper left)—all affirm organic design.

the upper story a series of individual suites. Behind is a guest house and pool, reached by a stairway sheltered by a continuous concrete canopy. The final effect is masterful in its arrangement of plastic elements. It has been justly called one of the finest modern houses in the United States, and by some among the finest in the world.

The building which ceremoniously announced Wright's return to the architectural scene was "Falling Water" (Figure 2·28), a week-end house designed for the Pittsburgh department-store owner Edgar J. Kaufmann at Bear Run, Pennsylvania, in 1936. This was the first reinforced-concrete house Wright had built, and its dramatic site offered him a superb opportunity. Over the natural waterfall he projected great reinforced-concrete cantilevered slabs that are anchored in the hillside behind and seem to float effortlessly out into space. The

The success of these two structures resulted in Wright's once again finding himself with almost more clients than he could cope with. His answer was to dip into the immense backlog of projects that had accumulated at Taliesin. "Our buildings cannot go out of fashion," he insisted. "They are not and never will be dated." [29] In this, of course, Wright chose to ignore what he perfectly well knew, that his designs were in a constant state of evolution.

A plan that suffered far less than most from delay, perhaps because its theme is more permanent, is the Beth Sholom Synagogue (Figure 2·38), still incomplete on the interior at the time of Wright's death in 1959. The origin here may well date as far back as the handful of steeply pitched roofs Wright used on his 1892 "bootlegged" houses (e.g., the Edmond house, La Grange, Illinois) during the years with Sullivan. The synagogue's more direct ancestor, however, is the tepee-inspired lakefront cottage for Lake Tahoe in 1922. This wigwam form was redesigned in 1926 as a monumental interdenominational church with a proposed double roof of glass, or plastic below glass. It was on hand when the Beth Sholom Synagogue commission came Wright's way.

The T square, triangle, and scale Wright confessed were the energizing instruments of his craft. "I like to take an idea, play with it, until finally it becomes a poetic circumstance," he once explained. [30] And as shocking as the powerful horizontals and thrusting verticals of his early years once seemed, they were not nearly so disquieting as the triangles, polygons, and hexagons of his middle period. In a kind of baroque exuberance, Wright jiggered plans this way and that to fit the controlling angular motif until even the beds became parallelograms.

Such extraordinary acrobatics had a highly significant reason behind them, however. Wright in his earlier plans had welcomed the centrifugal design which sent wings sweeping out into space like giant pinwheels or swastikas. But his experience with the low-cost "Usonian" houses in the 1930s and 1940s had presented him with a baffling problem: how to keep the bedrooms from trailing off like a handle or tail of the main structure. By using the more complex hexagons and octagons, Wright was attempting to reincorporate these projecting areas into the central mass. And as the forms became more and more multisided, Wright discovered that he was approaching the circle. In

2·31–35 S. C. Johnson buildings, Racine, Wisconsin, were Wright's first major office structures since the Larkin Building, thirty-four years previously, and demonstrated Wright's growth in the interim. The main Administration Building (opposite page) was erected between 1936 and 1939, the Laboratory (above) in 1947 to 1949. Laboratory contains within the glass sheathing a giant central stack from which floors branch out, affording spacious sunlit work space within. The disciplined, functional design is one of Wright's most pleasing.

2·36–39 Wright's structures often achieve an almost baroque exuberance of rectilinear form—for example, his chapel (top) and campus plan for Florida Southern College (above) or the roof of the Beth Sholom Synagogue, Elkins Park, Pennsylvania (below). By contrast, the Guggenheim Museum (opposite page) has the calm and serenity of an unbroken wave.

1939, with a project for the Ralph Jester house in Palos Verdes, California,[31] Wright took the next significant step of arranging the internal organization of space in circular form, topping the living areas with a floating rectangle.

Almost instinctively he recapitulated the entire architectural history of the spiral in his work. In a project for the Gordon Strong Planetarium on Sugar Loaf Mountain, Maryland, Wright had used the same spiraling ramp employed by Assyrian King Sargon II in 706 B.C., when he built a 6-foot ramp around his ziggurat at Khorsabad. By 1947, Wright was proposing a spiral ramp for a self-service garage in Pittsburgh, and in 1948 he internalized the ramp in the V. C. Morris shop in San Francisco (Figure 2·44). An even handsomer variation was the house he designed for his son David Wright in Phoenix in 1957 (Figure 2·23), in which the ramp, or ''serpent's tail,'' as Wright called it, swings upward through space to arrive at the second-level living quarters.

The most impressive use of the ramp in Wright's work is the Solomon R. Guggenheim Museum, a project which began in 1943 and was completed sixteen years later—six months after Wright's death on April 9, 1959. The museum was one of the hardest fought battles of Wright's life. When Wright's client Solomon R. Guggenheim died, the project passed over to a foundation; the director was far from sympathetic. The museum program, in the process, had changed from a permanent exhibition of the Guggenheim collection of nonobjective art to a series of changing exhibitions. As a result the building was woefully ill-equipped for what Wright called scornfully ''the museum business.''

To get his building finished—and Wright was as aware as anyone that time was running out—he willingly made compromise after compromise, the final result of which shows in terms of finish and detail. Yet despite these qualifications, the Guggenheim Museum stands today as a testament to Wright's powerful geometry, its heavy shell structure uncoiling effortlessly upward in contrast to the rectangular structures surrounding it.

While the greatest of Wright's projects, the Guggenheim Museum was by no means his last. At the time of his death, some thirty-seven projects (totaling 20 million dollars) were on the boards or

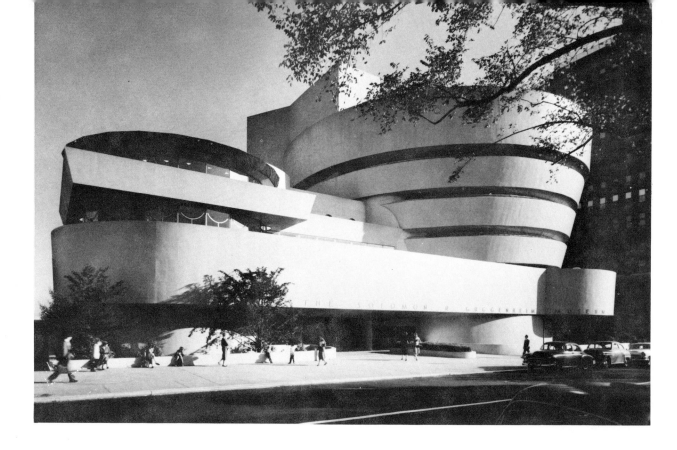

2·40–43 Solomon R. Guggenheim Museum, 1071 Fifth Avenue, New York (1943–1959), contains a great spiraling ramp mounting six stories, serving as a continuous gallery. The museum is Wright's final monument and most daring composition.

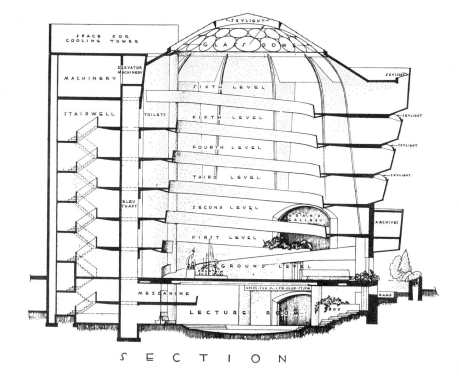

SECTION

2·44 V. C. Morris Shop (below), San Francisco (1948), demonstrated possible commercial uses for ramp construction five years after the original plans for the Solomon R. Guggenheim Museum were drawn.

being built.* The life force that so relentlessly drove Wright through seventy years remained strong to the end. The place Frank Lloyd Wright will hold in the history of architecture cannot yet be fully appreciated. "If this were an age like the Renaissance, . . . Wright would have been honored as the Michelangelo of the twentieth century," the architect Eero Saarinen has stated.[32] And perhaps it is only by summoning up such great artists as Michelangelo that we can have any perspective on Wright's total achievement. His life work (and much of it exists only in sketch form) is more complete than any corpus of work left by any artist or architect in history since Leonardo da Vinci. He was unquestionably the greatest architect of his time. A host of his innovations—the picture window, split-level planning, carports, skylighted kitchens and windows, and much of what is known as the ranch house—have enriched modern architecture. No list of contemporary monuments could omit such buildings as the two Taliesins, Unity Temple, "Bear Run," the S. C. Johnson Administration Building, or the Guggenheim Museum. Yet a final irony casts its shadow over Wright's reputation: He did not create the style and vernacular of his age. That task fell to younger men—architects whose creative gifts were disciplined to express the new spatial requirements and technology of the twentieth century.

*Taliesin Associated Architects, nineteen architects headed by Wright's son-in-law William Wesley Peters and chief draftsman John H. Howe, was formed shortly after Wright's death to complete projects and carry on Wright's tradition.

3 : **AUGUSTE PERRET :**

3·1 Maison Perret, Rue Franklin, Paris (1902–1903)

3·2 Place de l'Hotel de Ville, Le Havre (1948–1954)

3·3 Notre Dame, Le Raincy, France (1922)

Steel has been the most characteristic material in modern American architecture. In Europe, and particularly in France, reinforced concrete is the prime building material. The first great figure to exploit this new material in architecture was Auguste Perret (1874–1954), a dedicated Frenchman whose part in making reinforced concrete a major element in modern architecture in many ways parallels that of Louis Sullivan in evolving the skyscraper. Both men drew heavily on the accumulated engineering experience of their time. Both men were followed by brilliant disciples—Sullivan by Frank Lloyd Wright and Perret by Le Corbusier.

Perret's first significant building was the headquarters that he and his brothers erected in 1902 in Paris (Figure 3·1), a building which has since become a modern landmark, but which was so daring in its day that the *crédit foncier* refused even to grant it a mortgage. Behind its inception lay over a century of investigation of cements and concrete in France by men such as François Coignet, who patented concrete in 1855, and the French engineer François Hennebique, who in 1892 had patented his system of reinforcing concrete with steel rods and had then proceeded to make a fortune with his world-wide network of construction companies.

Perret always proudly referred to himself as a constructor, rather than an architect, and indeed structure was for him the essence of good building. "If the structure is not worthy to remain visible, the architect has badly fulfilled his mission," Perret maintained.[1] In his Ponthieu Garage in Paris he left the concrete structure unabashedly exposed, much as medieval architects had gloried in expressing every rib and vault of their soaring structures. True, a garage is not likely to be great architecture. This Perret cheerfully admitted. But he asked, "How can we build a palace, if we do not build our factories in the same way."[2]

Perret's chance to build something approaching a palace came in 1910 when he was called in to build the Theâtre des Champs-Elysées, a building which announced defiantly that reinforced concrete was a modern material capable of monumental effects. The structure, however, which far surpasses the theater as an architectural creation, is an economy project that cost barely $35,000, a part of

* Quotations in chapter headings are by the architect under discussion unless otherwise noted.

PIONEER IN CONCRETE

Architecture is what makes ruins beautiful *

3·4 Admiralty Research Laboratory, Boulevard Victor, Paris (1928)

which came out of Perret's own pocket. This is the church of Notre Dame at Le Raincy, a First World War memorial built at L'Ourcq.

Despite its restricted budget, the church which resulted is one of the handsomest in modern times (Figure 3·3). Within, the soaring columns rise unimpeded for 37 feet, giving order and measure to the space. The concrete screen that stands in place of the exterior wall is made up of five standard precast concrete grilles. Each bay has a small panel filled with stained glass designed by the famous postimpressionist painter Maurice Denis, with colors ranging from bright yellow at the entrance to a deep violet at the chancel. The total effect is a stirring experience. Quite justly it is called "The Ste. Chapelle of Reinforced Concrete."

To Perret's office shortly after the turn of the century came some of the most talented younger architects of Europe. "Perret had the temerity to claim that reinforced concrete was destined to revolutionize architecture," Le Corbusier, today France's greatest architect, recalled. "He was the only man who had found a new direction in architecture." [3] However, much as Sullivan and Wright found themselves not speaking to each other for years, so Perret fell out with Le Corbusier.

Perret was a classicist at heart. "Proportion is man himself," he insisted. "Style is a word that has no plural." In later years Perret was to be attacked also by even younger innovators, who felt that Perret had failed to exploit the plastic possibilities of this marvelous new material. "Perret's unconcealed aim was to build classic structures in concrete," Mexico's leading concrete-shell exponent, Felix Candela, has said accusingly. [4] The fact that Perret also attacked Le Corbusier in later years ("He is a clerk. He will pass," Perret whispered to Frank Lloyd Wright at a formal Paris architectural dinner) [5] begot bitterness in return. Le Corbusier pointedly said, "His authority, that authority which the younger generation conferred on him, he now uses against them." [6]

It may be that Perret's later black-listing by the emerging leaders of the modern movement has been an injustice both to Perret and to architecture. When Perret stated, "Architecture is what makes ruins beautiful," [7] he underlined the fact that modern architecture, even in these few decades, has *not* aged well. Perret pointed out, "A locomotive merely has character; the Parthenon has both character and style. In a few years, the most beautiful locomotive of today will be merely a mass of scrap metal; the Parthenon will sing forever." [8] It was taken at the time as an attack on the machine esthetic—almost machine worship—in vogue in the 1920s. Actually Perret was making a very telling distinction between design and architecture.

Curiously in much the same way that *art nouveau* has now staged its comeback, largely because its surrealist overtones and its sculpturesque quality seem a welcome antidote to the too finely drawn and ultrarational architecture of today, so Perret's classic tastes are once again finding a responsive chord. Such late Perret buildings as the Admiralty Research Laboratories (Figure 3·4), the Ecole Normale de Musique (1929), and the Mobilier National (1935) would now be ranked high among his finest works. It is significant, too, that it was to Perret that the French Atomic Commission turned for its Research Center at Saclay (1949).

In part the fact that Perret's structures, while modern in method, construction, and materials, seem to blend into an ageless past accounts for the revival of interest in his work. Today they seem, as even Le Corbusier has pointed out, "the continuation of the great, noble and elegant truths of French architecture." More important is the continuing work of rebuilding the center of war-damaged Le Havre, the major reconstruction project of postwar France and the last major project in Perret's long life. As it nears completion, including the great central *place* and Hotel de Ville designed by Perret in his final years, those very classic qualities that so long counted against him are now appearing as virtues. For what Perret has built is finer than what it replaced. The new order, logic, and general commodiousness of rebuilt Le Havre suggest that the great civic planning eras of the past are all now worthy of restudy as modern architecture moves into its mature years.

4·1 Unité d'Habitation, Marseilles (1946–1952), houses 1,600 residents. Le Corbusier sees this gigantic apartment block, raised on stilts, as the basic unit for future city planning. The facade is composed of narrow balconies of duplex apartments. Band of louvers (halfway up facade) and emergency exit (left) serve the two-story shopping center within the building.

4 : **LE CORBUSIER** : VISION AND FORM

The Middle Ages aspired toward the City of God, and the Renaissance evoked a more worldly ideal, the great age of classic Rome. The twentieth century too has had its great vision, which is no less poetic because it invokes science and technology. It is that of a new society founded on the machine's gigantic powers of production and man's ability to mold his own environment in the light of his own vision. That the machine must be the servant of a master designer, all architects have agreed. The cityscape that would result, however, has as many aspects as men have dreams. Sullivan saw a virile world of brotherhood expressing itself in a form world of tolerance and harmony. For Auguste Perret, the new age could do no better than to maintain the ageless and eternal forms of the classic tradition. Wright, the most visionary of all architects, saw form and function becoming one in a transcendental expression that would embody the democratic vistas of Emerson, Jefferson, and Whitman.

However, it remained for a Swiss-born Frenchman whom the world knows as Le Corbusier to seek salvation through art. His goal was to combine the unconscious esthetic of the engineers with the revolutionary discoveries of Western art from the time of Cézanne to Picasso. The result would be a new, modern environment as responsive to man's wishes as the airplanes, ocean liners, and automobiles that technology has made his everyday companions.

To this task, Le Corbusier brought a formidable combination of talents, for he is a man who acts as if architecture were a science, practices it as if it were painting or sculpture, and preaches it as gospel. When he could not build, he designed, not modest structures, but whole cities. When he found he had no patrons, he took his cause to the public, and in so doing he has become the greatest propagandist for modern architecture of the century. He may well be the first architect in history who has dared produce a master plan for a whole city (Paris) before he had built a single significant structure, and who, even today, has written almost as many books (over forty) as he has built buildings (under sixty).

And yet Le Corbusier's impact on the evolution of modern architecture is almost incalculable. A whole generation in Latin America, India, Japan, France, and Italy has read his books with a sense of revelation that no other architect has been able to transmit. His stylistic innovations—sun breakers, buildings set above the ground on tall columns—

*Architecture is the masterly, correct
and magnificent play
of masses brought together in light*

have become part of the vocabulary of architects the world over. His conception of the city of tomorrow where the skyscraper would arise as a mighty slab, freeing the surrounding area for green parks while traffic flowed safely by on segregated ribbons of concrete, has challenged a whole generation of city planners. It is a dream that now has taken on the mortar, stone, and concrete of reality. On the heat-blasted plains of the Punjab, Le Corbusier has had the profound satisfaction of beholding a whole new city, Chandigarh, arise as triumphant affirmation of his principles, and in the Brazilian capital of Brasília an equally dramatic demonstration of his concepts by his dedicated followers, Lucio Costa and Oscar Niemeyer.

Today, wherever reinforced concrete, and not steel, is the prime material for building, Le Corbusier is the presiding genius, one of the three great polarizing presences of modern architecture whose influence is matched only by Frank Lloyd Wright, with his great drama of space, and Ludwig Mies van der Rohe, who has elevated technology into an orthodoxy of refined steel construction.

The self-imposed rendezvous with destiny that has been Le Corbusier's chosen role since early man-

4·3 Pavillon de l'Esprit Nouveau, Paris (1925). This prototype for Le Corbusier's duplex apartments presents a facade of linear elements. Sculpture is by Lipchitz.

hood has also made him one of nature's prickliest individuals. The role of prophet is no easy stance to maintain in this century. And Le Corbusier, never one to bear fools gladly, has risen to heights of polemics when his plans have been rejected, his advice scorned, or his projects balked. Indeed, it is only by comparison with Le Corbusier's high sense of his own destiny and the magnitude of his final accomplishment that the bitterness of his defeats can be sympathetically comprehended.

When asked to draw a word portrait of Le Corbusier, his old friend and fellow Swiss, Siegfried Giedion, wrote: "Withdrawn, hard, inaccessible, warding off personal contact, as mistrustful as a mountain peasant. Nobody knows who he really is. In all probability these are only protective shells to shield his innermost depth from impudent interference. The innermost layer of the creative personality requires darkness, just as seeds do." [1]

E. Maxwell Fry, a former collaborator of Walter Gropius in the 1930s, wrote of Le Corbusier, after working on the housing units at Chandigarh, "What struck me in working alongside Le Corbusier—working 'with' being next to impossible—is his capacity for using creatively the fruits of cool analysis. I believe this to be a rare gift that sets him completely apart." [2] An American sculptor, Costantino Nivola, who made Le Corbusier's acquaintance in the 1940s and shared his studio with Le Corbusier, sees another aspect: "His approach to a problem is basically artistic. He did not force. He lets ideas come through. He thinks in terms of form." [3]

It is perhaps this last aspect of Le Corbusier, his concept of architecture as man's greatest sculpture, that will prove to be his longest-lasting contribution. For a generation that has abandoned nearly every great prerogative of traditional architecture —ornament, plasticity, and drama—the late work of Le Corbusier marks a new, challenging direction, one no longer based on sociology, on technology, or even on function, but on art. Architecture, as Le Corbusier has defined it, is ". . . the masterly, correct and magnificent play of masses brought together in light." [4]

Le Corbusier was born Charles-Edouard Jeanneret on October 6, 1887, in La Chaux-de-Fonds, a watchmaking town in French-speaking Switzerland. Both his father and grandfather were watchmakers (his mother was a musician), and young Jeanneret was early apprenticed to the trade of engraving watches destined for South American

4·4 Swiss Pavilion, University City, Paris, (1930–1932), enunciated Le Corbusier's use of stilts, curved forms, textured surfaces.

export. His escape came through a local art teacher named L'Eplatenier, who admired the youth's amateur sketches, enrolled him in the local art school, and awarded him, at the tender age of seventeen, a commission to design his house. "Probably hideous, but off the beaten track," Le Corbusier says of this early work today. With the money earned from his first architectural commission, young Jeanneret was able to leave Switzerland on a series of knapsack trips that took him to Italy, then Budapest and Vienna, and finally Paris, where he got an introduction to Auguste Perret, the pioneer in reinforced concrete.*

Jeanneret's fifteen months of apprenticeship (1908–1909) to the great Perret was the major formative influence of his long career, as important as Wright's years with Sullivan. For in Perret's office at 25 bis, Avenue Franklin, Jeanneret was at the very generative center of modern architecture as it was then evolving in terms of reinforced concrete.

An assignment from his old art school at La Chaux-de-Fonds, to make a study trip to Germany to examine the arts and crafts movement, brought Jeanneret to Berlin in 1910. For five months he worked there in the office of Peter Behrens, a monumental figure in German architecture, whose Turbine Factory and Small Motors Factory for the German electrical trust AEG (1909) were pioneering efforts toward creating new prototypes for factory construction. Jeanneret, at the time, was mightily impressed by the organizational strength of the German school, but as a Swiss with a touch of Paris about him he found ". . . the Germans lack a tradition and their hands are still unskilled." [5]

Le Corbusier did not tarry long in Berlin. With a Bern antiques dealer he next set off on a seven-month hiking trip through the Balkans. For Jeanneret it was a spiritual exploration of the past which reached its climax in Athens, where for twenty-one days he haunted the Parthenon. In Rome he discovered in Hadrian's Villa and the Pantheon ". . . the first example of Western planning on a grand scale." [6] The small, tight island called Switzerland now seemed too small. In 1917, at the age of thirty, he settled down for good in Paris, an intense, visionary young man with his way still to make.

The first years in Paris were bitter ones for Jeanneret. While living in seclusion at 20, Rue Jacob on the left bank, he attempted to manage a

*See Chap. 3.

construction company and failed miserably. He dabbled in mathematics; his soul yearned for art. The man who seemed to come closest to his ideal was a fellow Swiss, the painter Amédée Ozenfant. Under Ozenfant's tutelage, Jeanneret began painting at the age of thirty-one, turning out large, simplified images of geometric objects—briar pipes, bottles, spoons—that seemed to have achieved a kind of ideal form through usage, and yet corresponded to Cézanne's dictum that nature should be seen in terms of the great geometric shapes, the cone, the sphere, and the cube. Ozenfant at the time was sure that Picasso's work was beginning to show ". . . a preference for standards of the embroiderer and lacemaker . . . his grand manner degenerates into intriguing mannerism." [7] The time called for a new movement, to be called "purism," and a high goal, ". . . to convert [cubism] from an empirical art of personal expression to a new type of ordered, reasonable classical art." [8]

In Paris such an undertaking calls for a manifesto (*Après le cubism*), an exhibition (the first was held in the Galerie Thomas in 1918), and finally a magazine. Today purism is only a footnote to the history of modern art, but *L'Esprit nouveau*, the new art review that first appeared on October 15, 1920, is a landmark in architectural history, for it marked the emergence of a brand-new personality, Le Corbusier,* and some of the best polemical writing in the history of architecture.

"A great age has begun, guided by a new spirit, a spirit of construction and synthesis, guided by a clear concept." So began Le Corbusier's first article. In rapid order, this new spirit was briskly spelled out. It was to be seen in industrial produc-

*Jeanneret picked the pen name "Le Corbusier" from his mother's line, for his *L'Esprit nouveau* articles; Amédée Ozenfant also used his mother's name, Saugnier. The two were hyphenated on the original articles, but as Ozenfant rather ruefully tells us, "When the work was reprinted (as *Towards a New Architecture* in 1923), it bore the sole name, Le Corbusier." (See note 9.)

tion and in the machine. The palaces of the budding twentieth century were the great transatlantic liners. Architecture, on the other hand, was stifled by custom: "Architecture has nothing to do with the various styles!" Le Corbusier announced. "The styles of Louis XIV, XV, XVI or Gothic, are to architecture what a feather is on a woman's head; it is sometimes pretty, though not always, and never anything more." [10] By contrast, Le Corbusier argued, the engineers, in paying attention only to mathematics and economy, were producing masterpieces of design in grain silos and factories.

It was Le Corbusier's genius to see that these early industrial forms could be combined as architecture: "Let us display," Le Corbusier exhorted, "the Parthenon and the motor car so that it may be clear that it is a question of two products of selection in different fields, one of which has reached its climax and the other is evolving."

Once Le Corbusier had displayed the Parthenon and a Delage 1911 Grand-Sport on the same page, it was only a step to pointing out that "The house is a machine for living in." The furnishings of the sun decks of the ocean liners, the early London-Paris passenger planes, and the sleeping compartments of the *wagon-lits* all gave clues to the future furnishing of houses with lightweight, functional, and mass-produced units. "We must create the mass-production spirit. The spirit of constructing mass-production houses. The spirit of living in mass-production houses. The spirit of conceiving mass-production houses," Le Corbusier wrote. [11]

The "machine to live in" must have a serviceable chassis. While he had been teaching in Switzerland during the First World War Le Corbusier had worked out a basic reinforced-concrete frame which was to act as the space frame for his cubist-oriented organization of the house into such a mass-produced "machine for living." In 1922 he felt ready to begin implementing it with actual designs. Calling in his Swiss cousin, Pierre Jeanneret, as a partner, Le Corbusier set up headquarters in a former Jesuit monastery at 35, Rue de Sèvres on the Left Bank in Paris, and soon the two enthusiasts began turning out the first plaster models of the Citrohan House (the name is a conscious play on the name of France's best-known car, the Citroën), which they outfitted like a ship's cabin. In 1922 Amédée Ozenfant gave Le Corbusier his first commission, for a studio. Soon afterwards the sculptor Jacques Lipchitz, who had just then made his first big sales to the American Argyrol maker, Albert

Barnes, followed suit. "Don't spoil my pure walls," Le Corbusier begged, [12] urging that paintings be stored away out of sight *à la japonais* and brought out only on occasions to be looked at.

By 1925 Le Corbusier had enough experience to produce an even more daring exhibition structure, Le Pavillon de L'Esprit Nouveau, in which a rectilinear frame was set up, then carved out daringly to set up a pattern of contrasting voids and space (Figure 4·3). Paintings by Jeanneret (as Le Corbusier still continues to call himself as a painter), Juan Gris, and Fernand Léger, and sculpture by Lipchitz were added to underline the fact that here "Cubism is at home." The single tree on the site was allowed to grow through a circle cut in the roof, the first of such circles that soon became a cliché in modern architecture. The interiors were not furnished; they were "equipped" with standardized cupboards, built in or suspended from the walls.

The Esprit Nouveau pavilion became the basis of Le Corbusier's Five Points, enunciated in the following year as the essentials of modern architecture:

1. The free-standing support. Buildings are to be lifted from the ground on stilts, thus displaying the house as a piece of free-standing sculpture and freeing the ground level for pedestrian use.

2. Independence of the wall from the frame. The wall, no longer a weight-bearing element, is to be conceived of as a panel, open or opaque. Ribbon windows, carried around the corners, were preferred.

3. The free plan. The interior of the house was no longer to be honeycombed into small compartments but thrown open with one space merging into the next. (This concept Le Corbusier had first witnessed in Auguste Perret's office as a student. Wright had already extensively developed it in his prairie houses.)

4. The free façade. The concept of the façade as a sculptural plane, no longer expressive of the frame within (as Perret's buildings are) or even of the space within (as Wright's buildings), but a taut, flat plane, preferably of stucco and painted white.

5. The roof garden. Having cleared the ground floor of construction by lifting the building on stilts, Le Corbusier now added another dimension to the building by creating the flat roof as a garden, to be used for planting or for sculpture.

The building which incorporates all five elements is Le Corbusier's Villa Savoye (Figure 4·19), at

4·5–7 Unité d'Habitation, Marseilles, a reinforced-concrete apartment house with painted balconies (above) and sculptured roof garden show Le Corbusier's mastery of color and form.

4·8 Bold slab form of the UN Secretariat and Assembly, New York, carries out the concepts of Le Corbusier in the technology of America.

4·9–11 Notre-Dame-du-Haut, Ronchamp, France (1950–1955), probably Le Corbusier's most personal statement of the plastic possibilities inherent in reinforced-concrete construction. This small church serves as a hilltop chapel and focal point for pilgrimages. The interior (above) is an almost cavelike retreat; from the exterior pulpit (below, right) several thousand can be addressed, with the exterior wall as backdrop.

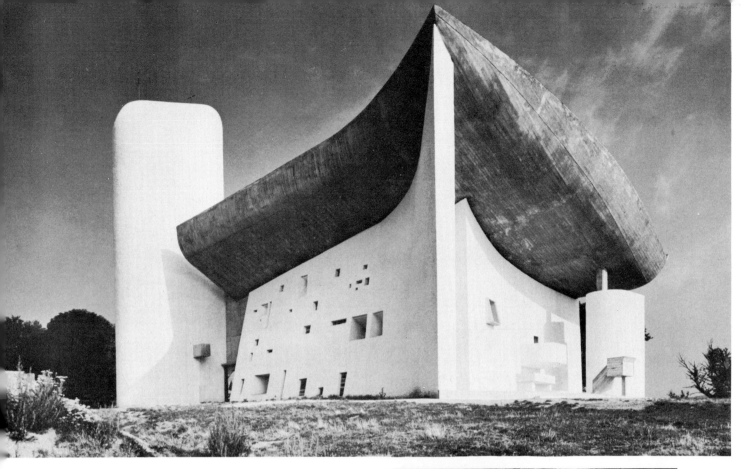

4·12–16 Le Corbusier's Chapel at Ronchamp evokes images of a nun's coif (above) or abstract sculpture of a man (below); interior roof suggests a tent form.

Poissy, a week-end house seventeen miles west of Paris. Unlike Frank Lloyd Wright, who had merged his prairie house into the site, Le Corbusier conceived of the house as "an object," emphatically a creation of man and painted a dramatic white to contrast with the background of forest greenery. To get away from the dampness, Le Corbusier raised the whole basic cube off the earth on stilts (*pilotis*). The owners were to arrive by car, driving under the *pilotis* to their front door, and the ground-floor curve was calculated on the turning circle of their automobile. Once inside, they would mount to the main floor (Figure 4·17), positioned above the earth, experiencing along the way the drama of moving upward through space on ramps connecting the main living area to the roof garden and culminating at the roof-top solarium behind a curved concrete screen. It was a progression half within and half without the building's structure. The basic discipline of the cube remained, as the square canvas is retained by the painter, but space now was reorganized around a whole new concept of interpenetrating spaces. The spell of geometric forms, pure mathematics, sharp delineation of materials produced a superb stage set, flooded with sunlight, and was all here to be seen and experienced. For a whole generation of modern architects in the 1920s it was the epitome of modern architecture.*

Le Corbusier's first major public building was the Swiss Pavilion (1930–1932) for the Cité Universitaire in Paris. It proved to be equally significant, a laboratory of modern architecture that, even today, architects are still quarrying. The building itself (Figure 4·4) is modest in function, housing some fifty students. The main residence block is elevated at either end on monumental *pilotis*, sculptural in effect. Inside, Le Corbusier incorporated a novelty of the time, photomurals, and set the office space behind a rugged wall of fieldstone. The stairways and elevator were housed behind a curved façade that announced a new direction in Le Corbusier's search for free form.

From the time Le Corbusier set up his practice as

an architect, he has been concerned with city planning. There is something heroic about his endless and futile assaults on Paris. Whole sections of Paris were to be leveled (though the Louvre would be spared), and in their place would rise great columns of widely spaced, sixty-story skyscrapers set in great open parks. Traffic would be separated from pedestrian ways. Le Corbusier's imagination roamed over the possibilities of remaking the capitals of the world. New plans were drawn up for Antwerp, Stockholm, and Algiers. In 1928 a new organization, CIAM (Congrès International d'Architecture Moderne) was set up with forty-two members from twelve countries present to bring the new day closer at hand. But just as Le Corbusier's plan for the new League of Nations Palace in Geneva was passed over (ostensibly because the plans were not drawn up in India ink!) and his grandiose Palace of the Soviets (which included a huge auditorium suspended from a free-standing parabolic arch) went unbuilt, so Le Corbusier's endless labor on city plans seemed for decades love's labor lost. However, they did become the imaginary landscape against which Le Corbusier set his prototype structures which ranged from "endless museums" to "palatial auditoriums."

Most important of all were the superblocks Le Corbusier envisioned as the housing units for the city of the future. These took various forms on Le Corbusier's drafting boards, changing as his theories developed from a cruciform plan (abandoned because he realized the north sides would receive no sun) to a huge slab raised on stilts and topped with roof gardens, playgrounds, and race tracks (Le Corbusier was a physical culture enthusiast at the time). The first of these great slabs ever to see the sun was, as fate would have it, built not in France at all but in Rio de Janeiro, where a team of Brazilian architects, including Lucio Costa and Oscar Niemeyer, erected the Ministry of Education and Health (1937–1943). Le Corbusier's role was one of initiator and guiding spirit. The second Le Corbusier superblock was the United Nations Secretariat, and again Le Corbusier's role was restricted to that of the master plan and adviser. The first opportunity Le Corbusier had actually to develop and oversee a residential superblock in person came at the end of the Second World War with his Unité d'Habitation, a large apartment house in Marseilles, the most important reinforced-concrete structure of the last two decades.

---

* The Villa Savoye was abandoned by the Savoye family during the Second World War, and then used as a haymow and storage for fruit crates. A world-wide protest, launched in the United States by the architect-photographer G. E. Kidder Smith and historian Siegfried Giedion, caused the Minister of State in Charge of Cultural Affairs, André Malraux, to suspend plans to raze the house to make way for a school in 1959. Said Le Corbusier at the time: "Houses can die as well as men, but if there's a way of saving them, so much the better." (See note 13.)

4·17–20 Villa Savoye, Poissy, France (1928–1930). Top to bottom: interior and exterior; gatehouse; Villa Savoye in its prime; Villa Savoye as it appears today.

The impressive structure that emerged after five years of construction is a massive reinforced-concrete block, 450 feet long, 70 feet deep and 180 feet high, which contains 337 apartments housing a population of 1,600 (Figure 4·1). Situated off the Avenue Michelet, some fifteen minutes from the center of Marseilles, it stands like some gigantic steamer in the midst of its 11½-acre park. As a piece of gigantic sculpture, it has few equals, yet each element in the over-all composition actually derives from the interior plan. The louvered, two-story section on the seventh and eighth levels are an "interior street," a built-in shopping area similar to Rockefeller Center's below-street-level shopping areas but raised above ground. The central vertical slab, perforated with small windows, is the interior stairway and elevator shaft. The honeycomb façade derives from the balconies, painted in primary colors. Supporting the tremendous bulk of the building are thirty-eight massive *pilotis;* topping the structure is a roof garden, with ventilator shafts, a children's playground, and running track (Figure 4·5), which Le Corbusier's plastic design sense raised to the level of pure abstract sculpture.

"It is my pride, my honor and my joy to hand over to you the Unité d'Habitation, the first manifestation of an environment suited to modern life," Le Corbusier proudly declared on October 14, 1952. But exactly how suited this isolated superblock is to modern life is far from settled, even today. At the time, Le Corbusier dated his conception to his visit at the age of twenty to the monastery of the Chartreuse of Ema, in Tuscany; and a taste for monasticism would certainly come in useful for an inhabitant of the Marseilles Unité.

The apartments are arranged as duplexes, with a 15-foot-high living room opening on a 4-foot-deep balcony. The master bedroom is long and narrow (13 feet); the children's rooms are a bare 6 feet wide; bathrooms and kitchens are windowless. Criticism has been intense, ranging all the way from no cellars for cheese to no privacy for sex. The interior shopping streets turned out to be unwanted by French housewives with a taste for going to market—a serious wastage of valuable interior space. And, for all the plastic expression on the roof top, children prefer to play in the adjacent park land. As for the rough finish of the structure, even Le Corbusier was willing to admit, "The defects shout at one from all parts of the structure!"

All of this is not to say that the Unité, apart from the awkwardness and high costs involved in any prototype, was not a qualified success. Le Corbusier conceived of such superblocks as being situated within the city—his plan for St. Dié shows eight such buildings—and presumably of much greater proportions. The Marseilles Unité fulfilled neither of these conditions. A second Unité, both more successful and less expensive, has been finished at Nantes-Rezé, one is planned for Briey-en-Forêt, and yet another has been constructed in the Charlottenburg section of Berlin. As a twentieth-century form, these massive slabs have now become accepted..

The greatest impact of these housing projects, however, has been from their dramatically sculptured exteriors. Their use of rough texture, dramatic color, *brise soleils* (sun breakers), rhythmical balconies, statuesque *pilotis*, and dramatic free forms on the roof gardens, all mark a clear break for Le Corbusier from his earlier concept of the façade as a thin, white, flat plane derived from cubism to architecture as a three-dimensional sculptural object. This new direction, involving both a new drama and a new brutalism, is the mark of Le Corbusier's latest work, particularly his Chapel at Ronchamp, one of the pivotal structures of mid-twentieth-century architecture, and the state buildings for Chandigarh, Le Corbusier's most ambitious architectural composition.

Haut-Lieu ("high place") at Ronchamp is at a last bastion of the Vosges Mountains overlooking the Saône Valley, and a natural gathering place throughout history. Pagan temples existed there in pre-Christian times; pilgrimage shrines have been endlessly erected and then destroyed by the wash of wars that have swept past. In the Second World War, the Chapel there was used as an artillery spotting post and demolished by shell fire. In the drive to make a truly twentieth-century art of church architecture, which was launched by the Benedictine Père Couturier, Le Corbusier was approached to rebuild a modest chapel for Notre-Dame-du-Haut, one useful as a shrine throughout the year and capable of handling crowds of up to twelve thousand during the great annual pilgrimages.

Le Corbusier responded heroically to this challenge, much as his master, Auguste Perret, had for another war memorial, Notre Dame at Le Raincy, after the First World War.* He began by visiting the site, filling his notebook with sketches. He had noticed during his youthful knapsack journeys that the axis of the Parthenon relates to the mountains of Greece and the Mediterranean. So, at Ronchamp, he sought out clues from the four horizons, aiming to capture "an acoustic component in the domain of form." As he designed, Le Corbusier thus strove to evoke a plastic image that would function as a sounding board for some great voice, receiving and hurling back into the void a mighty dialogue between nature and man. It is a highly mystical concept, but it brought forth Le Corbusier's most astonishing creation of sculptural forms to date.

The church itself is first seen by the pilgrim approaching on foot as a great coif rising on the brow of the hill. The clerestory towers with three chapels, similar in shape to the stacks used to ventilate peasants' houses on the Greek island of Ischia, rise above the shell roof, which is modeled on a crab carapace Le Corbusier had picked up on the shores of Long Island. The walls, made of rubble left over from the previous chapel, are covered with concrete stucco whitewashed to bring out its rugged surface. The actual supports are columns buried within, and appear only where the space between wall and roof is left open. The walls themselves, arbitrarily thickened for plastic effect, are pierced by irregular windows, in which glass carrying

* See Chap. 3.

4·21–23 Three important Le Corbusier buildings in Ahmedabad, India: Mill Owners Association Building (1954; opposite page, left), open-faced Shodan villa (1956; opposite page, right), and the massive unfaced-brick Art Museum (1955; below).

votive prayers, written by Le Corbusier, is inserted (Figure 4·12).

The main entrance to the Chapel is through a glazed door covered with one of Le Corbusier's designs. Exterior pulpits serve during pilgrimages; the interior floor, which, following the line of the site, slopes toward the altar, is ill lighted, dark and brooding. Only the chapels, which glow a brilliant red as the light funnels down from the clerestories overhead, relieve the austerity. Emphatically, this is no "machine for praying," but a magnificently modulated piece of sculpture. As a combination of painting, sculpture, and architecture, it expresses all three sides of Le Corbusier's artistic genius, a unity achieved through the synthesis imposed by one man.

The new capital city of Chandigarh is unquestionably the most challenging commission that Le Corbusier has had. For once Le Corbusier could control the evolution of the city plan. He was also given the four major structures—Supreme Court, Secretariat, Assembly Building, and the Governor's Palace—to design. Starting with a dusty plain and a few mud-hut villages on the westward slope of the Himalayas, he has developed for the first time his concept of a twentieth-century city and created a whole range of dramatic, volumetric forms that will probably rank as his greatest architectural masterpiece, or perhaps his greatest failure.

The division of the Punjab between India and Pakistan in 1947 awarded the ancient capital city of Lahore to Pakistan, leaving India's 12,500,000 without a central seat of government. India's Prime Minister Pandit Nehru first commissioned Albert Mayer, a former lieutenant colonel in the United States Army, to draw up a city plan. Assisted by another American architect, Matthew Nowicki, whose brilliant career was cut short by a plane crash on his way back from India, Mayer laid out a flexible city plan. But when it came to implementing it, the Indian government wanted an economy-minded architect outside the dollar area. In 1950 the choice narrowed down to Le Corbusier.

It took Le Corbusier only six weeks camping on the site to evolve his master plan for a city of 150,000 (first stage), which could expand later to 500,000. The impressive state buildings, he decided, would lie at the top of the slope silhouetted against the background of the distant Himalayas, with the civic center in the center and the residential quarters arranged in self-contained blocks down the slope. Factories, when they came, would be placed on the outskirts.

Le Corbusier used two basic systems to organize the site: the grid and the sector. The basis for the grid was Le Corbusier's system of segregating traffic, dramatized as the Seven Vs (from the French *voie*, or "way"): Superhighways were designated V-1, and the routes downgraded to V-6 (driveway) and V-7 (bicycle paths). Key routes for Chandigarh are V-3s (fast-moving traffic), which enclose a residential sector of approximately 240 acres, designed to hold some fifteen thousand inhabitants. These sectors, twenty-five in all, are inward-looking, semiself-contained neighborhoods, each facing on its own bazaar street, which runs

irregularly through the sector, with buildings on the shady side and off-street parking. At right angles to these are bands of open space, running from sector to sector, which are used for leisure and sports. Housing fills up the rest, in this case designed by his cousin, Pierre Jeanneret, and the British husband-and-wife team of Jane Drew and E. Maxwell Fry.

"No idea taken from folklore or art history can be allowed to weigh in an enterprise where buildings are constructed in mass concrete," Le Corbusier decided. "The whole problem here is one of construction. The esthetic which arises from this will be entirely new." [14] At the end of his first visit, Le Corbusier had what he terms a "revelation," namely that sun and rain are the two controlling factors: "The problem of shade can be taken as problem number one." Le Corbusier's solution was thus to make the roof both parasol and umbrella, the façade a continuous covering of sun breakers.

The first building to incorporate this parasol concept was Chandigarh's Supreme Court, a towering structure topped by a curving concrete roof, beneath which the façade is broken into a honeycomb of sun breakers (Figure 4·27). Within, the structure is hollowed out, much as was the Villa Savoye, to provide tremendous interior ramp accesses up through the building (Figure 4·26). The judges' chambers are decorated by large-scale Le Corbusier tapestry murals, brilliant touches of color which have not pleased all the judges, several of whom have asked that they be removed. From afar the building, with its reflecting pool, appears like an immense theatrical backdrop, a feeling heightened on approaching by the slashes of color incorporated into the recesses and sun breakers, and the drab, discolored end walls.

Le Corbusier's second building, the Secretariat, is actually eight buildings in one, housing the multiple ministries of government. It is a superblock to end all superblocks, with the access ramps this time placed on the exterior, and the façades enlivened and energized by Le Corbusier's apparently endless ability to improvise cubist forms as sun breakers and balconies, some two thousand units in all. Le Corbusier's plan for the Governor's Palace, with joyous sculptural cantilevers on the roof garden, and the Palace of the Assembly, its tapered hollow form rising to the open sky (Le Corbusier foresees a possible revival of sun festivals), will be culminating works when finished. The final stamp of Le Corbusier's hand will be a whole series of Le Corbusier sculpture to be erected on a 400-yard esplanade between the Parliament and Supreme Court. Here he plans to set up the "modular," the "Harmonic Spiral," and his favorite theme, "The Open Hand," the last a huge piece to be constructed of sheet metal mounted on ball bearings (to act as a weather vane) and coated with orange, white, and green enamel. The particular area reserved for this sculpturesque gesture of friendship has already been evacuated and dubbed, none too happily, "The Depth of Consideration."

Le Corbusier today could afford to rest triumphant if he were the sort to rest in any manner at all. A capital city is being raised under the sign of the future and in his name. The superblock he first

4·24–27 Chandigarh, new capital of the Punjab, is Le Corbusier's most ambitious project to date—a triumph over primitive methods and materials. To combat the sun, elaborate sun breakers were devised for the Secretariat, a superblock of eight buildings (left). In the Supreme Court, interior space was hollowed out to allow air circulation (below); court is topped by a concrete parasol (right). Project includes play sculpture (top).

4·28 In Le Corbusier's more recent work we find a strong tendency to emphasize the sturdy, masculine qualities inherent in roughly shaped reinforced concrete. In Unité d'Habitation at Nantes (1958; above) he has used such concrete to create textured, rhythmic forms that cantilever out over the river bed.

4·29–31 A strong but perplexing building is the Dominican monastery (opposite) at Evreux, France. Dynamic forms seem to glory in the uncompromising quality of raw concrete. The monastery contains an interior courtyard with a pyramidal oratory.

on precision, shallow cubist space, and volumes, Le Corbusier today has moved steadily in the direction envisioned in the 1920s has come to pass. Much as Frank Lloyd Wright in his later years was able to draw on a whole backlog of design, Le Corbusier is seeing projects such as his Endless Museum, conceived thirty years ago, built in India and Japan (Figure 4·23). Le Corbusier forms can be seen in Africa, South America, and Asia.

Far from being static, Le Corbusier in recent years has shown a whole new direction which seems at a number of points to contradict his own earlier premises. Beginning with a machine esthetic based

of sculpturesque form, rugged surfaces, deep recesses, and an almost primitive evocation of deep primordial emotions. It is significant that in one of his late buildings, the convent of La Tourette (Figure 4·30), the roof was left unplanted, to be seeded in good time by whatever trees, shrubs and flowers the winds and birds might chance to bring. Nature is no longer to be challenged but to be worked with, an almost Wrightian concept. In Le Corbusier's Brazilian Pavilion at the University of Paris, completed nearly three decades after his famous Swiss Pavilion, forms no longer rise effortlessly but lie heavy and massive—brooding shapes, brutal and unrelenting.

That this new direction in Le Corbusier's work flows logically out of his concern for sculpture is, of course, obvious. But it also points to a deep schism developing within the once solid ranks of modern architecture. On one hand Ludwig Mies van der Rohe has disciplined and refined steel until it has become in one of Mies's own phrases "almost nothing." Le Corbusier, on the other, seeks to overpower by the very mass and crudity of reinforced concrete. Either direction pursued by less than a genius can produce architectural sports of grotesque proportions, monstrosities either of total aridity and monotony in glass and steel, or of elephantine lethargy in concrete.

In times past such widening polarities have been danger signs, ushering in periods fraught with feverish temptations toward mannerism and eclecticism. But such widening polarities also announce the possibility of a new synthesis, one that may already be emerging, where steel will be used as sensitively as nerve fibers, and concrete, no longer gross and heavy, will be stretched until it becomes little more than a membrane. For architecture endures longer than man. And each end is in itself a new beginning.

5 : **WALTER GROPIUS** :

*Idea and experience will never coincide
in the center. Only art and action can
effect a synthesis.*

GOETHE (TO SCHOPENHAUER)

The new architecture could be seen emerging throughout Europe in the 1920s. In Germany the dominating figure was Walter Gropius, one of the century's great organizing geniuses. The role Gropius played vastly exceeded designing his own buildings, for though he was a pioneer in his own right and a superb coordinator, he was that rare personage, a natural teacher and leader. In Germany he gave a sense of unity and direction to the fusion of art, design, and architecture. In the United States, where Gropius arrived to teach at Harvard in 1937, he ushered in a new age for American architecture that can be compared in importance only to the impact of the 1913 Armory Show in the realm of American painting.

Significantly, the importance of Gropius's teaching cannot be identified with any one form. Once, comparing himself to Frank Lloyd Wright, Gropius explained why this is so: "I think of Wright as creating very unusual, dramatic beauty. I am interested in finding the common denominator—anonymous architecture, entity." Gropius believes such architecture can be evolved though synthesis and organization and predicts, "In the future,

there will be more teamwork—teamwork of the structural engineer, the acoustical engineer, the sociologist, and all the other people needed to arrive at a good conception. The Architect should be the coordinator." [1]

There has probably never been a more successful revolution than the one Gropius presided over, beginning in Weimar, Germany, shifting in 1925 to Dessau, and ending finally with a champagne toast in a remodeled factory on the outskirts of Berlin in 1933. The name of this triumphant movement was the Bauhaus (literally "building house"), and to designers and architects the world over it stands for one of the brightest periods of modern architecture's first heroic age, the school where artist, craftsman, and architect established the grammar of design suited to twentieth-century mass production.

Today the Bauhaus, much like the jazz age, has taken on the nostalgia of the newly remote. Even the Bauhaus school's proud slogan "Art and technology, the new unity" today seems self-evident. In a direct sense, the actual Bauhaus was the victim of savage repression by the Nazis. Today the actual

THE TRIUMPH OF AN IDEA

5·2 Bauhaus, Dessau, Germany (1926), most famous modern structure of the twenties.

Bauhaus buildings, once gleaming white examples of the best in modern design, have been capped with a fake gabled roof, and the sheer sheets of glass façades have been bricked up. The brilliant staff that once gathered there has long since scattered. Yet today there is hardly a poster, advertising page, sign post, label, or book jacket that does not owe something to their pioneering. In exhibition techniques, the Bauhaus established standards and methods that still dominate today. Its ''basic design course,'' which emphasizes close personal experience with the primary materials of building, is now an accepted part of architectural school curriculum. From furniture and textiles to architecture, the Bauhaus concepts have become the usable past for modern architects.

It is the fate of all architectural movements, however, that they tend toward a style, which in itself is a lifeless thing, a sort of abandoned carapace which proclaims that the organic life once housed within is now dead. As a result, the truly great achievements of the Bauhaus tend to become accepted, while its design clichés, such as flat roofs, ribbon windows, and asymmetrical organization of cubed masses, now obtrude. Today we no longer see modern architecture solely as the white box with chrome chairs and angular, abstract lighting fixtures. But if Bauhaus design seems frozen, its dynamic approach to design does not. As a methodology, the Bauhaus has spread to every land where modern architecture is practiced.

The man destined to give form and method to this idea was born in Berlin on May 18, 1883. His father was a high government official on Berlin's Building Commission. His great uncle had been an architect, and Gropius as a schoolboy had delighted in building every bridge described in Caesar's *Commentaries.* The family offered no resistance when, at the age of eighteen, he announced that he too intended to be an architect. But the Beaux-Arts system of education then being taught left Gropius profoundly dissatisfied. Over his father's stern objections, he left Munich's Technische Hochschule. He traveled first for a year through Spain, Italy, and Holland, then tried his hand at designing workmen's houses on his uncle's estate in Pomerania, a clear indication of the profound concern with the social aspects of architecture which has never been wholly absent from his thinking.

"When I was a boy, the mental climate was static, becalmed by an unshakable conception of eternal truth," Gropius once recalled. "I for my part was attracted to the struggles of Ruskin and Morris to reunite the world of art with the world of work, but I rejected their anachronistic denial of the machine." The one German architect who at that time seemed intent on finding an architecture that would express the machine, rather than deny it, was Peter Behrens (1868–1940). When Gropius joined the staff in 1908 at the age of twenty-four, Behrens had just received the commission to design a factory for Germany's AEG (General Electric Company) and redesign the products. Behrens responded by designing the massive AEG Turbine Factory (1909), in which the powerful concrete

5·3 Fagus Works, Alfeld-an-der-Leine, Germany (1911), announced the arrival of the glass curtain wall in architecture.

corner piers, central glass windows, and arched roof were highly expressive of the product being manufactured within.

Behrens's architecture attracted the best young architects in Germany. Ludwig Mies van der Rohe received his architectural training there.* Le Corbusier † arrived from Paris, talking of the great French architect Auguste Perret. Gropius himself rose to become the top draftsman, but it was soon apparent that his mind was taking an independent line of thought. A year after he arrived in Behrens's office, he drew up a memorandum entitled *The Industrial Prefabrication of Houses on a Unified Basis*, a pioneering rationalization of the application of mass production to housing units.

His first opportunity to build on his own came in 1911, when at the age of twenty-eight he drew the plans for the Fagus Works (Figure 5·3) with Adolph Meyer. A utilitarian structure designed as a shoe-last factory, it employed a traditional structural system of brick columns with steel beams supporting the floor. What made it revolutionary was the use of steel window frames and metal spandrels organized as a continuous façade, one which Gropius daringly carried even around the corners. For the first time in industrial architecture, the corner piers had been "dematerialized." The way had been opened for the development of a system of suspended glass curtain walls, which has since become one of the salient characteristics of modern architecture.

A rallying point for German designers, industrialists, and architects interested in raising the level of German machine-made products was the Deutscher Werkbund, a group formed in 1907. This naturally attracted Gropius, and he soon became a leading figure, designing the exhibition factory for the Werkbund's 1914 exhibition in Cologne (Figure 5·4). This building today has a curiously eclectic look. The low doorway recalls Frank Lloyd Wright, whose work Gropius by then knew (though he was more impressed by Louis Sullivan's skyscrapers). There are also notes from Peter Behrens. But the façade had now become a glass screen to keep out rain, cold, and noise. At the corners Gropius placed circular stairways sheathed in glass, architectural details no eye could miss. Although some exhibition visitors muttered about working like exposed goldfish, the building was an amazing

* See Chap. **6**.
† See Chap. **4**.

5·4 Deutscher Werkbund exhibition office, Cologne (1914), designed with Adolf Meyer. The building had a Wrightian entrance, was dramatized by glass-enclosed staircases.

tour de force at the time and established Gropius's reputation, at the age of thirty-one, as Germany's most promising young architect.

Gropius served as a German officer in the First World War with distinction, inventing a signaling device and surviving the pulverizing combat of the Western Front (he was once buried alive, another time shot down in an airplane). On infrequent leaves he learned that the Grand Duke of Saxe-Weimar was planning to make Weimar, Goethe's birthplace, a center of the arts. Henry van de Velde, head of the Belgian *art nouveau* movement, suggested Gropius as the obvious leader. Back at the front, Gropius drew up plans for unifying the Grand Ducal Academy of Fine Arts and the Weimar Arts and Crafts School into a "consulting art center for industry and the trades."[2]

On April 1, 1919, while gaunt war veterans roamed the streets and the German National Assembly debated whether it could, with honor, ratify the peace treaty, Gropius carried his plan into execution and founded the Bauhaus. Its first manifesto left no doubt that its aims were nothing short of revolutionizing both architecture and the state of design: "The complete building is the final aim of the visual arts. . . . Architects, sculptors, painters, we must all turn to the crafts."

"Art and technology, the new unity"—that was the slogan. Gropius was aware that the machine was slowly strangling the individual craftsman; a yawning gap was widening between thinking and doing, between the skilled designer who could conceive of a new form and the skilled carpenter or metalsmith who could execute it. What was needed, if the machine age was not to inundate society with ill-fashioned and malfunctioning objects, was a new kind of creative man, both designer and craftsman, one who could discipline and exploit the technology of machine production. The Bauhaus oriented its whole curriculum toward creating such modern-design craftsmen and in the process became the greatest laboratory for design and architecture in this century.

Gropius insisted that all beginning students work directly with materials in the shops. He instituted a revolutionary six-month introductory course in which students folded paper, sketched wood grains, experimented with color to learn the quality of pencil, brush, color forms. The aim of the course, first conducted by a Swiss painter, Johannes Itten, and later expanded by Herbert Bayer and Moholy-Nagy, was to startle the students into thinking inde-

pendently about form and materials. As Gropius was later to confess, "At the Bauhaus, we deliberately destroyed when the students set out to imitate. No, they must be themselves. The best teacher of all in this, I think, was Josef Albers. He would throw them in, and when they were drowning, then maybe he could help them, make them independent." For architectural students accustomed to designing merely on paper, this direct contact with materials and forms had an invigorating effect.

"As art is not one of those things that may be imparted, it depends on individual talent whether a design be the outcome of skill or creative impulse. But if what we call art cannot be taught or learned, a thorough knowledge of principles and sureness of hand can be." So Gropius faced the task of drawing up a three-year curriculum. To assist him he had one of the greatest faculties ever assembled, including, in the Swiss-born Paul Klee and Russian-born Wassily Kandinsky, two of the half dozen greatest artists of the first half of the twentieth century. Master of the carpentry shop was a young Hungarian, Marcel Breuer,* who in 1925 designed the tubular steel chair and was destined to become a leading modern architect and Gropius's long-time collaborator. Another Hungarian, Ladislaw Moholy-Nagy, made experiments with abstract pho-

* See Chap. 9.

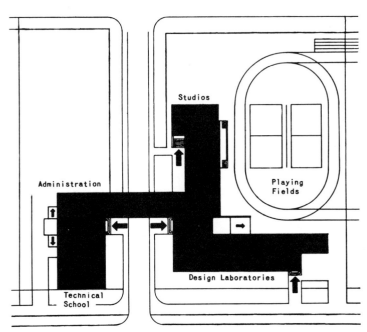

5·5–6 In the Bauhaus building, voids were given more importance than solids. Glass brought corners into light and white walls seemed to hover in space; planning was asymmetrical.

Studios

Administration

Playing Fields

Design Laboratories

Technical School

tography, including paintings made directly on film with light ("photograms"). Herbert Bayer experimented with typography, introducing techniques that are now standard in both book and magazine layouts and in commercial advertising. Cross-fertilizing the technical orientation of many of the faculty and students were painters like Josef Albers, who experimented with turning broken bottles into stained-glass windows, and Oskar Schlemmer, who in addition to decorating the buildings with murals, designed ballets. The result was an extraordinary atmosphere in which all traditional forms were questioned, and new materials exhaustively examined for clues to new and better design.

From this ferment emerged an esthetic based on lightness, clean lines, extreme functionalism.* Ex-

* Although Gropius's intention was not to found a conscious style, the Bauhaus production does reflect the esthetic of the de Stijl group then active in Holland, whose leader, Theo van Doesburg, lectured at the Bauhaus during its early period but never became a member of the faculty. Gropius has said, "Of course there was influence. And if you see it in Mies van der Rohe's floor plans, there is something in it. But Van Doesburg, who wanted to penetrate the Bauhaus, never really did. We had to have a certain harmony. Neither Klee nor Kandinsky wanted him; we all felt he was too theoretical. And he did no building. His three basic colors—what he called 'ground color' (red, blue, yellow, plus black and white) were influential, but really Piet Mondrian had more to do with that."

haustive attention was paid to designing each item, whether an ash tray or tapestry, for eventual machine production. For this was to be design for the machine age, and if today a host of Bauhaus-designed objects have passed into common usage, it is because this goal was constantly adhered to.

From the beginning the Bauhaus had insisted that the final aim of the visual arts was the building. When the Bauhaus moved to Dessau, Germany, in 1925—Weimar's enthusiasm having rapidly turned to open hostility—Gropius resolved that the Bauhaus should have its own permanent headquarters. These buildings (Figure 5·5) designed by Gropius became the living example of the new standards being pioneered by the Bauhaus and a prototype for larger industrial buildings still being produced thirty years later. The pinwheel plan is similar to the Fagus Works, with the buildings composed in functional groupings and connected by overhead passages, a favorite Gropius device. The larger areas were used as the design shops, dining areas with a dormitory, signaled by its projecting dormitories, in the rear. The glass façades Gropius introduced with the Fagus Works are now treated as major architectural elements, creating whole walls of shimmering glass and corners which offered the then novel effect of allowing one not only to see through them but also to see around them, much as cubist paintings sometimes presented

simultaneous views of the front and side of a head.

Since such asymmetrical planning has become commonplace, it is difficult to realize the initial impact of this new architecture in which there was, properly speaking, no front and no rear. In place of the formal balance of Beaux-Arts planning, unity is achieved by the standard bay spacings which set up their own rhythm. The surface of the building also has been transformed. Gone are the heavy corner piers and layer-cake embellishments at each story. Instead the concrete verticals seem to float like crisp, clean ribbons. The traditional factory structure has been metamorphosed into an envelope containing a new environment, machine-made and coolly functional. It created a form world where abstract composition takes the place of ornament, and uncluttered space, impersonal and unemotional, reigns supreme. Furnished completely with Bauhaus-designed objects, from the furniture of Marcel Breuer to light fixtures, the Bauhaus buildings proclaimed a new order in architecture. It was unquestionably the most important modern building of the 1920s, and a landmark in the emerging international modern style.

In 1928 Gropius decided to return to private practice, and after a quick trip to the United States, focused on the problem that had been his first love, low-cost housing. With Marcel Breuer, Gropius had already evolved a plan for a high-rise apartment

5·7 Berlin-Siemensstadt apartment house (1929), a line of 3½-room flats perpendicular to main thoroughfare to give maximum light and space. Designed after Gropius left the Bauhaus, it seemed stiff and military but was a vast improvement over rectangular blocks built around a dark court.

house in the form of a thin slab eleven stories high which would feature cantilevered balconies and a communal floor half way up the structure. This project remained for Gropius a will-o'-the-wisp for several decades, illusively evading his strenuous efforts to have such a structure erected. But in the Berlin-Siemensstadt in 1929, he was able to captain a group effort (Figure 5·7) which produced a series of relatively low apartment houses, placed at right angles to the street and surrounded by forest. Today they have a rather regimented look, but they were as fine as any pre-Second World War apartments built in Germany and suggest the brilliant architectural future Germany might have had.

Gropius, in fact, was facing a rapidly deteriorating situation within Germany. Hitler was coming to power, and in 1934 the Nazis made it clear that modern architecture (Hitler called it ''oriental'')

5·8 Exhibit designed with Joost Schmidt for the Non-Ferrous Metal Exhibition, Berlin (1934), dramatizes strength of metal.

had no place in the Third Reich. The same year Gropius transferred his practice to England, where his new partner became E. Maxwell Fry (who later was to collaborate with Le Corbusier in the building of housing units for Chandigarh, India).

By far the most important work Gropius produced during his three years with Fry in England was the design of Impington Village College (1936), in Cambridgeshire. This single-story complex used Gropius's familiar pinwheel pattern, placed the classrooms at ground level and one room deep off a single corridor. In many respects the plan, especially the classrooms, resembled the Corona School in Bell, California, designed the year before by Richard Neutra. Both schools found a responsive audience; Neutra established a new pattern for American school buildings, and Gropius set the pace for postwar school design in England.

In 1937 a whole new life opened for Gropius with the invitation to come to Harvard, first as professor of architecture and the next year as chairman of the department, a position he was to hold for fifteen vital years. It was a prophetic moment at the farewell dinner given by H. G. Wells in London when the noted critic Herbert Read declared, "Gropius belongs to the world." *

Gropius's task in the United States was to introduce a whole generation of eager young architects to the evolution of modern architecture in the 1920s and 1930s, and rarely has a teacher met with a more wholehearted response. Among modern architects today practicing in the United States, the front rank is still overwhelmingly composed of men who have been schooled by Gropius. "He was the first man who interpreted the industrial revolution to us in terms of architecture, in terms of design, in terms of community planning," one former student, Paul Rudolph,† wrote: "He constantly investigated the great potentials of industrial society and showed us how to assimilate them to our everchanging needs. . . . He has shown us a place in society and taught us that mechanization and individual freedom are not incompatible. . . . I shall always doubt that a lesser human being could have given us that new faith in our world." [3]

The theme of Gropius's Harvard training was stated in his belief "In an age of specialization, method is more important than information." [4] But in stressing that the method of approach must come first and the forms later as a logical outgrowth of the problem posed, Gropius found himself in the ironic position of warning his students against just those hallmarks of 1930 modern style (flat roofs, stucco façades, ribbon windows) he had been so influential in establishing but which were rapidly becoming shibboleths. "You are done with aping Europe," he told them, and vigorously criticized those who would make modern architecture a "style as snobbish as any of the older academic fashions which it aims to displace." Even functionalism, he found, was becoming equated with a mechanistic approach that was far from his intention: "Functionalism has only to do with material things," he pointed out. "There has always been a psychological side as well. Architecture starts beyond all practicalities. The prerequisites of the building have to be there. That is engineering. Architecture begins where engineering ends."

* See Chap. 17.

† The Bauhaus influence was also spread widely with the emigration to the United States of many of the key Bauhaus personnel, including Herbert Bayer, Marcel Breuer (at Harvard), Josef Albers (at Black Mountain College and Yale), Moholy-Nagy (founder of the Institute of Design in Chicago), Ludwig Mies van der Rohe (director of architecture at Chicago Illinois Institute of Design).

5·9 Gropius's house, Lincoln, Massachusetts (1937). International Style principles, with dramatically juxtaposed solids and voids, were adapted to the wood-construction tradition of New England. Open space became an integral part of the house.

Gropius, for his part, also discovered that the new cultural and technological environment of the United States was forcing him to adjust his basic precepts. His partner in Cambridge, Massachusetts, during this transition stage was Marcel Breuer (1938–1941), and the two men produced a series of houses and building projects which show a steady assimilation of new experiences.

Gropius's house (Figure 5·9) in Lincoln, Massachusetts, is an early and highly successful example. The volumes are still organized in a series of interpenetrating solids and voids, but the use of wood, employed as vertical sidings rather than horizontal clapboards, is new. So is the use of the outdoor screened porch, a fixture in traditional American houses but here exploited as an architectural unit rather than an appendage. Perhaps the most significant thing of all is the manner in which the house now reaches out into space to establish a reciprocal relationship with nature. In the New World the sense of freedom had made obsolete the necessity to armor the house against the outsider, a fact emphasized by a freely accessible exterior circular stairway.

In public housing Gropius and Breuer also showed a new flexibility in their awareness of site. The New Kensington, Pennsylvania, housing development (1941), which made use of the new wood vernacular the two architects had developed, was essentially a group of low-rise defense housing units. But the units were distributed unevenly about the hilly site in a far more relaxed and reciprocal manner than the military stiffness of Gropius's Berlin-Siemensstadt.

An even stronger proclamation of principles is the Harvard Graduate Center (Figure 5·10), built on a restricted budget between 1949 and 1950. For a university long committed to red brick and neo-Georgian design, it marked a bold move at the time. But for all the obvious pains taken in its design, it remains a curiously flat and unexciting series of buildings. The planning is open, with the dormitories linked by covered walks. The large common room is designed with steel and declares its special importance with a curved façade. Buff-colored brick has been substituted for white stucco, but the over-all effect is more a collection of modern art clichés than a restatement of principles

5·10–11 Harvard Graduate Center, Cambridge, Massachusetts (1945–1949), was conceived as a basically horizontal mass, with covered walks, cantilevered balconies for students' rooms (below), and interlocking horizontal elements in buff brick (above). Although an abrupt change from the university's Georgian-style buildings, the center looks more to the 1920s.

looking toward the future. Even the presence of paintings by Miró, sculpture by Arp, and screens by Josef Albers do not quite kindle the excitement that the architects had hoped for. The Harvard Graduate Center is the work of The Architects Collaborative (TAC), the younger architects Gropius assembled in 1946 to put into effect his cherished concept of group practice.* "I believe the result of a well-oiled team is greater than the sum of their ideas," Gropius states. "We tear each other's ideas to pieces, and nobody takes it on the wrong shoulder." Such a group-practice idea has worked well for Gropius, allowing him to be "job captain" on those projects he is particularly concerned with, at the same time guaranteeing that the architecture produced from the TAC office will remain at a consistently high level. TAC has been responsible for some of New England's best school building, including the Chandler Street Junior High School and the plan for Boston's New Civic Center, designed in 1953 with Pietro Belluschi, Walter F. Bogner, Carl Koch and Associates, and Hugh Stubbins, Jr.

* Composed of one Harvard-trained architect, John Harkness, and six Yale-trained architects, Norman Fletcher, Jean Fletcher, Robert McMillan, Louis McMillen, and Benjamin Thompson.

In this rather Orwellian "partnership of equals," Gropius has had to assume a major role on the most important projects, including the United States Embassy at Athens (Figure 5·12) and the nine-story apartment house in Berlin's Interbau development, the first major building Gropius has erected in Berlin in almost thirty years.

TAC's most exciting, and certainly most romantic, project in years is the design of the $70-million-dollar University of Baghdad on the banks of the Tigris (Figure 5·13). This project is doubly interesting because it marks Gropius's involvement with the whole new world of concrete-shell construction, a construction system he not only welcomes but suggests "may lead to the roof becoming the building itself, enclosing universal space, while the rest is flexible accessories."

While Gropius shows both great courage and capacity for growth, he finds himself in the position of the senior statesman whose policies have yet to be fully implemented: "Our generation is presented with the same challenge as were the founders of our Western Culture, the Greeks, when they deliberately buried the treasures and temples of their former existence under the triumphant symbol of their newfound freedom: the Acropolis. We certainly do not face our existence with anything

5·12   United States Embassy, Athens (1961), in Pentelic marble, has classic overtones.

5·13 Baghdad University, an Architects Collaborative project designed with structural engineer Paul Weidlinger. Reinforced concrete is used in post-and-lintel and shell structures like double-ended auditorium. University will eventually house 12,000.

like the same spirit.'' [5] For Gropius, the answer is for the architect, as coordinator, to redefine ends, rather than become wholly absorbed by means: ''We have amassed such a tremendous arsenal of techniques that their bristling display has nearly robbed us of our sense of balance,'' Gropius said when receiving the American Institute of Architects' gold medal in 1959. ''Our cities have taken on the look of a free-for-all, wild competition to engage the mind, heart and body of its populace, and all sense of propriety and discrimination seems to have been swept away by this unlimited technological dam-burst.'' [6]

As a preachment against the chaos of the present urban scene, few architects would gainsay Gropius's urgent plea for rational planning. Gropius's lifelong campaign to bring about a cohesion of effort directed at a common goal is too evident to need underscoring. It is one of the great losses in modern architecture that he has never been able to implement his various city-planning schemes. And yet Gropius's belief that design can be a cooperative effort at the level of a single building, or even a small group of buildings, is widely disputed. Architecture, perhaps, is not a matter for a committee. This conviction that the act of giving form in any art must finally depend on one artist's hand has become the rallying point for a significant sector of the younger generation to whom the Bauhaus is the New Academy.*

Gropius's undisputed contribution, however, has been as the method giver of the new architecture. Probably Ludwig Mies van der Rohe, in a birthday speech celebrating Gropius's seventieth birthday, stated it better than anyone: ''The Bauhaus was not an institution with a clear program. It was an idea, and Gropius formulated this idea with great precision. He said, 'Art and technology— the new unity.' He wanted to have painting, sculpture, theater and even ballet on the one hand, and on the other, weaving, photography, furniture— everything from the coffee cup to city planning. The fact that it was an idea, I think, is the cause of this enormous influence the Bauhaus had on any progressive school around the globe. You cannot do that with organization, you cannot do that with propaganda. Only an idea spreads so far.'' [7]

* See Chap. 20.

5·14 Pan Am Building, a fifty-nine-story behemoth atop Grand Central Terminal, is Manhattan's largest single building. Designed by Emery Roth & Sons, then revised by Walter Gropius and Pietro Belluschi, the structure reflects the cult of bigness, introducing a scale of building that may tax existing traffic facilities.

6 : MIES VAN DER ROHE :

THE ARCHITECT OF STEEL

A new look in architecture has spread across the United States today. Huge office buildings are wrapped in towering façades of glass held in place by delicate, geometric patterns of mullions and spandrels. These are the product of the most advanced technology on earth; into them goes larger and ever-larger expanses of glass tinted to defeat the sun, aluminum anodized all colors of the rainbow, and incredibly thin sandwich panels coated with plastics. In such buildings man can work in a nearly totally controlled environment serviced by soundless elevators, huge tunnels of conditioned air, miles upon miles of electrical wiring, and banks of incandescent lights.

The presiding genius, disciplinarian, and conscience of this new age of steel is the German-born Chicago architect Ludwig Mies van der Rohe, and his Seagram Building on Manhattan's Park Avenue is the most somber masterpiece of them all. His esthetic dictum "less is more" is today as well known as Sullivan's "form follows function." There is hardly an American architect of the second generation who has not felt the tonic effect of Mies's doctrine that in structure, and the expression of structure, lies the essence of architecture. In the midst of everyday shifts of style he stands as the greatest moral force in American architecture today.

It is doubtful if Mies van der Rohe could have been nurtured in any but a European environment, just as it is impossible for him to have realized his projects in any place other than the United States, the preeminent citadel of technology and steel. Even his birthplace, the ancient city of Aachen (Aix-la-Chapelle), where he was born on March 27, 1886, contributed to his education. As a young boy, he was taken by his mother to the magnificent ninth-century cathedral founded by Charlemagne, and there received his first lessons in architecture as he whiled away time during early-morning Mass counting the stones and tracing the joints.

Such a medieval environment combined with the devout religiousness of his mother may well have influenced Mies in a more profound way. Even today he infuses his thinking with a deep need for central principles, for a strict and almost predestined order of things. His favorite reading is the father of German mysticism, the fourteenth-century writer Meister Eckhart. St. Augustine's "beauty is the splendor of truth" remains Mies's byword. "I hope you will understand that architecture has nothing to do with the invention of forms," Mies tells his students. "It is not a playground for children, young or old. Architecture is the real battleground of the spirit. Architecture wrote the history of the epochs and gave them their names. Architecture depends on its time. It is the slow unfolding of its form." [1]

From his father, a stonemason, Ludwig Mies * learned the exacting standards of a stonecutter's craft. The necessity for discipline was doubly driven home when as a young boy he took his first turn at bricklaying. When one brick at the base was discovered to be slightly out of line, Mies was ordered to tear down the wall and begin over again. To this day, he is fond of saying, "Architecture begins when you place two bricks carefully together." The emphasis is on the word "carefully."

A broader world opened when, at the age of fifteen, he was apprenticed to a local architect. His tasks involved endless detailed drawings of Renaissance stucco ornaments. But in a desk drawer in the drafting room he discovered one of the *avant-garde* magazines of the day, complete with a bibliography of recent articles on art and architecture. Mies then decided to divide his pay, one half to his father, the other half for cigars (to this day an addiction) and books. "I have tried to find out what was essential in our time," he has explained. "Some people pray for this; I read for it." [3]

At the age of nineteen, Mies finished his ap-

---

* He added "van der Rohe," his mother's name, in the early 1920s to give his signature to articles in German periodicals a more impressive sound, remarking, by the way, "I certainly owe as much to my mother as my father" (see note 2).

prenticeship and set out for Berlin, first working with Bruno Paul, the designer then making some of the first mass-produced furniture. Three years later, in 1908, he joined the office of Peter Behrens, where Walter Gropius was in charge.* The three years Mies spent in Behrens's office was a period of great inner turmoil for all architects. "Our enthusiastic hearts demanded the unqualified, and we were ready to pledge ourselves to an idea," Mies wrote, "but the potential vitality of the architectural idea of the period [*art nouveau*] had by that time been lost." [4] In his search for "an idea" that could win his allegiance, Mies found indications of a new and more inspiring architecture in the works of the Dutch architect Hendrik Petrus Berlage (1856–1934). While carrying out a commission in The Hague, Mies went daily to visit Berlage's Stock Exchange, where the façade and inner walls were treated as flat planes in brick. Pillars and columns were presented as structural elements, without capitals; the steel arches that held up the great glass roof were austerely treated and painted in black for emphasis. Not only did Berlage's work magnificently exemplify the restrained use of brick but it also held an even more important message: The building, as Berlage himself pointed out, had

* See Chap. 5.

". . . the quality which distinguishes monuments from the buildings of today: quiet!" [5] Quiet is what most distinguishes Mies's own work to this day.

In 1910 Mies felt the impact of an altogether unexpected force in European architecture—that of Frank Lloyd Wright, whose work was then on exhibition in Berlin and had just been illustrated in a handsome folio by the German publisher Ernst Wasmuth. "The work of this great master presented an architectural force, clarity of language, and disconcerting richness of form," Mies wrote in later years. "The dynamic impulse emanating from his work invigorated a whole generation. His influence was strongly felt even when it was not actually visible." [6]

Apparently no sure synthesis of these various influences was yet possible, at least for Mies. He had just time to turn out two houses before the First World War began and he found himself in uniform. On his return from the Western Front at the war's end, Mies moved into a large, white-walled room, set up two drafting tables supported on wood sawhorses, and turned his office into a place of study. It was during these postwar years—from 1919 to 1924—that modern architecture actually evolved, according to critic-architect Philip C. Johnson.[7] Mies's own contribution to this crucial period lies largely in study projects which, although not actually built, crystallized architectural thinking, not only for Mies but for his whole generation.

The first three of these studies concerned the nature of the skyscraper and office building. He began with projects for an ideal skyscraper (Figure 6·2) and constructed a model covered with glass. When he hung it outside his office window, he made a significant discovery: "The important thing was the play of reflections and not the effect of light and shadow as in an ordinary building." [8]

In 1922 Mies moved on to examine the problems of a relatively low-rise office building, for which he developed a concrete structure with ribbon win-

6·2 Model for a glass skyscraper is a study project developed by Mies van der Rohe in 1920 to 1921 to test the effect of a glass-curtain-wall facade. Such a sheer cliff of glass was not actually attempted until the UN Secretariat was built in 1950.

6·3 Floor plan of a brick country house, a project never built, demonstrates how Mies combined free-standing walls in dynamic geometric patterns. Design reflects Frank Lloyd Wright and de Stijl esthetic.

dows that ran around the corners and made the floors appear as so many floating bands of concrete. Next Mies focused his attention on the problem of residential architecture, grouping the two-story elevation in a series of cubes. The floor plan (Figure 6·3) shows a pattern altogether unexpected in Mies's work up to that date—a pinwheel pattern reminiscent of Frank Lloyd Wright's houses. Walls, rather than enclosing boxes, project out into space. Interior partitions, instead of surrounding the space, now channel it much as a series of screens would.

In this structure a second influence besides Wright was now operative in Mies's thinking—that of the Dutch group known as de Stijl (literally, "the style"), headed by Theo van Doesburg, including as its most talented member the painter Piet Mondrian. In two respects de Stijl principles have carried over into Mies's later work: first, in his over-all site planning, which often has the beauty of a Mondrian painting, and, secondly, in the manner by which Mies lets horizontal and vertical structural members appear to slide by one another rather than abut. The esthetic effect of this use of structural members had been foreshadowed by the de Stijl architect Gerrit Rietveld, whose furniture seems to be held together by some mysterious magnetism.

The influence of these projects of Mies's, as well as his own work with the Deutscher Werkbund exhibitions, led to Mies's appointment in 1927 as building director for one of the most ambitious modern architectural exhibitions ever conceived: a complete housing project in Stuttgart's Weissenhof area, to which would be invited sixteen of Europe's leading architects, including Walter Gropius, Le Corbusier, J. J. P. Oud, and Peter Behrens. Mies himself built one of the largest apartment houses, in which he employed a steel skeleton as a structure and achieved a great variety of interior arrangements through the use of movable plywood partitions. The impact of the Weissenhof project

on architectural thinking was extraordinary, for it marked the emergence of a clearly discernible style with its own trademarks—flat roofs, white stucco walls, ribbon windows, flexible interiors.

The prestige of the Weissenhof housing project established Mies van der Rohe's name among the leaders of modern architecture and led directly to his most luxurious public commission in Europe, the German Pavilion at the 1929 Barcelona Exposition (Figure 6·4). This building, which the critic Henry-Russell Hitchcock has called ". . . one of the few buildings by which the twentieth century might wish to be measured against the great ages of the past,"[9] revealed to the world the elegance, polish, and dignity of which the nascent modern style was capable.

"When the Barcelona pavilion came up," Mies said, "we were faced with the representation of grandeur. The government was to receive a king, a dictator, an ambassador—important people."[10] The setting Mies provided for such pomp and circumstance was faultless. It was also uncompromisingly modern, both in materials and technique. As the floor plan shows (Figure 6·5), both the Wright and de Stijl influences were operative but severely disciplined. The unifying element had become the roof, a clear rectangle, and the larger Roman travertine base. A strict distinction was maintained between the structural and nonstructural elements. The columns were left free-standing and sheathed with chrome, so that they functioned as decorative objects in their own right. The partitions were nonstructural, declared by their fragile materials—etched glass of gray and bottle green. A free-standing wall of onyx was used in the hall, and another wall of handsome green Tinian marble was carried out from under the roof to enclose a sculpture pool, in which Mies placed a work by George Kolbe to bring the composition into harmony. At the age of forty-three, Mies van der Rohe had created a masterpiece.

The Barcelona pavilion, for all its grace, was a

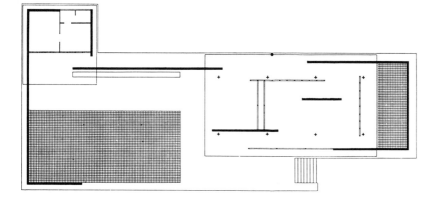

temporary exhibition building and was soon torn down. Architecture, however, inherited from it the loveliest of souvenirs—Mies's most famous piece of furniture, the "Barcelona" chair, perhaps the most beautifully designed object of this century. Today it is almost a permanent fixture in modern architecture, from the great office buildings of Manhattan to the Palace of the Dawn in Brasília. A commission that in 1930 promised far greater permanence was the Tugendhat house * in Brno, Czechoslovakia (Figure 6·7), after Le Corbusier's Villa Savoye, the most famous early modern house in Europe. The site itself, at the top of a sloping lawn, offered Mies an opportunity to exploit the view with floor-to-ceiling glass windows while masking the interior with solid walls on the uphill, approach side. The fame of the Tugendhat house, however, lies in its arrangement of the interior space, and in particular the 50- by 80-foot living area. This Mies left as one open space divided only by plane and curving partitions. The principal areas—living room, dining room, library, and entrance—are defined by the placing of a straight wall of onyx and curved wall of Macassar ebony.

6·4–6 German Pavilion at the Barcelona Exposition (1929) ordered its interior spaces geometrically by use of glass wall dividers. Separate structural columns sustain the roof.

* The hope for permanence was dashed in the Second World War, when it was first occupied by German troops and later bombed. Its present fate behind the iron curtain is not known.

6·7–8 Tugendhat house, Czechoslovakia (1930), was Mies's most elegant European residence and set standards of interior design for two decades. The open planning allowed for precise, formal groupings yet free flow of interior space.

"Mies gives as much thought to placing chairs in a room as other architects do to placing buildings around a square," Mies's biographer Philip Johnson has noted.[11] This is immediately evident in the study and living-room area (Figure 6·8), where the earlier Mies "MR" chairs are precisely positioned about the table, and a new chair, designed especially for this commission, is placed with equal precision in formal, ceremonial groupings to create the living room on the other side of the onyx wall. Equally arresting is the richness of the materials used—black and beige raw silk for the curtains, natural wool rugs, white vellum, with natural pigskin and pale green cowhide for the upholstery.

All this, combined with extraordinarily precise detailing (Mies even designed the tracks for the draw curtains), completes one of the great classic interiors of modern architecture. But it also required great austerity and restraint on the part of its owners. For where "less is more," clutter becomes almost a sacrilege. Perhaps few clients merit such superb architecture; certainly few could long tolerate such a goldfish-bowl existence.

Mies's triumphant surge to maturity at the beginning of the 1930s coincided with the steadily deepening world-wide Depression and the rise of Hitler. Both these facts were brought home to Mies by the fate of the Bauhaus. In 1930 he received an urgent visit from Walter Gropius and the mayor of Dessau, both begging him to take over the Bauhaus, which had steadily gone downhill since Gropius had left it in 1928. Reluctantly Mies agreed to "glue it together again,"[12] rented a factory on the outskirts of Berlin, and transferred all Bauhaus activities there. But it was already too late. Harassed by the Gestapo, Mies in 1933 ordered champagne and announced to the authorities that the Bauhaus would now, of its own free will, disband. This marked the end of a glorious chapter in the rise of modern architecture and exile for nearly all its founders.

Mies's opportunity to come to the United States came through a commission in 1937 from Mrs. Stanley Resor, wife of the president of the J. Walter Thompson advertising agency, to design a summer house in Jackson Hole, Wyoming. The friendliness Mies felt for America was warmly reciprocated by the architectural profession. John A. Holabird asked Mies to accept the position as director of architecture for Chicago's Armour Institute (later Illinois Institute of Technology), which he gladly accepted. On October 19, 1938, in the Grand Ballroom of Chicago's Palmer House, Mies was thus duly installed. It was an occasion as significant for the future of architecture in the United States as the appointment of Gropius at Harvard the year before. The event was given its tang of scandal, however, by Frank Lloyd Wright. Standing to address the audience, Wright said, "Now that Europe is taking over American architecture—and it serves them right, too—we can hope for ideals of an organic architecture to prevail. When these ideals do prevail, the entire structure of what we call education will lie down in the dust, and it will not even be a picturesque ruin. Organic architecture

6·9 Crown Hall, Illinois Institute of Technology, Chicago (1955), is in many ways the clearest statement of Mies's principles. The entire space is one great column-free room within which partitions may be placed to create areas of work or study. Such flexibility will make the space usable in other ways when functions change.

had to come from abroad. Be reconciled to that. I am. I give you Mies van der Rohe." [13]

As the applause subsided, Frank Lloyd Wright did the unexpected; he stalked from the head table and left in a sudden fit of pique. No one knew why. Mies had spent the weeks before at Taliesin as Wright's guest while he worked over his acceptance speech. The two men had spent hours in conversation. Pressed for an explanation in later years, Wright said, "I feel that the first setback for organic architecture, a true architecture of our own, was the Chicago fair of 1893. The second was the Bauhaus." [14] The breach steadily widened, reaching its climax when Wright peered at Mies's Seagram Building, called it "glassic architecture, an advertisement for a whisky company." As for Seagram's pools, Wright sniffed, "What are they? Puddles? First time I ever saw water misused as a material." [15]

The division between the two men is more than mere vanity; Mies in his understatement can be as arrogant as Wright, for all his rhetoric. It is a basic division in goals, methods, and ends of architecture —a polarity as strong as the age-old division between the classic and romantic. For Wright, architecture was a symphony embodying man's hopes and dreams; the machine was a tool for poets. For Mies, architecture was an expression of the essence of the twentieth century, in terms of technology,

science, and economics. The discovery of technology "can be compared only with the classic discovery of man as a person, the Roman will to power, and the religious movement of the Middle Ages," [16] Mies has stated. Architecture works with the given forms and strives to refine them. Just as Mies accepts the steel I-beam as it is extruded at the steel mill, he accepts the fact that twentieth-century cities will continue for a long time to be built upon the steel frame.

"The structural system is the essential element," he has said. "That, rather than craftsmanship, individual genius, or function of the building, determines its form. When we talk about structure, we don't say, 'What structure?' We just ask that it be a clear structure; that is all. If a new one is developed by the engineers, we are delighted to use it. The difference is that I really understand structure and don't deviate from it. I don't compromise. I'd rather sell potatoes than do that." [17]

No greater contrast exists than that between the campus which Mies van der Rohe designed for the Illinois Institute of Technology and Frank Lloyd Wright's University of Southern Florida (Figure 2·37). In Wright's work the free improvisations of T square and triangle are arranged to create an organization of forms responding to forms, space answering exotic space, until the final result stuns the sensibilities. Everything about Illinois Institute of Technology, however, is point and counterpoint, space against solid, vertical against horizontal, all maintained with a regular cadence that never falters.

The essence of I.I.T. is the grid of 24- by 24-foot spaces thrown like a net over the entire site. Each building is placed precisely in terms of these units, not face to face, but staggered so that they seem to slide, one past the next. The module for the buildings is equally rigid: Each bay measures 24 by 24 feet and is 12 feet high. "I had to decide on something that would not change, that would not be out of date by the time we had finished," Mies explains. "Structural architecture was the obvious answer. It doesn't cost as much, and it lasts longer. It is based on logic, not impulses." [18]

The vocabulary Mies developed as the common vernacular for the campus—buff-colored brick and exposed steel painted black—is deceptively simple. Each brick is placed with precision; the corners are studied with the intensity of an astronomer adjusting the Palomar telescope. Mies's stated goal is simply flexible and neutral space, but this does not mean that structure is denied its poetry. The very corner beams exposed with such exactitude are not structural (the weight-bearing elements are buried in the masonry wall); they fulfill the role of the classic pilaster, declaring the system of support within the building. Mies's corners involve some of the most beautifully proportioned details in modern architecture—or classic architecture, for that matter—but their essential role is disciplinary and esthetic, not functional.

By the time Mies van der Rohe had retired as director of architecture in September, 1958, Illinois Institute of Technology had eighteen buildings on its 110-acre site; another twenty to twenty-five buildings are required to complete the plan. But two buildings—the chapel (Figure 6·15), dedicated in 1952, and Crown Hall, the largest of the campus buildings, dedicated in 1955—are likely to remain the two structures in the whole complex by which Mies's genius will long be measured.

In designing the chapel, Mies was faced with the problem of what form it should take on a campus dedicated to science and technology. The answer was of necessity as equivocal as the role of religion itself in a science-oriented age: "A church or chapel should identify itself rather than rely upon the spiritual association or a traditional fashion in architecture, such as Gothic." His solution was straightforward—an enclosure measuring 60 by 37 feet, with the ceiling raised to 19 feet. The materials used were buff-colored brick, with glass from floor to ceiling. Floors are of gray terrazzo; the altar is a monolithic block of Roman travertine weighing 7½ tons. For the altar rail and cross,

Mies used gleaming stainless steel. "There is nothing spectacular about this chapel," Mies declared at its dedication. "It was meant to be simple. . . . In its simplicity, it is not primitive, not noble; and in its smallness it is great, in fact, monumental." [19]

Not all critics have been willing to follow Mies in his strong defense of the I.I.T. Chapel. Eero Saarinen's chapel for an equally scientifically oriented institution, Massachusetts Institute of Technology, indicates that elements of mystery, withdrawal, and reflection can suggest an entirely different form. Wright's Philadelphia synagogue evokes another set of intensely poetic responses, Le Corbusier's Ronchamp yet another. But for Mies, religion is no other-compartment of life, and his chapel, while it attracts few devotees, remains as a pristine, cool, and Euclidian view of the function of prayer, humility, and mystery in a technological age.

Few such hesitations greeted Crown Hall (Figure 6·9), the building which houses I.I.T.'s department of architecture and planning, surely one of Mies's great masterpieces. "Who else but Mies would think of suspending a roof from four gigantic girders, and then place the girders above the roof for all to see?" one architect exclaimed. Mies himself feels, "This is the first time that I have achieved really universal space in a completed building. . . . Other buildings on the campus . . . have at least some columns inside and so are not completely free." Why expose the girders? "It is a practical thing," Mies explains, "because it leaves the ceiling . . . free of interruption. But there is an esthetic reason too. A girder draws attention

6·10 Illinois Institute of Technology campus (1939–1958) is Mies's most nearly realized large project, entailing a master plan and eighteen completed buildings, all erected on a common module. Materials are exposed steel, glass, and buff-colored brick. The grid on which these buildings are designed emphasizes Mies's belief that "the spaces between buildings are just as important as the buildings."

6·13 Farnsworth house (right), Plano, Illinois (1950), is the purest statement of Mies's philosophy and gives point to his dictum that "less is more." The pavilion is refined to roof plate, travertine floor, eight I-beam supports, and glass walls.

6·11–12 860 Lake Shore Drive, Chicago (1951), is Mies's declarative statement of how high-rise structures should be expressed. The steel frame, painted black, organizes the facade by subdividing the glass walls. The two towers are set precisely at right angles. From within, the view is an exciting panorama of Chicago.

to the building and makes the design more interesting. A girder is nothing to be ashamed of!"

The space within Crown Hall is truly impressive. The main floor measures 120 by 220 feet of uncolumned space beneath the 20-foot-high ceiling suspended from the four massive exterior girders. Glass, partially frosted for privacy, encloses the building, which is essentially one great room. And it is toward such space, clear and unobstructed, that Mies has been striving. His reasons have, in fact, considerable historical justification. The street front of London's Regent Street and the façades along the Place de la Concorde have all remained unchanged over the centuries. But functions behind them have changed repeatedly. "You must design with that in mind," Mies points out. "Good design does not grow old."[20] Beginning with the open planning of the Barcelona pavilion with its freestanding walls, Mies has moved steadily in the direction of creating an architecture that would be in essence unobstructed space. This concept underlies Mies's striking Cullinan Hall addition to the Houston Museum of Fine Art (Figure 6·23) as well as his design, in reinforced concrete, for the Bacardi Company in Santiago, Cuba (Figure 6·22). Mies's plan for Chicago's Convention Hall, a project dated 1953, calls for a single space frame, square in plan (700 by 700 feet), to provide a single assemblage area for 50,000 people without any interior columns. As a basic guiding principle, Mies's concept of "universal space" is one of the most influential in mid-twentieth-century architecture. It also marks the end of the theory of functionalism as one of the strongest determinants in modern building design.

Much as Le Corbusier first developed a prototype house based on the esthetics of cubism, and then incorporated it in series to arrive at the beehive arrangement of his Unité d'Habitation in Marseilles, Mies van der Rohe evolved his concept of the house as a cube of glassed-in space; he then arranged the cubes vertically within the grid of a steel frame to arrive at his Chicago apartment houses. Underlying Mies's approach to housing is the same space concept used in his I.I.T. buildings, namely, that of open, usable space, unhindered by columns, where function can be defined by flexible room dividers and furniture grouping. Mies also insists that there be no division between the principles of industrial and domestic construction; these principles he carefully worked out in a summer house for Dr. Edith Farnsworth in Plano, Il-

linois (Figure 6·13), Mies's most important statement in residential architecture.

When the Farnsworth house was finished in 1950, it was described correctly as "a quantity of warmed and filtered air caught between floor and roof." *Architectural Forum* noted: "To many partisans of great architecture, it is the most important house completed in the U.S. since Frank Lloyd Wright built his desert home in Arizona a dozen years ago." In view of such praise, the house itself comes as something of a surprise—a kind of architecture that declares itself almost by its absence. In essence it is two raised platforms, justified in part as a protection against seasonal flooding from the nearby stream, each platform paved in travertine, one serving as the house, the other as the porch. To support the house cage, Mies set up eight 22-foot steel columns which are welded to the fascia beam above. The service core contains the kitchen and two bathrooms; a room divider separates the bedroom. Curtains are of raw silk; low cabinets (which also act as space dividers) are of primavera wood. As a pure composition, this is one of Mies's abso-

lute works.* It also suggests a public way of living unknown since the days of France's absolutist kings, when every private function from morning toilette to childbirth was performed in full view of the court. Obviously, as a solution to closely juxtaposed housing, such a display case is ludicrous. It is practicable only when the view itself can be considered the outer walls—which involves a considerable tract of land—or when such structures are stacked one on top of the other in skyscrapers.

The opportunity to expand into high-rise building came to Mies through Herbert S. Greenwald, a young theology student turned real-estater. Promontory Apartments, the first Mies-Greenwald venture, caused a wave of interest among Chicago architects; the next project, twin twenty-six-story apartment-house towers at 860 Lake Shore Drive. created a sensation (Figure 6·12). Here at last

* Such detailed planning, involving five years of work by Mies, can be deceptively simple. When Dr. Farnsworth discovered that the house cost $73,872 instead of the $40,000 she anticipated, she brought suit but eventually settled out of court.

6·14 Commonwealth Promenade, Chicago (1957), displays the vocabulary of construction developed and refined by Mies. As in Sullivan's skyscrapers, the building is raised off the ground. I-beams welded to the exterior serve as mullions to retain the glass, becoming at the same time decorative motifs. Small spaces are left between mullion elements to allow for heat expansion, more importantly to indicate that they are non-weight-bearing.

Mies was able to build an all-steel-and-glass skyscraper, the dream that had haunted him since his skyscraper sketches of 1920. The result, as Philip Johnson has pointed out, was to produce "a prototype for multi-story buildings which may become as influential in our era as Sullivan's skyscraper designs were in his." [21]

For the site on the shores of Lake Michigan, within easy driving distance of the Loop, Mies arranged his identical towers as two cubes deliberately set at right angles. "A clear block or tower is a clear shape," Mies points out. "This was the strongest form; it made the clearest shadow. The strongest shape for a building is the best shape for communicating strength." [22] The strength of the steel beams used allowed for apparent lightness, and to emphasize this Mies lifted the towers two stories high from their travertine base. Steel is apparent in the façade, with vertical I-beams welded to the steel frame where they can act as stiffeners and also serve as mullions for the floor-to-ceiling glass. In effect, Mies was borrowing his esthetic from the vocabulary of standardized steel shapes, thus forcing steel to produce its own decorative motif.

The apartment house at 860 Lake Shore Drive was not without faults. As a cooperative building, economies were considered necessary. Air conditioning, the *sine qua non* of a glass-walled structure, was omitted to make a $2,000-per-apartment saving, and the variety of sunshade devices required to make a glass building livable gave the façade a patchwork appearance, even though exterior curtains were of uniform material. Interior planning left some apartment owners with no choice but to leave their garbage cans at the front door. But these initial defects were easily remedied in Mies's next apartments. As structure after structure rose, it was only a matter of time before a bid would come from New York, the city of skyscrapers.

The commission, when it came, was for the Seagram Building on Park Avenue, a building certain to rank as one of Mies van der Rohe's greatest architectural statements To assist him, Mies appointed his former biographer, Philip Johnson,* as co-architect and the firm of Kahn & Jacobs to draft the working drawings. But to the astonishment of the assembled draftsmen, Mies's approach to design proved to be almost entirely cerebral. After listening carefully to the building's requirements for rent and office space, and then digesting

*See Chap. 15.

6·15 Illinois Institute of Technology Chapel (1952) is an austere structure deriving from Mies's belief that a religious edifice should be built with noble proportions and good materials. The altar is a monolithic block of Roman travertine; the cross is of stainless steel. Searching for a form to express the role of religion in a technological age, Mies emphasized structural clarity and precision but little of the mystery or withdrawal associated with contemplation.

New York's complicated building code, Mies withdrew to his hotel where he sat hours upon end quietly sipping whisky, enshrouded in a dense cloud of cigar smoke, until the design came clearly to his mind. To visualize it even more clearly, Mies ordered a model constructed of Park Avenue for the several blocks on either side of the building site, and then made his decision. "It was a clear conception from the start," Philip Johnson has said in admiration. "It was all there in Mies's first sketch. Once he had set it down, it did not change." [23]

The Seagram Building as it stands today at 375 Park Avenue is the finest steel skyscraper of the mid-twentieth century, a soaring, bronze-sheathed column rising thirty-eight stories from its 90-foot-deep pink granite plaza (Figure 6·20). It is also one of the most expensive (the estimated cost is 43 million dollars), the most precisely detailed (only $\frac{1}{16}$ inch tolerance was allowed in carrying out the 4 feet 7½ inches module, even in the interior office spaces and shower rooms) and the most elegantly appointed skyscraper Manhattan has ever seen.

The Seagram Building has its faults. The T shape, made necessary by the concrete sheer wall which acts as wind bracing in the rear, leaves an awkward distribution of interior space. Although the "bustle" at the rear (needed for additional office space) functions as concealment for the unsightly rear wall of the YWCA that stands behind Seagram's, it also encloses a vast interior area shut off from natural light. However, as a rigorously disciplined work of art, Seagram's is not soon likely to be surpassed. Fanatical attention was paid to precision and purity of design, even to the point of redesigning the door handles and mail chutes.

6·16–20 Seagram Building, 375 Park Avenue, New York (1959), is a thirty-eight-story bronze-sheathed tower piercing the Manhattan skyline (left). Facing 90-foot-deep plaza is pink granite (right, bottom), contrasting with the bustle of Park Avenue. Appointed elegantly within as without, Seagram is modern architecture's finest skyscraper and in many ways is a fulfillment of the form as first stated by Louis Sullivan.

Mies's genius for the austere use of rich, traditional materials has been noted before in such early works as the Barcelona pavilion and the Tugendhat house. With Seagram's, Mies was able to work with such materials on a monumental scale, from an architectural bronze the color of ancient bronze cannons, which sheathes the structure, to the severe, open plaza, which becomes both a great podium and an accent of calm in the heart of a busy city. To border the two sides of the plaza, Mies used a "permanent hedge" of green Italian marble set in massive blocks, each perfectly aligned. Within the cantilevered portico entrance, the massive elevator shafts rise like columns of Egyptian temples as the eye follows to the Picasso backdrop signaling the entrance to the 4-million-dollar Four Seasons Restaurant. Mass is everywhere apparent in this building, from the great columns that bring the structure to the ground to the welded bronze mullions holding the glass sheets in place. Throughout the Seagram interiors, mahogany paneling splined with stainless steel gives a rich glow to the stainless-steel furniture. By way of contrast, huge linear abstractions and swirling abstract-expressionist paintings decorate the interior walls.

Perhaps the most dramatic solution of all was the use of night illumination. During the day, Seagram's is protected from the sun by a specially made solar glass tinted a pink gray. At night, a luminous ceiling carried around the perimeter on each level of the building to a depth of 11½ feet is turned on by master switch; the great 520-foot façade glows like some gigantic Japanese shoji (Figure 6·16). As night architecture, Seagram's seems to reverse itself, changing from the weighty to the weightless, from light and shadow to a radiant, softly glowing image in which the interior lighting itself takes on the quality of a major structural material.

Seagram's, more than any other building, marks the realization of Mies van der Rohe as an architect. His emergence as a world figure was underlined by the award of the gold medal of the Royal Institute of British Architects (1959), the gold medal of the Architectural League of New York (1960), and the gold medal of the American Institute of Architects (1960). These awards are the highest the architectural profession has to offer; but even more significant is the spread of Mies's philosophy abroad. Increasingly as steel becomes available in other areas of the world, structures tend to reflect Mies's exacting discipline. Today, in the

6·22 Bacardi Office Building, Santiago de Cuba, shows Mies's plastic use of forms in an all-concrete building. Glass in this tropical site is recessed against sun. Podium supports structure.

world of steel, Mies van der Rohe stands as the great polarizing influence, just as France's Le Corbusier is the major architectural figure throughout that portion of the globe where reinforced concrete is the primary building material.

But the technological forces loosed by the industrial revolution are not likely to be harnessed by one man, or even by one logical progression of forms. Already a new world of concrete shells is arising—one that finds no place in Mies's strict vocabulary. Mies has taken his stand for objectivity and the clear expression of rectilinear steel structures. With a warning that in the future the space between buildings may be as important as the buildings themselves, Mies has elaborated his own system of architecture to the point where it can now not only function as sturdy prose but, in the hand of a master, serve the highest aims of poetry. It is an achievement matched in history by only a handful of the greatest architects.

6·23 Cullinan Hall (below), Houston Museum of Fine Arts (1959), applies the concept of unobstructed, universal space to the requirements of an art gallery, with moveable partitions arranged for each exhibition. Lighting is in floating ceiling.

7 : **ALVAR AALTO** : MASTER

Without the contribution of the Scandinavian countries, modern architecture, and indeed the whole range of modern design, would have been a far less vigorous and colorful movement. For this northern tier of countries thrives on extreme contrasts, from the long, nearly sunless winters to the long, daylight summers. Out of this testing ground of the spirit have come the hallucinatory images of the Norwegian painter Edvard Munch, the extreme theology of Søren Kierkegaard, the romantic pantheism of the Finnish composer Jean Julius Christian Sibelius, and the architecture of the great Finn, Alvar Aalto, whose work today places him among the three most important living architects of our time.

The very struggle for existence has always sharpened man's appetite for life, and in Finland this struggle has permeated every element of life. The durability of materials, the weave of cloth, the sharpness of the deadly *pukko* knife, the length of a ski must all be measured against the extreme situation in which they will be the key to survival. Good design therefore in Finland represents the distillation of the race's genius to endure. Here the standards that must be met are not the courtly elegance of eighteenth-century Versailles but the tough-minded, earthy tests of durability and function. It is, in part, for this reason that the crafts have hung on so tenaciously and remain a continuing inspiration for modern design.

And yet Finland, which achieved its independence from Russia only in 1917, has always guarded its deep commitment to European life. Nothing would be farther from the truth than to see these vigilant and often vociferous peoples as islands of provincialism one remove from the Lapps in united resistance against the industrial revolution. Nor does their intense nationalism rule out an equally fervent internationalism, as the Nobel prizes testify. The essence of the Scandinavian contribution is precisely its ability to synthesize the intensely local with the universal, creating an architecture with its own special vigor, simplicity, and durability.

A double focus is especially necessary to understand the highly individual work of Alvar Aalto, who seems at one and the same time both the master of such traditional materials as wood, copper and brick, and also a pioneer in reinforced concrete, the modern material *par excellence* in Europe. His free form design and undulating lines suggest the shapes of Finnish lakes, but they equally reflect the influence of such modern artists as Fernand Léger, Joan Miró, and the Rumanian sculptor Brancusi, all Aalto's personal friends. Aalto is both immensely tough-minded and immensely sophisticated. If Aalto retains the traditional Finnish steam-bath *sauna* and the massive, elevated Finnish fireplace in his designs, it is because he is convinced that they are as necessary to a full life as large expanses of glass, which he also uses freely. The final test of appropriateness for Aalto becomes its suitability for the man who will use the architecture. "Architecture, the real thing," Aalto has proclaimed, "is only to be found when man stands in the center. His tragedy and comedy—both." [1]

Alvar Aalto was born on February 3, 1898, the son of a surveying engineer in Jyväskylä, a town situated in the center of Finland, where wood is known as "green gold" and foresters are ranked as aristocrats. Aalto early decided to be an architect, fully aware that in Finland this profession, like that of poet and musician, ranks on a par with that of statesman and well above politician. Aalto also realized that the early romantic nationalism that had nourished such great Finnish composers as Sibelius, and the romantic aspirations expressed by Eliel Saarinen's Helsinki Railroad Station (1914), properly belonged to the nineteenth century. Modern art in the 1920s was what was being produced in Paris; modern architecture was the new International Style. It was the combination of these two sources that Aalto used in his first commissions.

The newspaper offices for the Turun-Sanomat in Turku were designed by Aalto in reinforced concrete, with strong, sculpted columns on the interior which show a lively intelligence at work. In 1928

BUILDER OF THE NORTH

Aalto also won the competition for the new Tuberculosis Sanatorium in Paimio, Finland, today a landmark in modern architecture and rivaled in size at the time only by Gropius' Bauhaus buildings in Germany.

The Paimio Sanatorium (Figure 7·2) is a youthful work; Aalto was only thirty at the time. But the finished building in no respect suffers from this. The program called for a hospital for 290 patients, with housing for nurses and doctors, in a wooded area north of Turku. Aalto organized the building in terms of far-flung wings, six stories in height, topped by a sheltered roof garden which trapped the sun and looked out over a superb view of tall pine forests. "Just before I did the sanatorium," Aalto explains, "I was in bed myself for two months with a broken leg I had gotten skiing. I tried to analyse the difficulties of life if you live horizontally. An ordinary room is designed for vertical human beings, so I designed the roof like

7·2–3 Tuberculosis Sanatorium, Paimio, Finland (1929–1933), was Aalto's first major commission, won in competition when he was thirty. Built with open balconies and roof garden, it was the pioneer of modern hospitals in Finland, and was at that time the largest example of modern architecture erected after the Bauhaus.

a wall and the wall like a roof.'' [2] To save the eyes of patients, he painted the walls an indefinite tone and the ceiling a darker shade. Hospital noises Aalto found disturbing, so he placed a slab of insulating board over the ceiling.

Aalto carried his analysis through to the smallest detail, including the doorknobs (designed to fit the hand but not snag clothing). Lights were adjusted not to shine in patients' eyes. Window ventilation kept drafts away from the beds. Wardrobes were made of light plywood hung from the ceiling, so that morning cleaning could be expedited. Even the washbowl was redesigned (Aalto noticed doctors were endlessly washing their hands) so that the basin received the water at a 30-degree angle without splashing.

The greatest care went into the roof garden. ''Three hundred patients is too big psychologically for a social group,'' Aalto points out, ''so we broke it up into groups of about twenty each who can be friends. This way the doctors can move the patients around until each one finds a congenial atmosphere. This can be important with a sickness like tuberculosis, which has social overtones.'' [3]

Aalto's second major building—also won through a competition—was the Library and Culture Center for Viipuri. As it turned out, it was even more audacious than the sanatorium, and much more difficult to build. For seven years the local officials fought it, pointing out, among other things, that it would destroy esthetically the nineteenth-century pseudo-Gothic church which shares the same square.* But the structure Aalto finally was able to build, with its carefully thought-out spaces, became the finest modern library in all Europe.

For the reading room at Viipuri, Aalto devised an ingenious lighting arrangement—fifty-seven conical light wells, each fitted with a prismatic diffusing glass, which refracted the light in evenly overlapping circles (Figure 7·5). Because the sun in Finland never rises higher than 57 degrees, no direct sunlight ever entered the 6-foot-deep openings. But what the Viipuri library today is mainly remembered for is its dramatic use of free, serpentine lines in a modern architecture that had hitherto made a fetish of rectangular spaces. For the lecture room (Figure 7·4), where the audience needed to be heard as well as the speaker, Aalto designed a wavelike contour ceiling, constructed of 30,000 knotless Karelian pine strips, which functioned as an acoustic baffle.

The use of such free form was a distinct innovation. Coming at a time when the first generation of moderns showed signs of going dry, it was hailed as a new freedom, somewhat similar to the biomorphic forms then to be found in the early work of Miró and the surrealists in contrast to the rectilinear forms of cubism, where the emphasis was primarily on shallow planes. Aalto's surrealism is skin-deep, if it is there at all. A more telling juxtaposition may well be the 60,000 Finnish lakes. At least the free-form glassware done by Aalto and his very talented wife, Aino (they married in 1925), bears a striking resemblance to air photos of the Finnish lake country.

Whatever the origin of the free, serpentine line, Aalto has exploited it with great skill and daring. In 1938 he designed the Forestry Exhibition Hall in Lapua in the North of Finland with an undulating log-stockade wall. In the Finnish Pavilion at the 1939 New York World's Fair Aalto went even further. Here Aalto not only used an undulating

* Today the arguments have been grimly canceled. The town was badly damaged during the Russo-Finnish war, and totally destroyed during the Second World War. Viipuri itself is now in Soviet territory.

wood wall for the photograph displays but also sloped the wall inwards (a logical device, since it made seeing the pictures easier from below). In the 1940s Aalto came to the United States to design the senior dormitory at Massachusetts Institute of Technology, finished in the late 1940s, in which the serpentine configuration is the central design element of the building (Figure 7·6). The form is justified in this case by the manner in which Aalto was thus able to give each room a river view.

The M.I.T. dormitory is highly expressive of his design philosophy with its honest but bare brick interior walls. The result is a bracing, Nordic, and somewhat chilly environment. But the building does not lack for fantasy, as the open-walled dining pavilion on the front shows. In fact, this dining area, gaily lighted from above by exterior lights, so appealed to Aalto that he once claimed that the main building merely served as a backdrop for it.

As early as the 1929 Paimio Sanatorium, Aino and Alvar Aalto had designed furniture as well as lighting fixtures to go with their buildings. Aalto has always pointed out, "I am not such a professional in the furniture business as you might think.

I'm not interested in furniture design in the ordinary sense at all, but only for specific purposes.'' Nonetheless, Aalto first became known outside of architectural circles for his chairs, which date from 1932. In a land where a woodsman can still fashion his own pair of skis, it was inevitable that Aalto should turn first to wood as the natural material for furniture. The huge Finnish plywood industry had provided Aalto with the material for his first chairs and cabinets. Aalto devised ways of stacking chairs, a major saving in both storage and handling. By 1935 he had learned how to feather the wood into splices which could be laminated where the curves occur, yet leave the wood whole where the form required this. In time, Aalto's chairs became continuous curves of laminated wood, taking on the serpentine forms that he had used so expressively in his architecture. Their natural finish, although it tended to wear poorly if given rough usage, provided a welcome touch in contrast to the cult of chromium. It is a tribute to Aalto's design genius that the taste makers of the era all found it fitting to sit in Aalto chairs, and indeed, the whole series of innovations in American design

7·4–5 Town Library, Viipuri (1927–1935), completely destroyed in the Second World War. The undulating acoustical ceiling (opposite page) was the first free-form design to be introduced into the strictly rectilinear architectural style of that time. The reading room (right) had fifty-seven light wells piercing the ceiling. Prismatic glass distributed the sunlight.

7·6 Everett Moore Baker House, Massachusetts Institute of Technology (1947–1949). The serpentine line on dormitory facade gives each room a river view. Rectangular pavilion is the dining room.

initiated in the 1940s by such architect-designers as Charles Eames and Eero Saarinen rest on the principles pioneered by Aalto.

Having been the white hope of the 1930s and the darling of the designers, it was perhaps inevitable that Aalto's high reputation should at some time slip a notch or so. This is exactly what happened after the Second World War. At the time it seemed as if Aalto's senior dormitory at M.I.T. might well be his swan song. The purposefully rough brickwork began to seem an anachronism. The austerity of the interiors had an enforced monastic quality which Aalto thought the right antidote for a young technical student who might be tempted by the drugstore or the movies. But the prevailing temper was toward an austerity of another sort, that of the stripped-down "skin-and-bones" precision of Mies van der Rohe * with exposed steel, sheer glass walls, and curtain-wall façades. Aalto was in danger of becoming architecture's forgotten man.

In fact Aalto was passing through a difficult time. In 1949 the death of his wife Aino, his partner for over twenty years (Aalto always insisted that all plans be signed with her name first), was a hard blow. Life seemed to Aalto as grass growing and dying, with little that was permanent or eternal. But, he added, while we are on earth, let us live in the make-believe world as if we had a purpose, ideals, a religion; architecture is the scenery and the place where we live. Architecture does not exist just to fulfill man's need for shelter, but also to fulfill man's belief in the nobility of his existence on earth.

Once back again in Finland where he could breathe deeply of his native forest air, Aalto's hardihood won out over depression and disappointment. What crystallized from this black period was a stern questioning of the all-out pursuit of technology. "Why put 40 per cent of the building's cost into air-conditioning?" he asked. "Raise the ceilings instead. Let in the air and give people more space." [4] Instead of stainless steel, he turned to rough stone and brick, striving perhaps for something monumental and yet lyrical, like the Finnish granite churches of the Middle Ages. The endless arrays of glass façades and synthetic metals seemed to him to be turning into a dead-end street; buildings with what he called "dollar grins" became anathema. "Grown-up children play with curves and tensions which they do not control," he grumbled. "It smells of Hollywood." [5]

* See Chap. 6.

7·7–8 Aalto's secluded "Experimental House," summer residence in the Finnish lake country, demonstrates his concern with contrasting textures. Wall is pierced to let in sun. Below, Aalto's home at Munkkieniemi, where free forms are exploited to provide a studio with pierced northern wall.

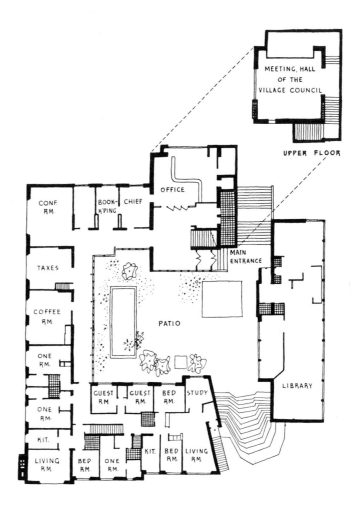

7·9–12 Säynatsälo Town Hall, Finland (1949–1953), a handsome demonstration of Aalto's town-planning principles at work. The civic buildings, raised above the noise and traffic of the street, are organized around a central patio reached by irregular grass-covered steps (opposite page, top) or, more directly, by stairs leading to the meeting hall (opposite page, bottom). A notable feature of the interior is the playful truss that supports the roof. The cantilevered brick portion of the meeting hall (below) is used as a visitors' balcony.

MEETING, HALL OF THE VILLAGE COUNCIL

UPPER FLOOR

CONF. RM.

BOOK-K'PING

CHIEF

OFFICE

TAXES

MAIN ENTRANCE

COFFEE RM.

ONE RM.

PATIO

ONE RM.

LIBRARY

KIT.

GUEST RM.

GUEST RM.

BED RM.

STUDY

LIVING RM.

BED RM.

ONE RM.

KIT.

BED RM.

LIVING RM.

7·13 Sunila sulfite mill, Finland (1937–1939 and 1951–1954), is a striking example of Aalto's sureness of design. Functional areas are well-ordered compositions in which broad horizontals have been masterfully juxtaposed with strong verticals.

7·14 Sulfite mill is a powerful industrial composition of elevator towers, conveyor belts, and massive concrete abutments.

Aalto's first clients were the large Finnish pulp mills, in particular the mill at Sunila owned jointly by five Finnish wood concerns, and for which he had already designed an extensive sulfite pulp mill. For these large concerns Aalto was able to construct whole communities, carefully zoned and placed in the landscape in a fashion that suggests that one of the Finn's prime inspirations must be the hill towns of Italy and the islands of Greece. What anti-Americanism he had built up while in the United States he was able to expend to his profit by designing Helsinki's Culture House for the Finnish Communist Party. Soon commissions for the Teachers School in his home town of Jyväskylä, an "Iron House" (an office block with shops) in downtown Helsinki, and a new Finnish Pavilion for the Venice Biennale arrived on his doorstep.

The urban building that best sums up the matured Aalto esthetic is the National Pensions Institute in Helsinki (Figure 7·15). With masses of dark red brick, copper, and black granite, it is both highly orchestrated and monumental. Aalto intended this building to be "the fortification of quiet." Great care was taken for the workers within. Clerical areas are kept horizontal to avoid up-and-downstairs traffic. Light floods the white work areas from the peaked glass skylights. The cascade arrangement of building blocks (connecting passages go underground beneath the elevated center court) lets the sunlight come deep into the structure.

But for Aalto, whose deepest inspiration comes from close contact with his own native soil, a forest site set in birches and pines seems to infuse energy into his design. There is no better proof than the Town Hall at Säynatsälo, built for a community of 3,000, most of whom work in the local plywood factory. The site itself is only a twenty-minute boat ride down the lake from Aalto's own summer retreat. But Säynatsälo's town fathers formally held a national contest; Aalto as solemnly entered and won.

Actually Aalto's client was both the town and local industry, the gigantic Finnish state-owned lumber concern, Enso-Gutzeit. Aalto was told that they would like something unusual which would attract notice and visitors (a wish that has more than come true). Aalto for his part saw a chance to put some of his own town-planning concepts to work. He began by programing the requirements: a town hall with a library and room for future expansion (Figure 7·11). "I wanted to make it a

town center, one that would gather in the people,''
Aalto explains, making a sweeping gathering-in
movement with his arms. ''I put a garden inside
and the inside is no longer neutral. I lifted up to
make a vertical difference between the traffic in the
street and the people meeting inside. The street is
full of gases from automobiles, heavy gases that
settle and we inhale. Vertical separation divides
the human being from the industrial traffic outside. We lift up the human being and put him in
a better world.'' [6]

The finished Town Hall is full of Aalto's signature details, from the homey touch of grass growing
on the informal stairway entry (Figure 7·9) to
the dramatic cantilever of the Town Hall within
which is the visitors' balcony overlooking the town-
council chamber. Wood is used exuberantly throughout, from the playful trusses of the ceiling to the
solid red pine furniture Aalto specially designed
for the interiors, and the window slats so set as
to allow a soft glow of indirect lighting without
glare (Figure 7·12). And despite the lack of symmetry, a hierarchy of forms is carefully kept. The
library is a strong horizontal, well lighted through
the side glass windows; the Town Hall towers above
the structure beneath its slanting ceiling much
as the keep of a medieval town commands its forti-
fied site.

Säynätsalo, which now attracts over a thousand
visitors a year, including an increasing number
of Russians, became something of a landmark in
Aalto's career.* In 1954, the day the building was
finished, he celebrated by marrying his second
wife, Elissa Mäkiniemi, a young staff architect who
had served as job captain on the project. Nearby,
Aalto has built his own summer residence, the so-
called ''Experimental House'' (Figure 7·7), on
the arm of an island so that at any time of day he
can race for the shore and find a sheltered beach
on which to swim. Behind it Aalto delights in building trial structures—one without foundations, another a free-formed wall, another an experiment in
solar heating. ''We put up a wall with a new material, leave it there for perhaps a year,'' he explains. ''I like to see how the material looks in
connection with nature.''

A much more finished structure is his new studio

* Aalto has defended it with considerable vigor against
what he considers unwarranted encroachment by commercial publicity. When a power company erected an offending
neon advertising sign, Aalto led a boat-raiding party to
the site and stoned the sign to smithereens.

7·15 National Pensions Institute, Helsinki
(1952–1956) shows Aalto's geometric style
applied to a large office structure. Organized around central court and pool, units
have setbacks to allow light penetration.

7·16 Black granite creates vigorous accents in the brick and copper of National
Pensions Institute. By breaking up the
masses, Aalto achieved a much-needed
human scale for this type of structure.

7·17 Lutheran Church, Vuoksenniska, Finland (1956–1959), a brilliant modulation of acoustic form by which the arch over the pulpit acts as a sounding board and suggests the sheltering wing of a guardian angel.

at Munkkieniemi, outside Helsinki (Figure 7·8), which along with his downtown office is where Aalto does most of his work. Much of it is still for Finnish clients, including in recent years several fine churches, such as the Lutheran church completed in 1959 at Vuoksenniska (Figure 7·17), in which all of Aalto's strengths, his flow of space, control of light, and sureness with volumes combine with a minute attention to detail. Increasingly, Aalto is being sought out from abroad. In 1957, he completed one of the several apartment houses in Berlin's Interbau. He has designed a library for Baghdad, a cultural center for Wolfsburg, Germany (home of the Volkswagen works), a museum for Denmark, a house and small gallery between Chartres and Versailles for the French art dealer Louis Carré, a semicircular apartment house in Bremen (it fans out from the handle, which contains corridor and elevator area), and a new opera house for Essen. The result is that today nearly half of Aalto's time is spent abroad.

Does this mark the beginning of a new Aalto school? The answer from his fellow architects is "No." "How can there be?" one asks. "You can't copy Aalto. When he comes up against a new problem, he finds a new solution." Aalto's influence on the architects who work under him is one of inspiration, not tyranny. One of his former pupils, for instance, is Jørn Utzen, whose prizewinning

design for the Sydney Opera House, with its volumetric shell forms, bears little resemblance to Aalto's work, unless it is the interior of the Vuoksenniska church.

Aalto's present importance, then, lies in another direction, namely the reintegration into architecture of strong, masculine surface textures and traditional materials. It is significant that both Aalto and Le Corbusier in the 1950s turned against the overly technological finishes of porcelain panels, stainless-steel casings, and aluminum, in favor of rough, unfinished textures. In both cases, too, their forms have become more massive, more monumental.

And yet between Le Corbusier and Aalto, once in the 1930s so close and now apparently again oriented somewhat in the same direction, there is still a chasm. Le Corbusier tends toward a monumentality that is sculptural, almost brutal, and increasingly his buildings, for all their inherent drama, seem like massive primordial backdrops for man's action. Aalto, by contrast, remains the ingrained individualist. "Probably architecture can do more to humanize life than any other art. At least I think so. There is a tendency in this direction today —even skin-and-bones structures sometimes can be good, you know—though perhaps it is not especially visible. I think the tendency will grow. We are at a turning point toward more emphasis on the human factor." [7]

Well-building hath three conditions:
commodity, firmness, and delight
VITRUVIUS

PART TWO # Modern in Transition

Flux, flow, change are dominant characteristics of mid-twentieth-century life. Our point of view shifts from the unseen world of the electronic microscope to the other side of the moon. Our time-space sequences range from pedestrian pace to several times the speed of sound. Our landscape is now identified by twelve-lane superhighways that bulldoze through mountains, forests, and the hearts of cities. Urban tracts are poured into place almost overnight, while stately residential avenues are declared obsolescent within two generations. It is a restless, explosive age, and architecture, which is called upon to give form and expression to this continuing revolution, is in itself in a highly dynamic state of evolution.

In this age of transition, the United States has proved to be the great design laboratory. In part this is true because of our abundant technology and atmosphere of freedom; in part, because the problems of a highly industrialized culture have emerged here first. The traffic-choked arteries of the American cities are now becoming a world-wide phenomenon; the skyscraper, which first evolved in answer to urban crowding, now marks the center of nearly every great city around the world. Already endowed with a vigorous native tradition of building and engineering, the American scene has also been immensely enriched by a prodigious influx of talent from abroad. But all over the world the task of creating significant forms expressive of this age is shared by members of the second generation, many of them former students of the first form givers, now coming into their own mature decades.

The responsibility confronting this second generation has brought with it some sobering second thoughts. The traditional graces of architecture—textural richness, contrast of light and shadow, and evocative sequence of spaces—have been slighted in the effort to match the accelerating tempo of technology. As the responsibility for revitalizing the whole environment inherited from the nineteenth century is met face to face, the architect's task has expanded from the organization of spaces within the envelope of the building to encompass the over-all sequence of spaces—streets, towns, and cities. The spaces between the buildings are now as much man's space, and thus the architect's domain, as those within the buildings.

The ultimate judgment which the future will pass on our age will be based on the cities we evolve. Already their components are emerging in the new cities such as Brasília as well as through such large ordered complexes as housing developments, large industrial parks such as General Motors Technical Center, educational facilities such as the United States Air Force Academy, and the shopping center. The emerging city may well grow to an organic metropolis that covers entire coastal and inland areas. And it can be monstrous unless the balance is found between man, the great constant of architecture as an art, and technology, the great impetus to architecture as the science of building. "Survival depends on design," Richard Neutra has said. He might well have added, "and so does man's sanity."

One of architecture's greatest hopes is the vitality to be found in this second generation, the vitality of men who are expanding, humanizing, and refining the insights and disciplines of the great founders with highly original solutions of their own.

8 : **RICHARD J. NEUTRA** :

THE NATURE OF HABITAT

Throughout the early decades of this century, the vision of America as the land of unexcelled architectural promise dazzled designers around the world. Gropius and Le Corbusier admired its technology, its skyscrapers, and motorcars from afar. Mies van der Rohe glimpsed its steel skyscraper skeletons and designed buildings that, though they were unbuildable in Germany at the time, would uncompromisingly capture the bare-boned beauty of steel. To Richard Neutra, in Vienna, it also seemed that "a grand industrial production like that of the U.S.A. was the true and promising quarry for the builders of the future." [1]

The infusion of foreign talent has enriched all strains of American cultural life, from the music of Milhaud to the mathematical genius of Einstein. But in few areas is this debt more apparent than in the twentieth-century American architecture. Richard Neutra might well have become the Alvar Aalto of Austria had he stayed in his native Vienna. Instead he was one of the pioneer European architects to undergo the difficult experience of adapting not only his personal life and practice but his whole esthetic to a different mode of life. He succeeded triumphantly. The school he established in California has produced some of the most handsome residences in the United States. And in recent years, using Los Angeles as a base, Neutra has emerged as a world leader, in climates varying from Europe to South America and Africa, urging architects toward a rational and sensitive approach to the nature of habitat.

If Neutra had not chosen architecture as a profession, he might well have become a brilliant psychologist. As it is, his early discovery of the physiological psychology of Wilhelm Wundt made him a profound environmentalist. To this day he has continued his research into the minutiae that affect man's well-being, from the jarring effect of bad acoustics to the soothing influence of color. Even the importance of peripheral vision and the rate of evaporation of moisture from the skin have architectural implications for Neutra. And his relentless elucidation of what he calls "biological realism" has resounded in untold benefits to his clients, who, in overwhelming numbers, have expressed their gratitude for an environment that is both functional and at the same time life-enhancing.

"I have always been an American," Neutra once exclaimed. Actually, he was born on April 8, 1892, into a well-to-do Viennese family, the youngest of five highly talented children. One brother became a neurologist; another an engineer and patent lawyer. His sister was an artist and married the director of Vienna's National Gallery of Art. In such a family, children were expected to be precocious. And Neutra at the age of eight already was entranced with the elegance of the Vienna subways designed by the famous Viennese modernist Otto Wagner, who later became his teacher. Another friend of the family was Adolf Loos, one of modern architecture's most effective pamphleteers. At the age of eighteen, Neutra decided to make architecture his career. Graduating first from Vienna's Polytechnic, after wartime service in the Austro-Hungarian mountain artillery he was graduated with honors from the University of Zurich. In the early 1920s, Berlin seemed a far more dynamic city than Vienna, and rather than return to Austria, Neutra sought out Erich Mendelsohn, at the time one of the most advanced architects in postwar Germany.

In 1922 when Neutra joined Mendelsohn, the German architect had just completed his highly expressionistic Einstein Tower and was rapidly moving toward the curved forms and low horizontals that marked his later work. With Mendelsohn, Neutra collaborated on the Berlin *Tageblatt* offices and on the planning scheme for the business section of Haifa (a plan which won the international first prize but was never implemented). But even in Berlin, Neutra was unable to erase from his mind the tourist poster he had seen by chance in Zurich in 1920, a poster that showed magnificent palm trees and a vast expanse of the blue Pacific with the legend "California calls you!" In 1923, recently married to his young wife Dione,

a talented singer and 'cellist, Neutra decided to answer the call and sailed for the New World.

Neutra worked diligently at coming to grips with his new environment, staying first with Jane Addams at Hull House in Chicago, and then working for the Chicago architectural firm of Holabird & Roche, engaged at the time on the Palmer House. True to his literary European background, Neutra kept notes as he worked at the drafting table and by the end of the year had compiled a book detailing step by step the planning and construction of the building. Neutra also searched out the nearly forgotten Louis Sullivan, then living out his last years on donations from his architectural colleagues. It was at Louis Sullivan's funeral in Chicago's Graceland Cemetery in April, 1924, that Neutra finally met Frank Lloyd Wright, the man who in European eyes loomed like a giant above the American landscape, and for whom, in fact, Neutra had already named his first-born son.

Perhaps Neutra, with his European background, was already too sophisticated to become the ardent disciple Wright expected. Although Wright generously invited Neutra and his family to live and work at Wright's combined home and office at Taliesin in Wisconsin, the two men soon found themselves in a bramble of ill-concealed antagonism, a situation from which Neutra disengaged himself after several months by moving to Los Angeles. There he joined forces with Rudolph Schindler, a fellow Viennese who had also worked with Frank Lloyd Wright, first as a draftsman for the Imperial Hotel, and later as supervisor for Aline Barnsdall's "Hollyhock House" (Figure 2·21). Together they staged an architectural exhibition which included their own work as well as Wright's. When the news of this three-man show (or "one-master-and-two-disciples," as Wright viewed it) reached Taliesin, Wright exploded and even in later years was fond of referring to it as "the Crucifixion between Two Thieves."

However ill-advised this youthful exhibition, Neutra eventually established friendly, if precarious, relations with Wright. But as a follower Neutra

8·2–3 Kaufmann "Desert House," Palm Springs, California (1946), is an elegant residence designed for Wright's "Falling Water" client (Figure 2·28–30). The drama is in the balance between the distant mountain and the man-made rectangular planes. Below is Kaufmann house plan.

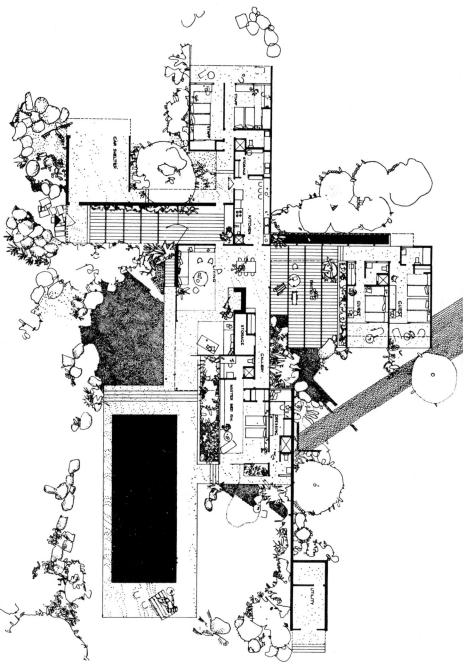

8·4–5 Lovell house ("Health House"), Griffith Park, Los Angeles (1927), made Neutra's reputation. An airy structure of light steel, it appears to float mid-air.

Neutra's deep concern with the triad of technology, psychology, and design is clearly stated in his first major project, the splendid house he built for P. M. Lovell in 1927 (Figure 8·5). The site itself was challenging, a precipitous hillside with a view over the Pacific Ocean and the ranges of the Santa Monica mountains. The ground plan is a paean of praise to outdoor living (hence the name "Health House"), with differentiated outdoor play and recreational grounds, including swimming and wading pools, tennis court, gymnasium area, and an outdoor stage for amateur theatricals, as well.

What gave the hillside structure its drama—it became known as Neutra's "floating house" almost as soon as the plans were first published in Europe in 1927—was Neutra's use of prefabricated light steel frame, hitherto reserved almost exclusively for industrial plants. True, Wright had used steel to give added drama to his cantilevered porches as far back as 1909 in his Robie house, but there it had been disguised beneath its wood sheathing. Neutra resolved to close the gap between industrial and domestic construction and reveal the steel skeleton clearly in its own right.

Since it was the first steel-skeleton house on the West Coast, Neutra could find no general contractor and had to undertake the task himself. It is a credit to Neutra's organization abilities that, although he had to deal with some seventy-two subcontractors, the actual steel framing went up in forty hours. To coat the outer walls, formed by triple steel casements and spandrels, Neutra used Gunite (concrete fired through an airgun). Not only was the concrete laid on with extraordinarily close tolerances, but it has withstood cracking to this day. Designed at a time when Gropius's Bauhaus was only two years old, Le Corbusier was still awaiting a major commission, and Mies van der Rohe had yet to build his first major residence, Neutra's "Health House" is a monument of modern architecture.

Recognition was quick in coming. Neutra found himself invited to deliver lectures at universities around the world. C. H. van der Leeuw, who had seen Neutra's work in Rotterdam, came all the way to California and agreed to finance the house in which Neutra and his wife still live. Neutra treated his own house as "a steppingstone to further the development of modern architecture, and of a general constructed environment that is wholesome for living." But as he rapidly discovered, "The family is probably the most difficult thing of all to handle and to discuss, from the point of view of

was lost to Taliesin forever. As Neutra in later years explained, "Because Wright is such a genius, he did not provide an art that anyone could satisfactorily imitate without diluting and harming the original. Wright is not a steppingstone. He is a born aristocrat—the Grand Seigneur."

At first glance both Schindler and Neutra seemed to have turned away from Wright's earth-hugging masonry structures toward the then emerging International Style of the 1920s as typified by the pristine white cubes of Le Corbusier or the hovering glass façades of the Bauhaus in Germany. In fact, the lessons of Taliesin had been well learned, to emerge later in the bold use of cantilevers (the structural "secret" of the Imperial Hotel in Tokyo), the contrasting ceiling and floor plan which creates endless spatial counterpoints, unexpected clerestories, strong horizontal lines, and even the use of such "natural" materials as rough fieldstone. At the outset, however, both Schindler's and Neutra's work were seen against the context of the modern architecture of Germany, France, and Holland.

design accommodation to management and group well-being.''

Actually Neutra's approach to clients is one of close empathy combined with scientific detachment. To get a good clinical picture of their lives, he requires them to make out a chart of their day's activities, their hobbies, lounging, and eating habits. ''The designer may never be found out, except on the day of judgment, that he has supplied his poor victims with a daily round of tiny or coarse irritations which threw them off balance,'' Neutra has declared. ''But not being found out does not mean the man and his deeds are not a peril. It is not the car which we see but the one we did not see that kills us. It is the little sore we overlook which later proves of an unsurmountable malignancy. Bad acoustics, for example, can lead to shouting, and this calls forth an argumentative mood. Like a doctor, the architect should examine the individual case; he should diagnose and prescribe for the neurophysiological requirements, find and improve biological deficiencies, counteract pathology.''

By this close attention to daily patterns, however, Neutra was able to score important design break-throughs. His Corona School, in Bell, California (Figure 8·6), for instance, replaced the multistory brick schoolhouse with a whole new environment for education, with flexibility replacing the rigid regimentation of school desks, sliding glass walls instead of incarcerating brick, and the outdoors as accessible as the indoors. In the Channel Heights Housing Project (Figure 8·7) he proved his design discoveries were projectable into low-cost units.

8·6 Corona School, Bell, California (1935), was Neutra's thoughtful and revolutionary design, allowing maximum flexibility on the interior and free access to the exterior.

8·7 Channel Heights Housing Project, San Pedro, California (1942–1944), applies modern design to the problem of low-cost housing. The cost per unit was only $2,600.

8·10 Tremaine house, Santa Barbara, California (1947; right), is placed in a setting of rock and oak, against which Neutra juxtaposes cantilevers and mitered glass.

8·8–9 Moore ranch house, Ojai, California (1950), overlooks a valley of orange groves and desert brush that leads to distant mountains. Masterful articulation of linear elements, the use of glass to eliminate dark corners, and the intimate relationship between inside and out make this one of Neutra's most delightful works.

But the area in which Neutra functions with greatest distinction is in private residential structures, buildings of such appropriateness, crispness of detail, and man-made beauty that they are among the delights and prides of modern architecture. Their example alone has inspired such former Neutra students as Raphael Soriano, Gregory Ain, and Harwell Hamilton Harris, as well as Robert E. Alexander, Neutra's partner since 1949, whose work has made the West Coast one of the architectural show places of the United States.

The choice of Neutra's best houses is of necessity an arbitrary one. The whole range from the Kaufmann ''Desert House'' and Tremaine house of the mid-1940s through the De Schulthess house in Havana, Cuba, and the Hansch house in the late 1950s is a remarkably sustained achievement. All of them bear Neutra's trademark—the clear articulation of structure as an energizing principle of design. Over the years he has achieved mastery of his clean-cut horizontals, which seem to float independently on incredibly thin supports. The distinction between interior and exterior has been all but abolished by the use of glass, both in mitered corners (an old Wright device to vaporize the traditionally dark corners) and as an all-but-invisible glass curtain wall that slides open at the touch of an electric button. Continuity between interior and exterior is maintained through carrying the same terrazzo flooring without change from living area to patio, so that the house, as such, becomes merely controlled environment caught behind glass between floor and roof.

Neutra was slow, however, to abandon the International Style's preference for thin metal supports contrasting with panels of white stucco or concrete. But in 1942 with the John B. Nesbitt house in Brentwood, California, he shifted his vocabulary to more traditional brick and redwood to create the beginning of a regional style. The first essay in new materials seems now embarrassingly gauche; mortar drips out between bricks like so much toothpaste. By contrast, the ''Desert House,'' which Neutra designed for Frank Lloyd Wright's client, Edgar Kaufmann, the Pittsburgh department-store owner who had previously commissioned what is perhaps Wright's finest house, ''Bear Run'' (Figure 2·28), is a much more vigorous handling of a very difficult problem.

While the Kaufmann ''Desert House'' (Figure 8·2) perhaps remains Neutra's most famous single house, it may well owe its fame as much to the handsome photographs of it produced at the hands

of Neutra's photographer Julius Shulman as to its actual design. The master bedroom (Figure 8·8) is remote from the living area, and accessible only by passing through the dining area and then down a long corridor. Indeed, even the seating arrangement, which gives half the guests a splendid view of the pool and presents the other half with a view across the dining area, across the patio court, and into the guest rooms, is hardly an inspired solution. On the other hand, Neutra showed himself adept at solving many of the problems of desert living, providing the platform around the pool with both heating and cooling installations, and incorporating aluminum louvers to shield the gloriette placed atop the building as a kind of sheltered roof pavilion.

The Warren Tremaine house (Figure 8·10) of the next year seems a much better solution, filled with elements of surprise (an underground gallery for prints and drawings opens unexpectedly on a porchlike garden) and exquisitely attuned to psychological responses. No other architect at the time, except perhaps Wright himself, would have worked with nature so carefully to provide the intimate view of boulder and oak that greets the eye in the morning from the bedrooms. Even the heavier use of concrete in column and roof slab (required by the unusual stresses of earthquake tremors) gives a quality of massive dignity and light and shadow. What is even more remarkable is that Neutra has

been able to manipulate this added mass without jeopardizing his proverbial genius for making walls seem magically to become nonexistent. Unquestionably, the Tremaine house is one of America's great modern residences.

This sensitivity to climate, to site, and to the necessity of providing practical solutions that not only work but can be artistically counterpointed has led Neutra toward difficult terrain and wide variances of climate; it has infinitely quickened his awareness of the whole rationale of habitat. Increasingly Neutra's work has taken him to Cuba, Puerto Rico, Venezuela, and, most recently, to the heart of Africa. The question remains, however, whether Neutra's full potentialities have as yet been totally utilized.

The goal that has hung tantalizingly just out of reach of architecture in this century is the authority to control man's environment in anything like its totality. As an architect who first embarked on his career as a city planner, this has been particularly clear to Richard Neutra. More than most, he is aware that though architecture can effect individual cures, its lack can produce biological disaster. The present plight of our traffic-choked cities, sprawling suburbia, and chaotic transportation proves that major design failures have been built into our culture. "Survival depends on design," Neutra has declared. His chance to prove it may be in the coming decades.

Architecture is not the materialization of a mood. Its objective is general usefulness, including its visual impact.

9 : **MARCEL BREUER** : THE

One of the first generation to graduate from the Bauhaus in Weimar, Marcel Breuer was in many ways a *Wunderkind*. At the age of twenty-two he was a full-fledged master of the Bauhaus and was put in charge of the carpentry section; at twenty-three he had invented the first tubular-steel chair. Chairs led to the design of storage walls. From there it was a logical step for him to package whole spaces for living, then on to stacking apartments in series to arrive at highly advanced schemes for the modern apartment houses.

Today Breuer is probably the most important single influence on the design of American houses, both through his own houses and those of his students. But Breuer has had one major handicap, namely, that he was for so long closely identified with Walter Gropius, founder of the Bauhaus. It was a problem Breuer did not really successfully solve until 1941 when he began his independent practice in the United States. From that time until such important projects as the Paris UNESCO Headquarters (Figure 9·1) Breuer did not so

much contradict his earlier work as expand the basic Bauhaus approach in a way that has made him, rather than Gropius, the major continuator as a builder in the Bauhaus tradition.

If today Breuer's buildings never oppose openly the early Bauhaus principles, they nevertheless leave hardly a proposition of the whole Bauhaus approach untouched. Functionalism is still master, but a master much tamed by a new and transcendent humanism. "The revolution against a bankrupt eclecticism in architecture has been won," Breuer now declares. "But in a revolution the shooting is not the final objective. A battle is certainly not just a battle for its own sake—not just *l'art pour l'art*. It is one thing to discredit outlived things, but it is another to replace them with better solutions that stand up under long-term

9·1 UNESCO Headquarters, Place de Fontenoy, Paris (1952–1958), is composed of the Y-shaped secretariat and conference hall, with sculpture plaza between.

BAUHAUS CONTINUED

wear and tear. Simultaneous with the sharply pointed action, with the oversimplification of the battle cry—there are human needs.'' [1]

A concern for human needs, of course, was always a part of the Bauhaus creed, but it never managed to surcharge the atmosphere to the degree that the concern with technology did. The point about even an early Breuer chair is not that it is comfortable (although it is), but that it is an exciting new use of a modern industrial material, esthetically conceived and adaptable to mass production. Much of Breuer's later development lies in reexamining not so much the credo of the Bauhaus as its psychology, with sharp focus on the most modern material (steel, concrete, glass, black linoleum) and intense, neomechanistic approach to design. Today Breuer would prefer natural concrete, rough ashlar, woven textures.

In planning a structure, the Bauhaus strove for the effect of a floating, gravity-defying structure. Today Breuer still turns on occasion to a floating box, but he has evolved earth-hugging structures as well. For the Bauhaus the ribbon of glass for a window was a hallmark. Today Breuer is moving toward the treatment of the whole façade as one plastic unity (rather than a layer cake so many stories tall). Indeed, the whole problem of glass has concerned Breuer intensely. Many of his stylistic innovations, from such simple elements as sliding windowpanes to complicated arrangements of sun louvers and projected panels of solar glass, have aimed at coping with the multiple problems raised by this material, which was a fetish of the founding moderns.

What makes Breuer's evolution of significant new forms fascinating to behold is that they evolve with such precision and logic from his own research. ''I try to develop the right, the best solution,'' he explains, ''Once I have found it in one element of a particular building, then I say, let's leave the problem. I vary it only when I can make what I consider improvements.'' [2]

This ability to master one element of design, digest it, then move on to the next problem has

marked Breuer's career right from the start. It may well have been this ability to think in terms of structure and space in both practical and esthetic terms that predestined Breuer to be an architect. Born the son of a doctor in Pécs, Hungary, Marcel Lajos Breuer rather fancied at first that he would be a sculptor. In the Austro-Hungarian empire the logical place to find out was, of course, Vienna, and there Breuer at the age of eighteen duly showed up at the Academy of Art. He stayed exactly thirty minutes. Then he heard of the exciting new Bauhaus which Gropius had just opened at Weimar. Its combination of esthetics and practical training was just what Breuer longed for. He showed up in time to register with the second entering class of 1920.

At the Bauhaus Breuer naturally gravitated toward carpentry—a significant fact in view of his role decades later in the United States in almost single-handedly making wood once again a ''modern material''—and became one of the first of the Bauhaus students to be trained in both practice and theory. When at twenty-two he became a master of the Bauhaus, he was put in charge of the carpentry department.

In the sometimes esoteric atmosphere of the Bauhaus, Breuer's voice rings out with a no-nonsense note. A record of an evening discussion at the Bauhaus has Breuer saying, ''Even if I try, I see no chaos in our time. That some painters can't make up their minds whether to paint naturalistically, abstractly or not at all does not mean chaos. Our needs are clear enough; the possibilities are limited only by ourselves. The main thing is to lend a hand where something needed is lacking and to move with whatever forces we can command toward a singleminded economical solution.'' [3]

Breuer seems to have caught fire in the creative atmosphere of the Bauhaus. ''How far can you bring the tension and still have unity?'' he asked. His first chair used straight rectilinear forms, slightly tapered, and a stretched webbing of red, blue, and yellow, an early indication of Breuer's interest in pure colors. For his first bed he tried

9·3–5 Breuer's key works after leaving the Bauhaus were the Dolderthal Apartments (1934; left, top), his tubular steel chair with wood frame and cane seat (1928), and the Harnischmacher house (1932).

exploit the possibilities; the Mannesmann Works, for example, refused to furnish pipe for further experimentation. But the very impersonal quality that at first put off users was central to Breuer's evolving esthetic. "A piece of furniture is not an arbitrary composition: it is a necessary component of our environment." He lectured his students: "In itself impersonal, it takes on meaning only from the way it is used or as part of a complete scheme." Breuer also drew from this a lesson for architecture: "Let our dwelling have no particular 'style,' but only the imprint of the owner's character. The architect as producer, creates only half a dwelling; the man who lives in it, the other half."[4]

The year 1928 was crucial in Bauhaus history. Walter Gropius decided to leave the Bauhaus and go into private practice. Breuer, a very close follower, also decided to set up his own office in Berlin. For a young designer of twenty-six it was a courageous act, and there were few commissions to live on. With the slim earnings from his furniture, Breuer decided to profit from his enforced holiday and traveled through southern France, Spain, North Africa, and Greece on a grand architectural tour.

Twice during his travels in these early years Breuer came back to execute commissions, once at the request of modern architecture historian Siegfried Giedion to design the still modern-looking Dolderthal Apartments (1934) in Zurich with the Swiss brothers, Alfred and Emil Roth, and again to draw the plans for his first modern house for the Harnischmacher family in Wiesbaden. This last villa in particular is a highly creditable achievement for an architect aged only thirty (Figure 9·5). A tense, vital design in steel and concrete, it is almost nautical, with bridges, open decks, and the use of steel cables as wind bracing for the roof terrace.

The rising tide of National Socialism spelled slow strangulation for modern architecture in Germany, and in 1935 Breuer went to London. There he joined forces with F. R. S. Yorke to design an exhibition pavilion in Bristol for Crofton E. Gane, a project that marks Breuer's suddenly awakened interest in natural materials, particularly stone. For the British manufacturer Jack Pritchard, Marcel Breuer designed a series of laminated-wood chairs and tables (known as the "Isokon" series), in which he used a veneer of birchwood to create free-flowing curves, thus returning to his experi-

experimenting with molded plywood decades before laminated wood chairs became the rage. Of all Breuer's projects probably his most famous single project was his tubular-steel cantilever chair, a striking simple concept that has become a classic of modern design.

The conception for the single, continuous chromium frame came from Breuer's admiration of his first bicycle, the sudden realization that the curved, chromium-covered handle bars were a magnificent and hitherto undeveloped technological element for furniture. He developed a whole series of them, beginning with one made of crossed webbing slung within the chromed-steel frame and finally arriving at his 1928 version, a severe cantilever with two simple panels of natural caning in black, bentwood frames (Figure 9·4).

Such simple ideas can start a revolution in design (as witness the endless copies), but they are difficult to patent. Nor was there any rush at first to

ments some thirteen years before at the Bauhaus. Breuer also turned to city planning, and, in what seems a startling leap into the future, he designed a model project, "Civic Center of the Future," for the British Cement and Concrete Association. As a grab bag of ideas this 1936 project is packed with new concepts (including the Y-shaped office building that Breuer was not actually to build until the UNESCO Secretariat in 1958.)

One of Gropius's first acts after he had been appointed chairman of Harvard's department of architecture was to invite Breuer to join the staff. Breuer and Gropius, as new arrivals, were fascinated to discover new possibilities in the already existing vernacular of American building. Two elements immediately fascinated them: the clapboard construction of the exterior walls and the screened-in front porch. Even the traditional layout of a New England farmhouse held interesting lessons for them, with its centrally located fireplace, departmentation of space that could be closed or opened, and front hall. Breuer recalls that after touring his first New England farm house he suddenly felt he had been given the clue to Frank Lloyd Wright. Wright, who in his later years was known to swat house flies at Taliesin, calling them "Gropius," "Breuer," and "Mies" by turn, agreed, "Breuer is right."[5]

Actually Wright's antipathy to such Bauhaus figures as Gropius, Breuer, and Mies is basic. "A building is a man-made work, a crystallic, constructed thing," Breuer has declared. "It should not imitate nature—it should be in contrast to nature. A building has straight, geometrical lines. Even where it follows free lines, it should be always clear that they are built—that they did not just grow. I can see no reason at all why buildings should imitate natural, organic, or grown forms."

This clear, ringing statement orients Breuer's own approach to one of his own first American houses, the Chamberlain cottage (Figure 9·6). As in Le Corbusier's Villa Savoye (Figures 4·17–20), the living area is raised from the earth, giving the owner a view out and over the surrounding New England landscape. The wood siding, arranged vertically rather than horizontally as in the traditional clapboard pattern, gives a crispness and definition to the form. Of course this is a cottage, not a villa, but nonetheless Breuer has given detached elegance and drama (with its cantilevered porch) to what would normally be a simple camp structure.

9·6 Chamberlain cottage, Wayland, Massachusetts (1940), designed with Gropius, shows a fusion of modern with New England. The cottage has a cantilevered screened porch and precise vertical siding.

9·7 Robinson house, Williamstown, Massachusetts (1956), is an outstanding example of the architect's mature style. The house is binuclear in plan, with a deep eave sheltering the west wall of glass; stone wall "furniture" projects into space.

Breuer, however, is not irrevocably wedded to the house on stilts. Perhaps the typical American experience of raising ebullient children in a usually maidless household turned his attention to the problem of providing some separation of activities. Breuer's mind naturally works in opposites—living versus sleeping, night versus day, sun versus shadow. The result was a radically different house plan for the Robinson house in Williamstown, Massachusetts (Figure 9·7). Here a clear division of living and sleeping is made, with the adult side of the house (living room, dining room, music area, and kitchen) grouped on the right (Figure 9·6) and the dormitory area placed on the left. Connecting the two is the narrow entrance hall. The result of this binuclear plan is an H form, set beneath a butterfly roof, which has set the pattern for a whole series of future Breuer houses.

The Robinson house reveals many other aspects of Breuer's thinking about American housing. The structure is earth-hugging, although the view out over the low valley makes this far from oppressive. In fact, the large glass wall expanse (shaded by the overhang of the butterfly roof) is conscientiously oriented to include the view of the rolling foothills of the Green Mountains. Space is now sculptured beyond the strict perimeter of the walls by out-flung masonry walls; glass, wood, and stone are set in rhythmical harmony. On the interior, too, textures and contrasts are given a new prominence —woven rush rugs, stone fireplace, natural-finish wood.*

What can well be considered the ideal Breuer house—a structure that combines all Breuer's key concepts—is the Starkey house in Duluth, Minnesota (Figure 9·8). Set on a rocky hillside site, it is raised on stilts and thus provides an exhilarating view out over Lake Superior from the floor-to-ceiling windows of the living area. At the rear, however, the house is anchored, or more properly speaking, moored to the ground level by gangways. Underneath, the slope of the site provides a covered paved patio with open fireplace for cookouts on ground level, with a stone bench extending out into space.

It is in the interior planning, however, that Breuer has most carefully worked out the series of

interlocking interior spaces to provide a pattern of living. Breuer used his H plan to divide living and sleeping area (Figure 9·7), including a sound-proofed playroom with skydome above for the family's five children. The hallways are paved in stone, impervious to rubbers and overshoes. The living area makes maximum use of the sliding-glass-window view over the lake for both living room and dining room. The kitchen, with teakwood counters and formica walls, is connected to the living room by way of a pass-through. A porch, with sliding panels, facing on the south, makes an outdoor alternative for dining in summer. The louvered sunshades—a kind of horizontal trellis—are an early solution to the sun-on-glass problem. Here Breuer has also included panels of solar glass, which intercept the heat rays before they can reach the window glass proper.

"Color is the last point to be reached," Breuer says. "And I've always said, if you can paint something white, why do anything else? White is marvelous! But if you are going to have color, let's achieve the utmost in effect and contrast. I want the reddest red, the bluest blue, the yellowest yellow. I want the strongest use of color, the utmost in tension." Here the porch panels are in primaries, a vermilion red, cadmium yellow, white, and gray. On the interior, Breuer experimented with silk panels of cobalt blue on the interior (blue, he has discovered, is the more ethereal color, good day and night, whereas red in space changes everything to pink; yellow loses color at night, can give a sickish hue).

It is in the details that an architect's signature can be read, and a Breuer house is full of them, from such small items as the exposed steel rods at the base of the columns ("Where there is structure, it is always nice to express it") to the nautical exposed rigging of the porch and gangways, and the juxtaposition of such natural materials as the Philippine-rush carpeting in the dining room with the Breuer-designed table in natural-finish walnut. Perhaps the nicest touch in the Starkey house is the centrally positioned fireplace, which is both a warm focal point and a sculpturesque object in space. The monolithic form of bush-hammered concrete, with black buzzard and white marble chips for texture, seems to have been carved out of space, with openings giving a sense of mystery and a view beyond. It is primarily in his stairways (constructions in space) and fireplaces (forms in mass) that Breuer's sculptural impulse has found

---

* A somewhat similar structure, with butterfly roof and split-level interiors, was exhibited in Manhattan at the Museum of Modern Art's sculpture garden in 1949, where it attracted some seventy thousand visitors and probably did as much as any other structure to set off the boom in split-level dwellings that were the rage of the 1950s.

9·8 Starkey House, Duluth, Minnesota (1955), makes dramatic use of the broad lake view. The side facing the lake is one continuous wall of glass, with open area beneath used as a covered patio. There is a pronounced nautical flavor in the ramps suggesting gangways, connecting the structure with the site. Taut details in pure colors, such as sliding sun panels, lend a trim over-all appearance. The stone paving and rush mats provide textural warmth.

9·9 Ceramic wall designed by Miro creates an open patio for UNESCO's Salle des Pas-Perdus.

9·10 UNESCO Headquarters, Paris (1952–1958), designed with B. H. Zehrfuss and Pier Luigi Nervi, is Breuer's best work. Foreground sculpture by H. Moore.

9·11 South facade of UNESCO employs a variety of sunshade devices lending sparkle and crispness to the vast expanse of wall. Brackets support large panes of solar glass which intercept the sun's rays and cast a filtered shadow into the offices. Reinforcing the glass are horizontal louvers, while vertical slabs project from the wall in a staggered pattern. The design is both functional and decorative, but its efficiency was largely negated when the contractor, for economy reasons, refused to install the air conditioning planned by the architects.

its ultimate outlet. As one critic pointed out, "If there were a Fireplace Club, Breuer would be automatically elected president."

"Building seems to be a national passion in the United States," Breuer has remarked. "Here any housewife knows what a two-by-four is, or a plumbing fixture. In Europe this is known only to experts. Maybe this is a hangover from the pioneering past. And don't underestimate the Americans' feeling for space. They have an exact image of how space will look. A European will ask, 'How will the façade look?' or 'How will the wall be decorated?' An American immediately guesses, 'That will be about 30 by 20 feet,' and wants to know, 'Now where do I sit?' In other words, the American walks right through the plan, visualizing it as he goes."

Breuer believes that this inborn space sense allied with a natural independence accounts for the excellence of much private housing in the United States. But, he sadly adds, such is not the case with public housing. "As soon as this independent American becomes a member of a committee or a council, he becomes cautious," Breuer has found. "He doesn't want to stick his neck out and he doesn't want to hurt the other guy. This comes from his political training, his sense of how to get along. Of course, with industrial buildings, you get good design early. There's a boss, the president of the company, or what not, and he gets what *he* wants. But in public building—do we yet have a really modern town hall? However, there has been a break-through with schools. It seems that modern is cheaper. It is the cost factor that broke down the resistance."

Breuer's own break-through into the larger arena of architecture also came through school and college commissions. In 1950 he designed a dormitory for Vassar College; in 1952 an arts center for Sarah Lawrence College, and since then has worked on St. John's Abbey, Hunter College, a 107-house faculty unit for Princeton's Institute for Advanced Studies, as well as a high school in Litchfield, Connecticut, and Torrington, Connecticut, and more recently a factory for the Torrington Manufacturing Co. in Van Nuys, California. Breuer still keeps two to three houses on the drafting boards of his Manhattan office, if for no other reason than that they are the best discipline for his fifteen to twenty draftsmen. "A house has so many problems that if you can design one well, you can design anything," he once remarked. But increasingly Breuer finds himself involved in the major problems confronting architecture today. The event which pushed Breuer into the limelight was his selection as the American representative on the three-man design team to draw up plans for UNESCO's new 9-million-dollar headquarters in Paris.

The decision of the United Nations Educational, Scientific, and Cultural Organization to build a new secretariat and conference hall for itself in Paris offered twentieth-century architects an opportunity equaled only by the League of Nations and United Nations Secretariat in New York. The UN, too, had acquired considerable experience by constructing its own building in Manhattan.*

But bureaucracy seems to cultivate architectural confusion, in this case involving three false starts,

* See Chap. 10.

9·12 East facade of UNESCO requires less shade and is treated more simply. In foreground: Japanese garden by Noguchi.

a cumbersome superstructure of authority, flowing from UNESCO's administrative board to a Committee of Five ("Les Cinq") composed of France's Le Corbusier, Brazil's Lucio Costa, the United States's Walter Gropius, Sweden's Sven Markelius, and Italy's Ernesto Rogers. Under "Les Cinq" were "Les Trois" who were to do the actual design.

The first inkling Breuer had that he was being considered came while he was sitting at the Café des Deux Magots on the left bank one summer afternoon. He noticed Walter Gropius strolling by, and hailed him. Next to saunter along was Eero Saarinen, a consultant on the UNESCO project. Told of the general muddle that had occurred (an initial scheme by the French architect Baudoin had been rejected and a decision had been made to call in an international team), Breuer was asked if he was interested. A few weeks later in Italy he was notified he had been nominated, along with Italy's Pier Luigi Nervi* and France's young Bernard Zehrfuss. In July, 1952, the three met for the first time when the contract was signed.

From the start "Les Trois" found themselves in remarkable agreement. "This building has to give architectural expression to an international organization, and to an organization that is more than functional—it has cultural and scientific aims which are practically a modern religion," Breuer stated. "It needs more than a functional solution." The decision was made at the start to divide the complex into two major structures, a Secretariat office building and a Conference Hall. The structure was to be reinforced concrete. As Nervi pointed out,

* See Chap. 22.

"Reinforced concrete has been used only as a building material for bridges, factories, and other heavy construction, and even then it is usually covered up. Courage has been lacking to use it architecturally. Stone is considered the 'noble' material. Now concrete has come into use as an architectural material. It too has become noble."

Actually, Breuer already had the solution for the Secretariat up his sleeve. In a 1936 project titled "Civic Center of the Future," Breuer had first introduced the Y-shaped building. Reexamined in terms of UNESCO's requirements for office space for its 1,080 permanent employees, it made more sense than ever. No decision passed "Les Cinq" without grueling criticism (Zehrfuss later wearily remarked, "Corbu alone was as active as ten commissions"), but Breuer made a good case for his form. Its curved facade proved a felicitous complement to the half oval of the Place de Fontenoy. The Y shape provided windows for a maximum number of offices, and yet the gentle curve of the structure gave each room a sense of privacy from its neighbors, impossible, for instance, in an X-shaped structure. Even more important, the rounded Y shape was most massive at the central core, thus providing interior space for elevators, stairways, and toilets.

Breuer's series of sunshade devices, necessary to shield the 7-foot-tall sliding glass windows, included vertical travertine slabs, a horizontal lattice, and extended solar glass (Figure 9·11). These were meant as strictly functional elements, a fact Breuer emphasized by varying the devices according to the amount of sun, actually leaving part of the Place de Fontenoy façade devoid of any sunshade elements at all. In effect, however, they are highly decorative, giving a dazzle and sparkle that enlivens the whole façade.

Breuer's return to Europe as a practicing architect (he made nearly sixty Atlantic crossings while working on UNESCO) after an absence of twenty years resulted in an unexpected spate of commissions from European clients, now wealthy with the post-Second World War prosperity and eager to sample United States technology from a man who they knew would instinctively understand the requirements of a European client.*

* Among his first clients were the Harnischmachers, who had given Breuer his first commission in 1932. The original house was destroyed in a Second World War air raid. To replace it, Breuer designed another house, this time using fieldstone and including a pergola!

9·13 Hunter College Library, The Bronx, New York (1959), uses hyperbolic paraboloids, each 60 by 60 feet, to span the roof. At the rear is a classroom structure.

The Van Leer Office Building (1959) in Amstelveen, Holland, offered Breuer a chance to try his double-Y-shaped office structure. The building is full of mature Breuer trademarks, for instance, the suspended bridge leading from the two-story lobby to the second floor. The landscape is carefully cultivated (the site has been made partially into a civic park). The exhilarating introduction to reinforced concrete that Breuer received while working with Nervi on UNESCO shows up in dramatic concrete canopies and the folded plate roof of poured concrete over the lobby—the new plasticity that has become the mark of the architecture of the 1960s.

For the Bijenkorf Department Store (a name meaning literally "Beehive") in Rotterdam, Breuer was given the prize corner on the city's main shopping thoroughfare. Since a department store, stated functionally, is merely a large showcase, Breuer decided to employ a basic box design. On the exterior façade he elaborated an over-all pattern of hexagonal blocks of travertine, patterned with staggered, slitlike openings. In doing this, Breuer was moving away from the desire to express structure by revealing its floor-by-floor organization in favor of treating the façade as one over-all pattern. This indicates a major shift in architectural goals for modern architecture, one that derives from what Breuer calls "the all-important change in our lives: We have learned to move faster—faster than anyone ever moved before. We no longer see little details, disconnected or detached from the over-all picture. We see continuities."

This new experience of space, of space in motion, space in flow, is for Breuer the essential challenge of modern architecture. "The nature of space within our buildings or between them is indeed the reality of architecture," he says, and points to the world of reinforced concrete as proof of a new, emerging substance to mold space within. "Here is a completely plastic medium," he says, "concrete for compression, steel for tension in one new material . . . not only bones alone, but bones, muscles and skin combined." [6]

Following on UNESCO, Breuer has begun to make increasing use of the possibilities of reinforced concrete in a multitude of stimulating ways. For Hunter College's Bronx campus, Breuer evolved a hyperbolic paraboloid roof (Figure 9·13) which looks like a tied mattress from the air, a series of six umbrellas (each 60 by 60 feet) in profile. To guard the glass on the exposed side he has designed a honeycomb grille of utilitarian open

12-inch flue tiles, somewhat reminiscent of the Bijenkorf façade.

In St. John's Benedictine Abbey, in Collegeville, Minnesota, a combined monastery and school, the first monastic wing is already built. Its new church is a striking structure which incorporates Nervi's folded slab (Figure 9·14) and the honeycomb tiles of Hunter College, and adds a dramatic new element, a 99-foot-tall cantilevered bell banner that will act as a reflecting surface for light, sending it back through the grille into the church from the north, and will serve as an inspiring symbol and mark the main entrance of the abbey.

Such a bold, sculptural gesture is indeed a long distance along the road which began with the sleek, glittering metal of Breuer's first chromium chair, and yet it has been traversed by Breuer without break in logic or essentially contradicting the fusion of form with function which lies at the essence of the Bauhaus's concept of space. No less than Le Corbusier's Chapel at Ronchamp or Eero Saarinen's TWA terminal, Breuer's St. John's Abbey announces that, as modern architecture matures, it has only begun to create the form world which will mark the twentieth century in the future history of architecture.

9·14 The chapel of St. John's Abbey, Collegeville, Minnesota (1961), with a beehive facade, has a 99-foot-high bell banner at the entrance. The bell banner acts as a reflecting surface, sends light into church.

Our architecture reflects us, as truly as a mirror
LOUIS SULLIVAN

10 : **WALLACE K.**

10·2 Trylon and Perisphere, symbol of the 1939 New York World's Fair. Spire and sphere forms may have been suggested by the campanile and domes of St. Mark's in Venice. Harrison's bold plastic handling has made them original and memorable.

The twentieth century has been richly endowed with innovators, men of genius who have practiced their profession as a great science and preached it with revolutionary zeal. But as a profession, architecture also has need of another type of man, one who has a bit of the poet and dreamer about him but whose vision is always tempered by a realistic appreciation of the conditions under which he is operating—the money available, the client he is working for, the factor of time.

Just such a role has been played by Wallace Kirkman Harrison, youngest of the seven architects who designed Rockefeller Center in the 1930s and a key figure in every major New York project ever since. He is the author of the famed Trylon and Perisphere symbol of the 1939 New York World's Fair, director of planning for the United Nations Secretariat and Assembly, chief architect of the Lincoln Center for the Performing Arts, and chairman of the Design Board (assisted by Gordon Bunshaft and Edward D. Stone) for the 1964 New York World's Fair.

Few men in this century have been so deeply immersed in the realities of building and planning, or have so consistently maintained high standards of excellence against what often has seemed overwhelming odds. The balance sheet Harrison draws from this wide experience, however, is corrosive. Praised as a great coordinator, he has been known to explode, "Group architecture is a mess!" Cited as a bold innovator in skyscraper design, Harrison wonders aloud if he has yet to produce a single masterpiece. But, to Harrison's great credit, he has seen to it that architecture is more than accommodation, adjustment, and compromise. "I have always tried to move forward to something better," he once said thoughtfully, "even at the risk of being wrong. That way you are certainly ahead of the man who is right and doesn't do anything."[1]

The truth is that Harrison is a maverick. The difference between Harrison and other mavericks is that Harrison is a practical one. It is a combination rarely seen, but it is made to order for the

HARRISON : THE ARCHITECT AS COORDINATOR

mid-twentieth century. It has also given him a rough-and-ready quality that sets him off as a kind of self-educated chief bosun, although in fact he is highly educated, a vigorous amateur painter who has numbered among his close friends both France's Fernand Léger and Finland's great Alvar Aalto. He was born in Worcester, Massachusetts, on September 28, 1895, the son of the superintendent in a local iron works. When his mother died, Harrison at the age of fourteen went to work for a local contractor. By the time he was eighteen he had become a junior draftsman, and at twenty he moved to New York to work for the great conservative firm of McKim, Mead & White.

Harrison studied architecture at night, managed eventually to pass the stiff entrance examinations to the Paris Beaux-Arts, and later finished his education abroad with a two-year traveling scholarship around Europe. Back in the United States he worked his way through the leading architectural firms of Manhattan, eventually got his chance to work on his first skyscraper, the twenty-three-story Pennsylvania Power & Light Company Building in Allentown, Pennsylvania, and earned a junior partnership in the firm of Helmle, Corbett & Harrison. When this firm was chosen to be a member of the group of architects to design Rockefeller Center in 1929, Harrison had his chance to contribute to the building project that still stands out as one of the most successful urban complexes of this century.

The two giants who dominated the Rockefeller Center planning were Harvey Wiley Corbett, an architect who insisted buildings must have "thrill appeal" (and who incidentally had been one of Harrison's teachers), and Raymond Hood, the man whose career summarizes the entire rapid maturing

10·3 Lincoln Center for the Performing Arts, the largest group project which Harrison has been called upon to coordinate. To be completed by the mid-1960s, the center includes (left to right) Philip C. Johnson's Theater for the Dance and Operetta, Harrison's monumental Metropolitan Opera House, Max Abramovitz's Philharmonic Hall, and (blocked in at right) the Repertory Drama Theater with Library Museum, by Eero Saarinen and Gordon Bunshaft, and Pietro Belluschi's Julliard School of Music.

104

10·4–5 Rockefeller Center, New York, a sixteen-building city within a city and one of the most successful urban complexes of the twentieth century. Above, central slab of the seventy-story RCA Building, with the International Building and General Dynamics Building at right. Below, air view shows new Time-Life Building at far right.

of skyscraper construction in the United States. During the two crucial decades between the completion of the 52-story Woolworth Building in 1913 and the 102-story Empire State Building and Rockefeller Center in 1933, Raymond Hood had changed from a talented designer to a national leader. With John Mead Howells,* Hood had won the world-famous $100,000 Chicago Tribune Tower design competition in 1922, with a building that was topped with Gothic tracery. Then almost overnight he had switched to the side of the "moderns." Indeed, Hood's two Manhattan skyscrapers, the Daily News Building with its lucid, crisp verticals, and the McGraw-Hill Building, which emphasized the repetitive horizontals, were at the time, with Howe & Lescaze's Philadelphia Savings Fund Society Building, the finest skyscrapers since Sullivan's.

After the death of Hood in 1934, Harrison formed a partnership with Hood's partner, the Swiss-born engineer André Fouilhoux, and the brilliant young designer Max Abramovitz. One of their first commissions was to design the keynote symbol for the 1939 New York World's Fair. Harrison made 1,036 sketches before hitting on the final design—one he admits "you find in everything from pornography to architecture." The result (Figure 10·2) was the 700-foot high Trylon and 200-foot-diameter Perisphere. It was one of the most memorable theme symbols ever executed, although typically Harrison to this day insists the decision to lop off the top 20 feet of the Trylon (for economy reasons) was nothing short of "a disaster."

After the Second World War, Harrison found himself increasingly, though not exclusively, concerned with the Rockefeller interests. As far back as 1926, he and Nelson Rockefeller became, in a manner of speaking, brothers-in-law (actually the brother of Harrison's wife, David Milton, had married Nelson Rockefeller's sister Abby. Over morning coffee at Rockefeller Center's Gateway Coffee Shop the two had planned such projects as the twelve-story Rockefeller Apartments and the 12-million-dollar Hotel Avila in Caracas.

During the Second World War, Harrison had gone to Washington, D.C., to serve as Director of Cultural Relations under Rockefeller, then Coordinator of Inter-American Affairs. It was this close working relationship that brought Harrison into

* Son of the author William Dean Howells and nephew of William Rutherford Mead, founding member of McKim, Mead & White.

the Rockefellers' last-minute bid to keep the United Nations headquarters in Manhattan, a rapid behind-the-scenes thriller that involved an $8,500,-000 pledge by Harrison in the name of John D. Rockefeller, Jr., to the real estate developer William Zeckendorf for the 17-acre plot between Forty-second Street and Fiftieth Street on the East River.

With Harrison as director of planning, the next task was to pick a representative group of ten architects to form the design team. ''We couldn't pick Alvar Aalto, who's a wonderful architect, because Finland wasn't a member of the UN,'' Harrison has since explained. ''We had to pass up Mies van der Rohe and Walter Gropius because they were too closely identified with prewar Germany.'' [2] This left France's Le Corbusier as the big question mark. It was with considerable trepidation, but with a sense of justice, that Le Corbusier was named.

In retrospect it seems as if Le Corbusier, who had been ruled out of the League of Nations competition on the flimsy grounds that his plans had been submitted in the wrong kind of ink, must have been waiting in Paris with his bags packed. He arrived in January, 1947, two months before the others, and by April, when the first meeting was held, he already had sixty pages of his sketchbook filled with analyses and plans for the building. In one sense, there was nearly universal agreement that the Secretariat would, because of site limitations, have to be a high-rise building. In fact, an already built prototype existed: Rio de Janeiro's Ministry of Education and Health (Figure 20·8), for which Le Corbusier had provided the original impetus, although the actual design had been carried out by a group of Brazilian architects, including Oscar Niemeyer, Brazil's representative on the UN planning group.

It is the nature of all international bodies to engage in politics, and Le Corbusier's commanding prestige plus his volatile temper and messianic cast of mind, made him a natural leader. Oscar Niemeyer, whose plan for orienting the buildings around a court is today considered by many architects to have been superior, yielded to Le Corbusier's scheme. The Soviet architect-engineer Bassov took strongest exception. Looking at Le Corbusier's slab structure set off the ground on stilts (*pilotis*), Bassov snorted, ''Chicken legs. Nokay!''

10·6 UN architects—back row (left to right), Sven Markelius (Sweden), Le Corbusier (France), Vladimir Bodiansky (France), Wallace Harrison (United States), G. D. Soilleux (Australia), Max Abramovitz (United States), Ernest Weissman (Yugoslavia), John Antoniades (Greece), and Matthew Nowicki (Poland); front, Ssu-ch'eng Liang (China), Niemeyer (Brazil), N. D. Bassov (Russia), and Ernest Cormier (Canada).

10·7 UN Secretariat and Assembly (1947–1952). Monumental glass-wall slab is thirty-nine stories high. At right can be seen the Assembly dome, which allows added interior height. The low block at center is the Conference Hall.

Actually, as Le Corbusier later took pains to point out, the final scheme was essentially his. But Harrison was appointed to execute the building. It became a nightmare task as the lack of financial credit of the UN became apparent. Next the Korean War broke out, bringing with it steel shortages and soaring construction costs. Harrison found himself in the position of trying to erect a building with melting sugar cubes.

To meet the need for economy, four committee rooms were dropped from the low Conference Building. The Assembly, originally conceived as a wasp-waisted structure with two auditoriums, was reduced to one auditorium. In the course of redesigning it no less than nine times, each revision more drastic than the last, the auditorium roof was dropped 15 feet, with a dome inserted to compensate for the lack of height, and the north lobby was reduced in width by 20 feet. Interiors, too, suffered, as terrazzo and carpeting were substituted for marble, fabric for wood, and painted concrete for plaster.

Essentially the drama of the UN lies in its massive thirty-nine-story Secretariat with its sheer curtain wall of glass set dramatically overlooking the East River. To design such a façade, actually 2,700 windows held by a tracery of aluminum

which could withstand winds of literally hurricane force, was a daring undertaking. Its successful completion is an engineering feat for which Harrison deserves full credit, as he does for introducing the first thermal glass. The United Nations Secretariat announced the arrival of the monumental slab and the hung glass curtain wall, with its startling reflectivity. It did not solve the problem of insulating the wall from the sun, as Le Corbusier underlined with some asperity when he criticized it for not incorporating exterior sun breakers (*brise soleils*)—an icicle hazard in Manhattan. Harrison, summing up his own feelings at the time, said, "The world hopes for a symbol of peace. We have given them a workshop for peace."[3]

The problem of the enclosing envelope for the skyscraper, obviously, is one that architecture has not yet heard the end of, as the later efforts of men like Edward D. Stone and Marcel Breuer (both of whom incorporate grilles as architectural air conditioning) indicate. Harrison's experimentation with the skin of the skyscraper has also been intense and adventuresome. For the Davenport, Iowa, offices of the Aluminum Company of America, Harrison had in 1949 first tried sheathing a structure in aluminum. Far more daring, however, was the ALCOA Building in Pittsburgh (Figure 10·8), a thirty-story tower in which aluminum was used in nearly every conceivable way, from hinges and window frames to hardware, including the spectacular 6- by 12-foot precast panels with which the entire building is sheathed. The Socony Building on East Forty-second Street, New York, is a far less successful attempt to use a novel prefabricated-metal-paneling system, in this case stainless steel. Indeed, the restlessness of the pattern, carried out over forty-two stories, is just garish, and the attempt to reintroduce a steel arch at the entrance is even less successful.

Manhattan's Corning Glass Building on Fifth Avenue, on the other hand, is elegance itself, as nearly a complete glass composition as the art of building will allow. The nature of the client, famous for Steuben glass, of course suggested exploiting glass in much the way ALCOA suggested aluminum. But Harrison and his partner Max Abramovitz managed to give this structure a glittering, ethereal quality that uses glass as a huge reflecting mirror to its nth degree. Even a few glaring errors of taste (e.g., the banal Fifth Avenue entrance and the much ado about very little in the plaza area) do not keep this from being one of the

10·9 The Time-Life Building, forty-eight stories, is the latest addition to Rockefeller Center. Exterior columns clad in limestone harmonize well with the older structures.

10·10 Oberlin College Auditorium (1953) gives the acoustic form strong plastic expression. Marble exterior is a prototype for Harrison's Metropolitan Opera House at Manhattan's Lincoln Center.

better skyscrapers in the tautly wrapped tradition of Lever House and Harrison's own east and west UN façade.

The Time-Life Building, the seventeenth structure of the Rockefeller Center complex and the first to jump across the Avenue of the Americas (Figure 10·9), clothes the vertical columns in limestone, the basic curtain-wall material used throughout the Center. Again the play of vertical masses against a low-lying slab used in Corning Glass is carried out. But the structure is also adventuresome, consisting of vertical piers carried up the full 587 feet on the exterior, which adds a dramatic verticality to the structure and a rhythm to the façade that was lacking in the monolithic flat walls of the older structures. This, of course, has a dollars-and-cents reason, namely, freeing the interior wall of its usual piers. Unhappily, the arrangement of interior modular spacing fell short of exploiting this generous space.

Skyscrapers, while they are doubtless Harrison's most obvious contribution to the Manhattan cityscape, by no means are the total output of the large Harrison & Abramovitz office. The firm has been almost as busy with college buildings, hospitals, industrial showcases. An outstanding example is the Oberlin Auditorium (Figure 9·10), in which

10·11 First Presbyterian Church, Stamford, Connecticut (1959), an essay in reinforced-concrete-slab construction. Vast spaces filled with chipped cathedral glass are carried up to the roof in a splendor of colored light. Structural engineer: Felix Samuely.

Harrison experimented with a big curved masonry-covered wall, fitting it to the acoustic requirements, to create a handsome structure that fuses form and function with striking effect.

An equally successful project, and far more impressive because of its scope, has been the campus buildings for Brandeis University, particularly notable for its delightful grouping of three small chapels designed by Max Abramovitz. Nor has Harrison & Abramovitz been caught napping in the shift toward reinforced-concrete structures. The University of Illinois Assembly Hall, a gigantic double shell that will seat up to 20,000, owes most to Max Abramovitz, himself an alumnus of Illinois (1929). The First Presbyterian Church in Stamford, Connecticut (Figure 10·11), is a personal project of Wallace Harrison's. Here folded-concrete slabs and lattices are used to create a space frame filled with cathedral glass from Chartres, carrying out Harrison's desire to "use new materials and new construction methods to create a place of worship with some of the splendor of colored light found in the great Gothic cathedrals."

The most challenging commission to come Harrison's way since the UN was his appointment as coordinator of design for the Lincoln Center for the Performing Arts. This project, which again centers on the Rockefellers, is estimated to cost some 90 million dollars before it is completed, and will cover a 12-acre site between Sixty-second and Sixty-sixth Streets between Broadway and Amsterdam Avenue on Manhattan's hitherto rather seedy West Side. And again it places Harrison reluctantly in the role of coordinating his fellow architects, an impressive list made up of such talented designers as Eero Saarinen, Gordon Bunshaft (for Skidmore, Owings & Merrill), Philip Johnson, and Dean Pietro Belluschi of M.I.T.

As early as the site-planning stage, however (Figure 10·12), it became apparent that the whole scheme was becoming infused with a nostalgia for a Renaissance plaza (like St. Mark's in Venice), with the equally Renaissance temptation for each architect to outdo the next. A unified scheme along the lines of a massive superblock, perhaps pierced with interior courts, which Gordon Bunshaft proposed, was blocked by the New York Philharmonic, which insisted that its structure (designed by Max Abramovitz) could no longer be delayed. This decision to go ahead piecemeal thus forced the project in the direction of a central open plaza, one that seems almost gridlike with its extensions. Around it, the architects are forced to design as individuals, a perilous procedure.

Even Harrison's own plans for the new Metropolitan Opera House also testify to the underlying restlessness of architecture today. Perhaps Harrison's term "new baroque," used to describe his preliminary Metropolitan Opera House project (Figure 10·14), is as useful as any in describing the romantic, questing mood. If dazzling conquest of space was to have been the keynote of Lincoln Center, then the modern means for accomplishing it, namely, vast shell structures, have not been called upon to provide it. A far greater failure than the stylistic uncertainties of Lincoln Center would, of course, have been the inability of one of the greatest cities on earth to organize itself toward such a potentially enriching civic enterprise. Not the least of the contributions of Harrison, the man who gets things done, is that Lincoln Center is becoming a reality. As for its stylistic weaknesses, Harrison, more than any other architect, is aware that the slow distillation of style is a luxury that the realities of today may not always allow. As so often has happened in the past, the challenge is to build now, and as well as possible. "When you leave the drawing board and start getting your hands dirty," Harrison observes, "you stop thinking of buildings as a challenge to create absolute art. You're happy to settle for good buildings that get built, in the hope that they will lead to progressively better buildings."

10·12–15 Lincoln Center, emerging in the 1960s, illustrates the strong neoclassic direction taken by American architects in designing structures of a monumental scale. Below (left to right) are Philip C. Johnson, Max Abramovitz, Eero Saarinen, Pietro Belluschi, and Gordon Bunshaft inspecting a model of Philharmonic Hall with Harrison (at the extreme right).

11·1 Edward D. Stone's United States Embassy, New Delhi (1959), was designed as a salute to Indian culture and American prestige abroad.

All revolutions are shot through with irony, perhaps the greatest of which is that the revolution actually succeeds. In architecture, the present is such an era. There has probably never been a more complete and total rout in the battles of styles than the obliteration of the whole Beaux-Arts. The noisy battlefield of the early decades of the twentieth century has become silent and empty. And yet the peace does not quite live up to its advance billing.

Today a new specter stalks architecture, the monotony of endless glass façades. The problem of how to bring back to architecture some of its traditional elements of ornament, the play of light and shadow, and tactile elements of delight is one that obsesses the present generation who flock out of nostalgia to Venice's Piazza San Marco and pin pictures of the Doge's Palace by their drafting boards. In the 1960s this hungering after beauty has found an unexpected champion in Edward Durell Stone, a man whose early career had cast him as one of the foremost American modernists but whose continuing love of the great classic monuments of the past gave him the inspiration to break the fifty-year taboo against ornament. He has returned to such classic prototypes as the Greek temple (in the United States Embassy in New

Delhi), the Pompeian house (in the Graf house, Dallas, Texas), even the mammoth Colosseum (with the United States Pavilion in the Brussels World's Fair). With a love of richness unmatched since the turn-of-the-century neoclassicist Stanford White (1853–1906), Edward Durell Stone stands in the vanguard of the New Romantics.

Edward D. Stone was born on March 9, 1902, in Fayetteville, Arkansas, a small (population 18,069) university town and county seat. It was there, at the age of fourteen, that Edward D. Stone began his architectural career by winning $2.50 for his prize-winning birdhouse in a local lumberyard competition. Stone's winning entry, as he recalls it, was "something straight out of Bernard Maybeck, a modest shelter for bluebirds, covered with sassafras branches." [1]

Stone's introduction to great architecture came when he went east to Boston to visit his brother, James Hicks Stone, fourteen years his senior and a practicing architect. The grand tour began with McKim, Mead & White's Boston Public Library, went on to H. H. Richardson's Trinity Church, and wound up in Manhattan, where his brother led him blindfolded to the middle of Brooklyn Bridge to give him his first view of Manhattan's skyline

11 : **EDWARD D. STONE** :
THE NEW ROMANTICISM

11·2 Stone and his wife Maria in Venice.

Architecture is what buildings do to you

WALT WHITMAN

11·3 Museum of Modern Art, New York (1937–1939), Manhattan's first major building in the International Style. Insulated glass facade, street-level opening, and punched-out penthouse roof are style notes carried over from the 1920s.

through the spidery web of bridge cables. On his own, Stone went on to Washington, D.C., stood entranced with the Pan American Building's tropical courts, colored tiles, and exotic macaws. "I decided that if architecture can be like this, then this is what I would really like to do. By the time I got back to Fayetteville, that hotbed of tranquillity, the die was cast."

Stone left Arkansas for Boston, got a job as an office boy for 10 dollars a week and signed up for night classes at Boston's Architectural Club. Soon he won a scholarship at Harvard. Design was Stone's special talent, and it was prized above all others in the Beaux-Arts system. Stone was able to finish two years of design at Harvard in one year. But faced with a long series of engineering courses, Stone threw his slide rule on the floor, announced he was off to M.I.T. to study with Prix de Rome winner Jacques Carlu. After one year he won the Rotch Traveling Scholarship and, still without a degree, Stone set off for a two-year trip through Europe, living on the Ile Saint Louis in Paris one winter, next to the clock tower of Venice's Piazza San Marco another. The "romance of the classic" held Stone entranced, but as a young architect with a career to make, he sought out the

handful of modern structures—a theater by Erich Mendelsohn, Mies van der Rohe's Barcelona Pavilion. He arrived back in New York in 1929 with $12 and the conviction that modern architecture would sweep the United States.

"It was an exciting time," Stone recalls. "People were jumping out of windows on Wall Street, and the new Waldorf-Astoria was going up on Park Avenue." The world into which Stone plunged was caught up in a stage of architecture best described as "modernoid": columns that met the roof without capitals, and thin wood veneers carried round corners. Stone hailed them all enthusiastically and did his best to get them incorporated into the Waldorf-Astoria (his first job in the United States as a draftsman), including a romantic trellised ceiling for the Waldorf's Starlight Roof. Within two years he had moved over to the Graybar Building to join the architects designing Rockefeller Center. There, on the first day, he found himself caught in the dispute between Hood and Corbett over whether the central RCA Building should be a flat slab (Corbett) or have setbacks (Hood). Stone voted for the slab.

Stone arrived late in the Rockefeller Center project. His own work, primarily on Radio City

11·4 A. Conger Goodyear House, Old Westbury, Long Island (1938), was a precise, elegant structure built in the modern style. Free-form table is by Isamu Noguchi.

Music Hall, merges into what was essentially a team effort. But at the time there was no more vital group of architects at work than those assembled at Rockefeller Center. When the Music Hall was completed, Stone, like most architects, floundered in the Depression, sometimes turning out lighting fixtures and advertising layouts for a living. But with a commission from Richard H. Mandel in 1935, Stone designed one of the first modern houses in the International Style to be seen in the United States.

The great taste-making institution of the late 1930s was the Museum of Modern Art. But when the Museum of Modern Art decided to use American architects, the fact became apparent that there was no American of international stature available (Frank Lloyd Wright at the time not being "modern"). The answer was a compromise: Philip L. Goodwin, a good but conventional architect (and member of the Museum Board) was chosen in tandem with Edward Stone, the outstanding design talent in the modern style who was alive at the time.

The resulting structure has proved to be a remarkably workable building. A monolithic cube on the exterior enclosing open loft space, with movable partitions within, it remained essentially unchanged until a vastly expanded collection necessitated an addition designed by Philip C. Johnson in the 1960s. The building, as a matter of course, was set on *pilotis* in the style of Le Corbusier, a glass curtain wall on the floor level (Figure 11·3), thus putting an end to the palatial staircases leading to massive skylighted barrel vaults which McKim, Mead & White had favored. Stone would have preferred a façade of marble; the director, Alfred Barr, Jr., wanted at least a minimum of natural lighting.

The solution to the problem was finally found in a clear, translucent wall of laminated glass which shed a soft, alabaster glow within. On the top an elegant free-form, glass-enclosed roof garden was sheltered by a roof (Stone has always liked a lid, or termination, to a building), pierced with open holes, an equally Corbusian motif, in this case suggested by the museum's director of architecture, John McAndrew.

Stone's success with the Museum of Modern Art was capped by a commission from A. Conger Goodyear, the founding chairman of the Museum's board of directors, for a small bachelor pavilion set on a hill on a promontory of Old Westbury, Long Island (Figure 11·4). In styling, this flat-top structure echoed many of the details of the Museum of Modern Art's penthouse; freestanding columns supported a cantilevered roof, behind which was placed a screen of glass. The flat planes of the roof were carried outward, an echo of Frank Lloyd Wright's turn-of-the-century prairie houses, now refined and metamorphized by European architects. The dining room, a circular structure encased in glass bricks and a curving picture window, boasted a Calder mobile suspended from the ceiling; the living room, the first of Isamu Noguchi's free-form tables. Details throughout the building—from the arboretum entrance to the bathrooms in butterscotch-colored marble—are sumptuously executed. For smartness and elegance in the then modern manner, the A. Conger Goodyear house in Long Island is one of the finest houses in the United States, now slightly dated but eminently livable.

The Second World War provided Stone, as well as dozens of other architects, with the first opportunity to plan on a large scale. In Stone's case his tasks as a United States Army Air Force office boy were planning the permanent installations for such airfields as Maxwell Field, Fairfield Suisun (now Travis) Air Base near San Francisco, Muroc (now Edwards) at Los Angeles, prototypes for the Eastern Seaboard Terminal for transport planes built after the war.

Immediately after the war, a commission to build El Panama Hotel (Figure 11·5) in the tropical

climate of Panama gave Stone a chance to explore another large and complex form. A hotel virtually without corridors, without windows, and without doors, El Panama proved a stylesetter for the tropics and has since been copied for resort hotels from Hawaii to Istanbul. It was designed to be only a single suite in thickness, with open-balcony corridor to the rear and individual cantilevered balconies fronting each room, an arrangement that turned each room into a breezeway and gave the exterior its elegant beehive façade (Figure 11·6). The ground floor was essentially lobbyless, with bar, restaurant, and reception desks merely areas enclosed in a glass screen, the only air-conditioned area in the building, and handsomely landscaped by San Francisco's Thomas Church.

The University of Arkansas Fine Arts Center * was in many ways a pivotal building for Stone. There were hints of Stone's later devices in the hung metal-mesh ceiling of the theater; the open brickwork (which also had been used in the Goodyear house and El Panama) pointed toward Stone's later use of the precast-concrete grille. What was holding back Stone's architectural career at this point was his harum-scarum reputation as a practical joker and devotee of the Martini pitcher. When a bathtub in the hotel in Little Rock, Arkansas, was found brimful of yellow Jello, the man-

*This won an honour award from the American Institute of Architects. Stone's Museum of Modern Art and El Panama Hotel had both won Architectural League gold medals.

11·5–6 El Panama Hotel, now El Panama-Hilton, Panama City (1946), was a style setter for hotels in the tropics. The ten-story structure is only one suite deep and acts as a breezeway for trade winds. The honeycomb facade (below) is composed of many individual private balconies.

11·7–9 United States Embassy in New Delhi, a new approach to architectural richness in government buildings. Textural qualities appear in pergolas for servants' quarters, gold-mesh screen over the interior water court, gold-leafed columns, and polished terrazzo grille on the facade.

ager in a panic called for the FBI. Those who knew Stone was in town could have named the culprit.

On June 24, 1954, Edward Stone married Maria Elena Torch, a diminutive, peppery Cleveland girl, some twenty-five years his junior.* At Maria's insistence, Stone became a teetotaler. Overnight Stone changed from a man his acquaintances described as "an unmade bed, a kind of one-man slum," into a somewhat sheepish figure of elegance. The effect on Stone's architecture was even more dramatic.

Three days after his marriage, Stone turned his attention to his newest commission, a new United States Embassy for New Delhi, India. For years Stone had cheerfully confessed, "At heart I am a classicist." As the ideal solution for a great public building he had in mind the classic Greek temple. In a few quick strokes on the back of a brown manila envelope, Stone set down the plan and elevation for the new embassy, a building destined to become one of the most exciting structures in modern architecture (Figure 11·9). The plan is simplicity itself, a rectangular structure with deep overhangs supported by thin steel columns covered with gold leaf. Within is a great interior atrium, or court,

* A second marriage for Stone. He has two sons, Edward, Jr., and Robert Vandiver, by his first wife, Orlean Vandiver.

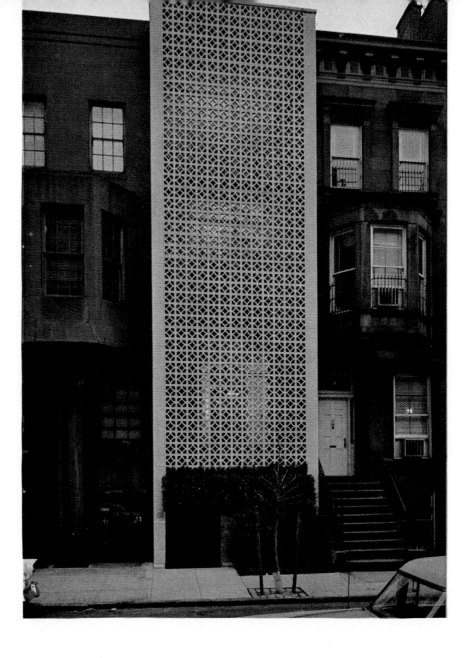

11·10 Concrete grille popularized by the New Delhi Embassy was used for the facade of Stone's Manhattan residence, a converted brownstone. Grille provides privacy in daytime, at night becomes a lacy stone curtain with romantic Arabian overtones.

11·11 Stuart Company, Pasadena, California (1958), uses Stone's grille as the front facade for a light industrial plant (vitamins). The 400-foot-long facade is enhanced by lighting, fountains and pools.

11·12–13 Palo Alto-Stanford Medical Center, Palo Alto, California (1957–1960), a 19-million-dollar complex, is organized around a 10-acre quadrangle which is bordered by a 300-foot-long colonnade. The poured concrete is given a rich, Wrightian surface.

converted into a floating garden. Overhead, as a sun-filtering device, Stone used the same metal mesh he had experimented with in the Arkansas Fine Arts Theater.

An inspection trip to view the New Delhi site, however, convinced Stone that his original idea of using a curtain wall of clear glass around the building was highly impractical. With temperatures as high as 120 degrees Fahrenheit, even automobiles left in the open turned into untouchables within minutes. Casting about for a local solution, Stone seized on the stone grilles prominent in Moslem temples and used as an element of adornment on such monuments as the great Taj Mahal. The actual design for the grille, a combination of squares and circles, was something, as Stone admits, "you can find in any handbook of ornament." But cast in hand-polished terrazzo and studded with gold knobs, it produced a stunning effect, ages old in origin but startling and new when employed by a major modern architect.

The success of the New Delhi Embassy was overwhelming. Overnight the grille became the most discussed topic in architecture. Stone began to use it in a startling variety of ways, as a 400-foot front façade for the Stuart Company in Pasadena, Calif. (Figure 11·11); as the front for his own remodeled brownstone in Manhattan (Figure 11·10); to enclose a luxurious Texas mansion outside Dallas; and as a major element in some half dozen university campuses. It was a dazzling display, but it raised some pertinent questions. Snorted one rival architect, "Architecture is more than putting up drapes in front of a house to hide it."

"But the grille is not a whim," Stone maintains. "It solves a basic problem inherent in all glass buildings, the problem of direct rays striking glass, which gives heat and glare. Shading glass from the outside is not new. French shutters and Italian blinds are a way of accomplishing the same end. Niemeyer's Ministry of Education and Health in Rio used *brise soleils* (sun breakers). A glass house is lovely if you own the view. But otherwise you are exposed to your neighbors in your pajamas. The grille is a basic architectural principle, as sound an idea as two steel columns with glass between them."

It was clear that in pointing out the defects of a hung glass façade, Stone was touching a sensitive nerve. The desire to etherealize the former formidable masonry wall into pure glass (or, as one critic has suggested, the desire to expose oneself)

has been so strong among modern architects that venetian blinds, green and then gray solar glass, and finally deep insets have been welcomed as long as the glass itself could be exposed. By making a frontal attack on this desire for exposure, Stone ruffled more tempers than he soothed. Significantly, Stone soon realized that the grille is not an end but a means. In his latest work the grille appears, but judiciously, as a signature, much like Le Corbusier's *brise soleils*.

In retrospect, the hullabaloo may have masked Stone's real position, namely, his belief that it is time for modern architecture to relax a little in favor of ornament and, secondly, his return to classic models for inspiration. It is in this sense that Stone's solar grille comes finally into perspective, not as a major organizing device for architecture, but as an element of design, both functional and highly decorative in its exploitation of light and shade. But the essence of architecture, as Stone knows well, lies in the organization of space, rather than in surface detail.

The United States Pavilion for the 1958 Brussels World's Fair is a striking example of Stone's flair for design and his use of classical models as a source of inspiration. The ground set aside for the United States Pavilion was a triangular plot which included several magnificent trees in a natural amphitheater. To dramatize the site, Stone devoted nearly half the area to an open plaza and reflecting pool. For the structure itself, Stone turned to Rome's Colosseum. In classic times, this Roman landmark had been rigged by Roman sailors with a great cloth velarium, or overhead canopy. Stone decided to capitalize on this idea, but instead of nautical ropes, Stone naturally turned to modern steel cables.

The circular pavilion was spanned with a plastic roof supported by cables radiating out from the center tension ring much in the manner of a bicycle wheel. The span required was 350 feet across, and the suspension roof developed surprising tensions. To support the center ring, some 63 feet across and weighing 25 tons, the steel cables were put under 100-ton tension. To surround the pavilion, Stone used a bowed, 42-foot-tall wall of transparent plastic, held in tension by a lattice system of steel straps. The finished structure had the effect of a translucent drum through which light filtered on the eleven giant willows left intact on the site, revealing a glittering mesh ceiling suspended from the lower spokes of the wheel. Despite the disap-

11·14 United States Pavilion for the 1958 Brussels World's Fair. The dramatic, drum-shaped structure with transparent, latticed walls capture the gaiety of good exhibition architecture. It is set off by a 250-foot reflecting pool and the pluming fountains.

11·15 Stuart Company interior carries the gaiety of exhibition architecture into office spaces. Entrance is from balcony above; company pool for employees is at left.

pointing displays, the structure itself had all the joy and exuberance required of great exhibition architecture (Figure 11·14).

Architecture through association, especially the nostalgic recall of the Renaissance and classic Roman and Greek monuments, has a long tradition in American architecture, running from Thomas Jefferson through Greek Revival buildings of the mid-nineteenth century and today enshrined in nearly every capital building across the land. Stone readily acknowledges such influences in the formation of his own taste. He has never regretted the student hours spent copying details from D'Espouy's *Fragments de l'architecture antique:* "Those great monuments of the past were an inspiration, not to imitate, but to enrich your vocabulary. The Pompeian house and the romance of the classical—why, I harken to them even now."

Stone even goes so far as to doubt that Gropius's revolution at Harvard was altogether a good thing. "A whole generation was brainwashed," Stone comments, "and this has resulted in a kind of architectural illiteracy." Stone's own uninhibited romanticism—he calls it "moxie"—at times undoubtedly lays him open to the charge of being a counterrevolutionist. "Every time I look at Mies van der Rohe's Seagram Building, I think what a jewel McKim, Mead & White's old Racquet Club is across the street," he quips. "At one time, like all young architects of my generation, I thought of Washington, D.C., as a chamber of horrors. Now I'm not so sure but what it isn't a pretty pleasant

city to look at. I even have a liking for those
wonderful columns in the middle of the National
Gallery. They, at least, have an atmosphere of
permanence about them.''

Permanence, grandeur, rich ornamentation—
these are qualities that have tended to elude
modern architecture. To achieve this sense of permanence, Frank Lloyd Wright built the Guggenheim Museum with such strength that he boasted
not even an atomic bomb could demolish it. Mies
van der Rohe, in giving the Seagram Building
its bronze sheathing, in effect equated his latest
architecture with sculpture. Stone's solution has
been to evoke the great enduring monuments of
the past, while keeping a foot in the modern
camp by using the most advanced materials and
structural methods.

The New Orleans International Trade Mart
project quite consciously summons up memories
of Bernini's Rome. The Huntington Hartford Gallery of Modern Art (Figure 11·16) evokes the
palaces of Venice (although in a manner that seems
somewhat heavy-handed.) The Palo Alto–Stanford
Medical Center, read in plan, is a completely modern organization of a complex hospital area. But
in elevation it recalls the great sequences of open
courts and fountains of baroque Rome at the same
time that its patterned concrete, rather consciously
Mayan in origin, picks up the reinforced-concrete-
block system originated by Frank Lloyd Wright in
such early California houses as ''La Miniatura.''

This reliance on historical evocation is a highly
significant trend in American architecture today.
Increasingly structures in reinforced concrete and
even in glass, steel, and aluminum recall Bernini's
colonnades, Italian loggias and pavilions, Greek
temple forms, and Renaissance palaces. Does this
romantic recall herald the return of the Beaux
Arts? A case can be made that something of the
sort is involved. If so, it is a movement fraught
with peril. Truth to material and the expression of
structure on which modern architecture rests are
not stylistic whims but the realities of building that
have emerged in response to the needs and potentialities of our time. Stone's dissent is directed more
at the bleakness and coldness of much contemporary
architecture. His strength, as well as his weakness,
is that he is among the first of the modern architects
unabashedly to evoke the past and to bring back
lost richness of surface and familiar forms.

11·16 Columbus Circle Museum, New
York, 1961, was commissioned by Huntington Hartford, Jr., as a modern-art gallery.
A ten-story building of reinforced concrete, its marble exterior is in marked
contrast to Stone's design for the Museum
of Modern Art (Figure 11·3). Here the
facade gives no clues as to interior space
divisions. Rich pierced corners and open
two-story balconies (behind which will be
located offices and restaurant) are reminiscent of such Venetian monuments as the
Ca' d'Oro and Doge's Palace; also evocative are porphyry and verde-antique medal-
lions set in place above lower columns.

12 : SKIDMORE, OWINGS
& MERRILL :

Anonymity is not unprecedented in architecture. We have only scattered references to the master builders of the Gothic cathedrals and none at all for many of the finest works of Greece and Rome. Today the problem of attribution becomes difficult for quite another reason—the emergence of huge architectural firms whose "umbrella practice" may involve literally dozens of architects plus dozens more of engineers, project supervisors, and landscape artists.

Such an architectural firm is Skidmore, Owings & Merrill. Working primarily on large industrial, educational, and commercial projects, it has exploited the potentialities of Mies van der Rohe's structural clarity and the formal dynamism of Le Corbusier's work, and applied the team approach advocated by the Bauhaus with astonishing success. However, it should be pointed out that this firm is far more than the three men of its name. Actually it has fourteen general partners,* some fifteen associate associates, and thirty-nine participating associates. With principal offices in Manhattan, Chicago, San Francisco, and Portland, Oregon, staffed by over a thousand draftsmen, planners, and engineers, it is a giant among the large architectural firms. Its record of buildings over the past

* Including co-founder Nathaniel A. Owings and architectural engineer John O. Merrill. Louis Skidmore, the other founding partner, retired in 1955.

decade totals well over a billion dollars and includes such architectural landmarks as Manhattan's Lever House, the trend-setting office structure that inaugurated the 1950s, and the United States Air Force Academy, one of today's most impressive assemblies of modern architecture on a vast scale.

S.O.M. has stayed primarily within the field of large commercial structures as a matter of choice. It designs no houses at all. Or, as one partner remarked, "We prefer to deal with the husbands, not the wives." Skidmore, Owings & Merrill is preeminently the Big Firm for Big Business, one that can deliver the whole package that architecture has become today, from site planning to structural engineering.

This highly successful collaboration of architecture and big business began, implausibly enough, over a 45-foot-tall pyramid of vinegar bottles. Louis Skidmore, a dapper young M.I.T. graduate who had just returned from Europe, where he had been traveling on a Rotch Fellowship, had landed the job of being chief designer at the 1933 Chicago world's fair. He had just ruled out the exhibit plan submitted by the H. J. Heinz Co. of "57 varieties" fame. The reaction was instantaneous. "Who," roared President John Heinz, "is this wax-mustached bozo in the raccoon coat and ear muffs who has turned down my exhibit?"[1] Skidmore duly trotted around to mollify the Pickle King and con-

THE TEAM APPROACH

vinced him that he should change to a show of historical kitchens, the shelves of which could, of course, be stocked with Heinz products. Heinz in due course became one of S.O.M.'s oldest and most loyal clients.

Skidmore's acquaintance with the 700 corporations showing their wares at the Chicago fair placed him in an enviable position to capitalize on the forthcoming 1939 New York World's Fair. He had in the meantime formed a partnership with his brother-in-law, Nathaniel Owings (Cornell, 1927). It was agreed that Nat Owings would range the Midwest for commissions; Skidmore would be based in Manhattan. To fill out the staff, J. Walter Severinghaus (a housing specialist), Robert W. Cutler (hospitals), William S. Brown (prefabrication), and Gordon Bunshaft (design) were added to the staff, followed by a top engineer, John O. Merrill.

This team was the hard core Skidmore and Owings meant to use as a task force to regain for modern architecture its role as the creator and coordinator of big projects. The two partners were also determined that the hallmark of the new firm would be an uncompromisingly modern style. Their first chance came when Oak Ridge was established as the center of the Manhattan A-bomb Project. S.O.M. got the contract and soon found it took the full time of John O. Merrill and a staff of 450

12·1 Skidmore, Owings & Merrill senior partners (opposite page) gathered at the Florida home of Louis Skidmore (far right). Reading clockwise: William E. Hartmann, Nathaniel A. Owings, John O. Merrill, Gordon Bunshaft (with pipe in mouth), James W. Hammond, Robert W. Cutler, John B. Rodgers, Walter A. Netsch, Jr., J. Walter Severinghaus, William S. Brown, the late Elliott Brown, Edward J. Mathews, and counsel Marshal G. Sampsell. New partners later added: John O. Merrill, Jr., Fred W. Kraft, and David H. Hughes.

12·2 Lever House, New York (1952). A vertical slab set on a broad horizontal base and enclosed in a slick glass curtain wall, it set skyscraper style for the 1950s.

12·3 Brooklyn Veterans Hospital (1950; left) is a thin, seventeen-story slab oriented to provide a maximum view of the ocean.

12·4 Joan Miró mural, commissioned for the Terrace Hilton Hotel in Cincinnati, adds richness to an austere structural style.

architects, engineers, and draftsmen to complete the 160-million-dollar project.

The postwar building boom found S.O.M. poised at the starting line and ready to go. The Veterans Administration Hospital in Brooklyn (Figure 12·3), Lake Meadows Housing Development in Chicago, and Manhattan House in New York allowed them to show off thin-slab structures which struck an almost belligerently modern note. A commission for the Ford Motor Company in Dearborn, Michigan, gave them the big office complex they had been aiming at; the Terrace Hilton Hotel in Cincinnati (Figure 12·4), a chance to prove that modern art, in this case a mural by Joan Miró, complemented their rather austere, stripped-down, "skin-and-bones" style.

Building on such a rapidly expanding scale requires not only having partners capable of hustling in the business, men with the right contacts at the right time. It also requires on-the-spot job supervision by architects, a fact which tends to thin out the ranks of even the biggest firms. But the pituitary gland that controls the growth and development of any firm is its design section, for it is on the drafting boards, in day-and-night ordeals, that architecture is made. And S.O.M. had, in Gordon Bunshaft, one of the top talents of this generation.

Gordon Bunshaft was born on May 9, 1909, the son of a Russian immigrant merchant, in Buffalo, New York, a city which boasts Frank Lloyd Wright's historic Larkin Building and several of his biggest houses, as well as Sullivan's masterpiece, the Guaranty Building. However, Bunshaft seems to have actually acquired his love for architecture on the Sunday afternoon trips he and his father would make around town to view the new buildings going up.

Studying at M.I.T. Bunshaft found the Beaux-Arts system in full flower, but, significantly, he proved best at handling the massive, structural Romanesque forms. He became so expert, in fact, that he won the much-coveted Rotch Traveling Fellowship, which provided $3,000 for a two-year study tour of Europe.* Back in New York he worked briefly with Edward D. Stone, then with designer Raymond Loewy, before joining Skidmore, Owings & Merrill in 1937. It was the second year of the firm's history. The staff in the New York office added up to a grand total of six.

"I am making you chief designer," Louis Skidmore told young Bunshaft. "But I'm not telling anyone. You prove it." For Bunshaft, endowed with a bull-in-the-china-shop attitude and a consuming love for design, this was a red flag. In short order, his weight was felt throughout the drafting room. His colleagues recall, too, that Bunshaft's enthusiasm for design also put a severe strain on client relations. When H. J. Heinz was being shown a model of a newly designed factory, Bunshaft interrupted the suave presentation by remarking, "You'll take it this way, or you won't have it at all." Fortunately, Heinz was all too happy to take it as it was.

Much of the work then under way was for the 1940 New York World's Fair. It fell far short of Oscar Niemeyer–Lucio Costa's Brazilian Pavilion or Sven Markelius's Swedish Pavilion, but it was a start. Perhaps the first structure that clearly declared Bunshaft's architectural talent was the reception room designed for the United States Navy's Great Lakes Training Station, both functional and dynamic, and a strong contrast to most run-of-the-mill wartime construction.

War is almost always a marking-time period for architecture. Crash programs, scarcity of materials,

---

* An honor also won by two of Bunshaft's future employers, Edward Durell Stone (Chap. 11) and Louis Skidmore.

12·5 Pan American Life Insurance Company, New Orleans (1952), is an early and highly successful S.O.M. reinforced-concrete structure equipped with paneled sun breakers.

and the feverish atmosphere militate against a high level of design. For Bunshaft it did, however, provide an opportunity to revisit Europe. As a major in the United States Corps of Engineers stationed in Paris he found Le Corbusier and enthusiastically toured the just liberated city with him. The building that struck Bunshaft most was Le Corbusier's Swiss Pavilion at the University of Paris (Figure 4·4), its curved façades lifted high on massive stilts (*pilotis*). But back in the United States after the war Bunshaft said, ''This is really a steel-building country. We are really the only country that builds that way. That's the thing about Mies van der Rohe. Here's a German who comes to America and expresses this steel-building country better than anyone else. Mies keeps on in a consistent development. That's why he is the central force.'' [2]

The first dramatic structure to rise in Manhattan embodying Mies van der Rohe's principles was Lever House (1952) on Park Avenue. Designed by Gordon Bunshaft, it proclaimed that modern architecture could be an exalted industrial product, trimly packaged in sheer glass and aluminum (Figure 12·2). Its initial success was stupendous. Here was a building using only 25 per cent of the air space allowed by Manhattan's building codes, to provide a pedestrian plaza, the first to be incorporated into a major building site since Rockefeller Plaza in the 1930s. It made the all-glass curtain wall, delicately delineated by thin mullions and spandrels, the ordering device for the façade of high-rise office buildings, and opened the way for Park Avenue to become the new area for prestige building. As time passes, it appears that Lever House was of more seminal importance than even the United Nations Secretariat in ushering in the tall, glass-sheathed slab as the style-setting prototype of today's office building.

The twenty-one story Lever House was designed as a tower of light which could frankly be a show place for the soap manufacturers, Lever Brothers, then headed by Charles Luckman, a businessman trained as an architect. The cost of keeping such a huge mirror bright and sparkling was considered negligible compared to the advertising value of seeing the immense panes of glass being sudsed down in good Lever Brothers soap by window washers suspended in a special gondola.

The influence of Mies van der Rohe was readily apparent in Lever House, but equally important was the influence of Le Corbusier. A good deal of

the beauty of Lever House comes from its juxtaposition of high tower and low horizontal element which serves as office space and provides a colonnade and enclosure for the open court. The top of this low-lying wing is a roof terrace which provides a welcome view for the company restaurant on the third floor, which is signaled on the exterior by a notched inset that runs around three sides of the main tower. The use of stilts (*pilotis*) and the highly successful attempt to set up a balance and tension between high vertical and low horizontal are far more in the spirit of Le Corbusier than of Mies van der Rohe. It is probable that this sculptural intent would have been more widely recognized had Lever Brothers carried through with the original scheme for a sculpture garden by Isamu Noguchi on the plaza level.

This Corbusian spirit, however, is all but lost in the succeeding structures designed by Gordon Bunshaft for Skidmore, Owings & Merrill. The Manufacturers Trust Company's Fifth Avenue branch (Figure 12·6) is a near-perfect essay in Miesian discipline and form, basically a glass cube within which the banking elements are placed. The first

12·6 Manufacturers Trust Company's Fifth Avenue Branch, New York (1954), first glass bank to stress light and openness.

12·7 Heinz Company Research Laboratory, Pittsburgh (1958). Reception room in the center of functional factory space creates a startling area of light and color.

of the "glass banks," it marked a daring move away from the dark, massive structures and heavy Renaissance detailing up to then considered psychologically appropriate for the secrecy and safety associated with money and high finance.

Bunshaft, in the Manufacturers Trust Company's Fifth Avenue branch, exploited openness, light, and the structural strength of steel in every way possible, from the monumental panes of clear glass and the white marble walls to the cold cathode tubes hung behind the thin, corrugated plastic ceiling. The result was to give the whole structure an almost hallucinatory appearance of floating, a sensation boldly reinforced by the cantilevered mezzanine which approaches the interior glass walls without touching them. Manufacturers Trust Company is significant also for its use of modern art to contrast with, and counterpoint, the architecture. Paintings are used throughout the upper private offices and dining area, including works by Miró and Léger. But art is also used dramatically in the public areas, including a massive welded screen by Harry Bertoia which runs the length of the mezzanine and mobile sculptures dancing airily at the top of the escalators. Perhaps the prime symbol of all for this new day of banking was the vault itself, moved from the basement to the front ground floor and there proudly displayed as a glittering, machine-made object.

The Connecticut General Life Insurance Building was S.O.M.'s first opportunity to plan a huge horizontal complex in open country. Some sense of how this 19-million-dollar building came into existence gives one of the best insights into the total approach to architectural problems that typifies mid-twentieth-century architecture.

First there was the client, Frazar B. Wilde, a Connecticut Yankee whose own personal taste ran to the genteel neo-Georgian residential style. But as a businessman his advice was, "You'd better not invest your money in a carriage factory." [3]

"Let's take our time with the basic thinking," he said. "We can hurry later on." As a preliminary, Connecticut General in 1952 sent teams of vice-presidents fanned out on scouting expeditions to look over potential architects. From among the six firms originally selected, S.O.M. got the final nod, with the proviso that designers Gordon Bunshaft and William S. Brown (the Lever House team) be assigned to the project.

The selection of the site was made from among the half dozen available on the outskirts of Hart-ford, Connecticut. Then, as attention shifted to graphs of present and future space requirements within the structure, S.O.M. realized three things: first, that the vast clerical spaces must be easily expandable, while executive space would remain relatively static; second, that to attract young high school girl clerks out of Hartford (the site is 5 miles distant), there would have to be a humane, even glamorous setting with plenty of shops, restaurants, and recreation facilities; finally, that the clerical work involved in a mammoth insurance company bore a striking parallel to a mass-production assembly-line flow diagram. The finished building is almost literally a translation of these requirements into space: a low three-story clerical area, which can be added to as needed, and a higher and separate executive tower. The lower level of the main block could house open recreation rooms, beauty shops, and a theater, and to give this a sumptuous, open feeling the restaurant was removed to become a separate unit. A basically horizontal ordering of spaces facilitates the flow of paper work from desk to desk.

For the first two years on the project S.O.M. kept away from "architecture" as such and concerned itself primarily with planning the creation

12·8 Painter Stuart Davis's "Combination Concrète," in the Heinz Company Research Laboratory, is a splash of color in vivid contrast with the understated dècor.

12·9–12 Connecticut General Life Insurance Office, Hartford, Connecticut (1957). A 470-foot-long facade of reflecting glass (above) looks out over a landscaped terrace, with cantilevered dining room seen in the distance. The rigorously modular construction, in units of 6 feet, allows for flexible office space (left, below) and gives a sense of light and airiness that is heightened by superb use of modern office furniture. As a foil to the architecture, Isamu Noguchi created "The Family" (right, below).

of space envelopes. In the fall of 1954 approval was given to a block model which emphasized the low, horizontal masses. Now came the moment for developing the building in detail. The module selected was the 6 by 6 feet required by a clerical worker at her desk. This could be repeated in both floor and ceiling pattern (Figure 12·10). Spacings between columns were opened to 60 feet along the 470-foot façades. Specially treated green-tinted glass was used to lighten the air-conditioning load (Figure 12·9).

To relate interior to exterior, and keep each desk 30 to 35 feet from sunlight, four great courts were then punched into the building. Glass and specially anodized aluminum with highlights of stainless steel were used throughout to keep long-time maintenance costs low, it being one of Wilde's goals to have a building in which daily maintenance costs would be negligible for at least fifty and preferably seventy-five years. It soon became clear that the building was becoming hollow space, not solid. In certain lights you could see through it, in others it became a mirror reflecting the moods of weather and the country. As one S.O.M. partner remarked, ''A thunderstorm or a sunset is quite an excitement up there. Often you can't tell where the sky leaves off and the building begins.''

To keep form and function in harmony with costs, a $100,000 mock-up of a section of the building was specially built, where each new idea could be tried out, tested, and approved. A constant running reassessment and stage-by-stage approval between Wilde and S.O.M. required a staggering total of 500 conferences. Here architecture had to justify itself at each stage of the way. How would the vast clerical areas be humanized? Bunshaft proposed playful screens and bright colors, brought in Knoll Associates to design furnishings, and the sculptor Isamu Noguchi to design the interior courts, promenade, and a special sculpture group (Figure 12·11). How to enhance the natural setting? A swamp area before the building was dammed to make a lake, one which not only boasts white and black swans for the delight of office picnickers but which also is a cooling vat for the air-conditioning system.

Now came the time to exploit the forms, tighten up the discipline of the detailing. The result was the exquisitely designed panels, cantilevers over a reflecting pool, and disciplined promenades. No detail became too small to investigate. Some eighteen hundred desk handles were redesigned. To select the right cherry wood for paneling the cafeteria approach, about twenty cherry tree samples

12·13–15 Reynolds Metals Company, Richmond, Virginia (1958), is almost classic in its ceremonial approach, severe rectangular, partially enclosed court, and reflecting pool. Magnolia tree and red-brick courtyard paving evoke traditional Virginia themes. In contrast, twentieth-century aluminum sun louvers, controlled by an astronomical clock, open and close in rhythm with the shifting sun.

were tried out; even the drawstrings on the vertical venetian blinds were scrutinized at length. The labor paid off handsomely. Connecticut General became a splendid example of the precisely machined elegance in which American architects lead the world. It was picked as one of the "Ten Buildings in America's Future" at the time of the American Institute of Architects' one hundredth anniversary, and received a first honor award from the AIA, as well.

It is the essence of group practice that carefully worked out solutions in one building can be passed along as the starting point for the next. An out-standing example of such accumulative experience is the Reynolds Metals Company headquarters in Richmond, Virginia (Figure 12·14). The court principle which existed in embryo in Lever House and came of age with Connecticut General is here exploited to the utmost. The entire building is built around a central brick-paved court, open on two sides and approached by a formal reflecting pool. Another structural complex, one which makes even more dramatic use of bold, horizontal planes and massive interior courts, is the United States Air Force Academy (Figures 12·16 through 12·19).

12·16–19 Air Force Academy, Colorado Springs (1959), a 133-million-dollar complex at the base of the Rockies, built to house full cadet corps of 2,520. Chapel (below) uses aluminum-sheathed tetrahedrons.

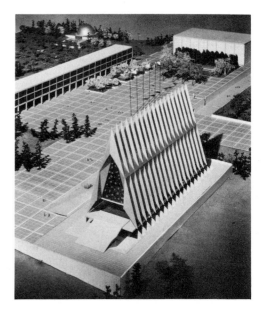

The pressure for office space and high urban land values which first forced the skyscraper upwards has been a continuing trend in American cities, and as the architectural firm preeminently at the disposal of big business, S.O.M. has continued a steady evolution in its development of the high-rise office structure. One of the proudest examples is the Inland Steel Building (Figure 12·20), designed in the Chicago office of S.O.M. by William E. Hartmann (M.I.T., 1938), and Walter A. Netsch, Jr. (M.I.T., 1943), and primarily responsible for the Air Force's tetrahedron-shaped chapel in aluminum and glass. Inland Steel is as expressively *steel* as Bunshaft's Reynolds Metals building is *aluminum*. The exterior supports of the Chicago skyscraper are sheathed in stainless steel, as is the adjacent elevator tower, which makes Inland actually two buildings in one. In San Francisco, the Crown Zellerbach Building (1959) shows a similar treatment by the main West Coast branch of S.O.M. Largest of all is the 60-story Chase Manhattan Bank in Manhattan's Wall Street area (Figure 12·22), a massive superblock that outdistances even Le Corbusier's flamboyant dreams of the early 1920s.

S.O.M.'s new family of skyscrapers, with strong perpendicular lines and the expansive use of glass, aluminum, and steel, bear more than a passing resemblance to one another. Even superficial style notes such as vertical venetian blinds and unpolished plate glass for room dividers quickly filter from one S.O.M. office to the next. But as strikingly handsome, logically programed, and efficient as these structures indisputably are, they have not gone uncriticized. From town planners there is grave questioning whether S.O.M., which has now erected three skyscrapers on one side of Manhattan's Park Avenue (Pepsi-Cola, Lever, and Union Carbide), each with a different height, different façade, and different module, can be altogether exonerated from the charge of bringing on the same kind of visual chaos that afflicted Bologna in the days when it was known as the city of a thousand towers.

The criticism that strikes closer is the one voiced by a Chicago architect who said, ''S.O.M. took Mies's stainless-steel standard, warmed it up, and sold it as a prestige package to the American businessman. That's all to the good, but now *rigor mortis* is setting in. They're becoming a conservative force in American architecture—they've stopped inventing.'' Or as another architect re-

12·20–21 Inland Steel Company, Chicago (1958). Exterior supporting columns rise for nineteen stories. Secondary structure (above, right) houses elevators; interior (below) has sculpture by Seymour Lipton.

12·22 Chase Manhattan Bank Building, lower Manhattan (1961). A massive super-block, its sixty stories top Woolworth Building; open plaza equals Venice's San Marco.

marked, "S.O.M.'s work is marvelous, but isn't it just another slice of the same handsome bologna?"

One possible indication that S.O.M. is not eternally committed to the strictly Miesian vocabulary as it was enunciated in Lever House is the John Hancock Building in San Francisco (Figure 12·23). This is a fourteen-story building of reinforced-concrete structure in which the walls (both exterior and central service core) are weight-bearing. The façade is of a rich, gleaming gray Minnesota granite. The mass of this structural system is transferred to the ground through haunched arches at the second-floor level to the columns on the ground floor, where they form a pedestrian arcade. A parapet of precast panels at the top shelters air intakes and window-washing gondola tracks, giving a positive silhouette and termination to the building. The effect of this building, designed by Edward Charles Bassett in S.O.M.'s San Francisco office, is curiously reminiscent of the massive masonry structures of the Chicago skyscrapers, such as John Wellborn Root's Monadnock Building, that date from Louis Sullivan's time.

What may be an even more promising direction is the use of reinforced concrete using prestressed, prefabricated elements. Certainly two buildings so far designed by Gordon Bunshaft with the structural engineer Paul Weidlinger point to dramatic new possibilities. The first of these was the Banque Lambert (Figure 12·27), designed for a leading Brussels banking family. The site, directly opposite the Palais Royal on the Avenue Marnix, suggested to Bunshaft that a structure sympathetic to the traditional architecture of Brussels, as exemplified by the rich Gothic and Neo-Gothic façades of the Grand' Place, would be more appropriate than another Lever House.

12·23–25 John Hancock Western Home Office Building, San Francisco (1960), marks a shift away from S.O.M.'s decade-long tradition of steel-frame structures. Using the more plastic forms of reinforced concrete, the building is faced with charcoal-gray reflecting granite and incorporates pedestrian passageways, landscaped roof gardens, and traditional balconies.

12·26 United Airlines Terminal, San Francisco (1958), shows massive girders cantilevered out from central reinforced-concrete columns. Inspiration for the structural design was derived from the work of Nervi.

12·27 Banque Lambert, Brussels (1961), recalls the splendor and dignity of a Renaissance palazzo. Precast concrete elements establish the rhythm of its facade. On top is a penthouse occupied by the owners.

The heavily patterned reinforced-concrete building that resulted strongly recalls a Renaissance *palazzo*, topped in this case with a sumptuous penthouse. Even more impressive is Gordon Bunshaft's Yale Rare Book Library, which has precast-concrete structural elements set with panels of dark, honey-colored onyx. Within the central motif is a six-story stack of rare books that rises from subbasement to near ceiling height. (Access to the stacks is through interior elevators.) Priceless manuscripts are displayed in this cathedral light filtered through stone rarely used in architecture since Byzantium, and even then never on so vast a scale.

The evolution that began with Lever House and reached its climax with Chase Manhattan's sixty-story skyscraper and the far-flung United States Air Force Academy make an exciting sequence of twentieth-century structures. The Banque Lambert in Brussels and the Yale Rare Book Library may well be a new departure from which will evolve an even more exciting architecture, but one no less strictly disciplined. "I believe in a disciplined approach based on intelligent planning," Gordon Bunshaft says. "Architecture is serving the needs of the people using the building. And something more, which is taking the materials and exploring and exploiting them for their maximum excitement. A bold idea, plus precision, care, and thought, make a good building."

13·1–2 Eero Saarinen's General Motors Technical Center, Warren, Michigan (1950–1957), has been called an "industrial Versailles." A gigantic complex of twenty-five structures grouped around a central lake, it is elegantly designed in strict Miesian discipline, combined with warm enamel finishes and a spectacular styling dome.

13 : **EERO SAARINEN** :

UNITY WITHIN DIVERSITY

In many ways the most interesting of the second generation of modern American architects is Eero Saarinen, son of Eliel Saarinen, one of Finland's most talented architects. The range of Eero's styles —all modern in one way or another—is so vast that his colleagues have a hard time guessing what the next Saarinen building will look like. If modern architecture were already an enshrined academy, it might well be that Eero Saarinen would be considered a mannerist and an eclectic. For he has designed whole industrial complexes such as the 100-million-dollar General Motors Technical Center in the discipline of Mies van der Rohe, then turned on his heel and created the circular chapel at Massachusetts Institute of Technology (Figure 13·3), employing the rough brickwork and interior wood detailing of Alvar Aalto.

Fortunately, modern architecture is still in a continuing state of evolution, and it seems to be Saarinen's secret that he, more than most of his contemporaries, recognizes that the valid approaches to modern architectural problems are vastly more varied than any single-minded approach would indicate. "We must have a structural reason as well as an esthetic reason for everything we do" is a favorite Saarinen watchword. And in giving esthetics its just due, Saarinen provides himself with a rich cultural background to draw from, one that will help him suggest the pleasant relationship of a Danish village to the sky when he comes to design a Lutheran College, or the grottoes of Capri when he deals with reflecting water. By stressing that in structure lies the probity of architecture, Saarinen has exploited systems that vary from the refined "skin-and-bones" style of Mies van der Rohe to the billowing forms of reinforced-concrete vaults in the TWA terminal at Idlewild International Airport, New York (Figure 13·4).

For Saarinen, to design a building is to make an architectural statement. A building must not only solve the problem presented in terms of site and function. It must go beyond that, and declare a new principle, open a new direction, and in some way advance the frontier of architecture. This de-

13·3–4 Eero Saarinen uses space and form with great originality, as can be seen in his treatment of light in the Kresge Chapel, Massachusetts Institute of Technology (1955; opposite). Suspended screen by Harry Bertoia reflects light filtered from overhead skylight. TWA Terminal (right) is Saarinen's most ambitious use of plastic form.

sire to explore new forms and solutions has made Saarinen resort to an exhaustive approach to each architectural problem, spending as much as $12,000 in expenses and drawing as many as 200 elevations for a competition that guarantees only $4,000 in expenses. It is a price, however, that Saarinen cheerfully pays. "The expensive thing," he points out, "is to make *architecture*." [1]

It was this exhaustive approach to each problem that caused one architect to refer to Saarinen's modest-sized office in Birmingham, Michigan, as "an office always *en charette*." In borrowing this old Beaux-Arts expression, which refers to the *charette* (cart) which dragged late-comers to the annual competitions at the end of an all-night's work, he meant to imply that Saarinen runs his ninety-odd draftsmen as if every commission were a competition. For all offices, going *en charette* is a now-and-then occasion. But for Saarinen it is a way of life. It is an approach, however, that has paid off rich dividends, both in pioneering new techniques (Saarinen's porcelain-enamel panel sealed with a neoprene "Zipper" gasket is a case in point) and in remarkably handsome structures, established Saarinen as the architect who most often makes the move first for his generation.

One great advantage Eero Saarinen has over most of his colleagues is that he was literally born into architecture. His father, Eliel Saarinen, was the most famous Finnish architect of his day, famed for his romantic Helsinki Railroad Station and Finland's National Museum. In the great, rambling thirty-eight-room lodge where Eero was born on August 10, 1910, life revolved about the 90-foot drafting room where his father worked, and his mother, a sculptress, wove at the loom or helped build the meticulous scale models with which Eliel Saarinen designed whole cities.

From these models, Eero Saarinen learned a valuable lesson he has never forgotten: "Always design a thing by considering it in its next larger context—a chair in a room, a room in a house, a house in a neighborhood, a neighborhood in a city."

13·6–8 Cranbrook School, Bloomfield Hills, Michigan (begun 1927; top), was Eliel Saarinen's major American commission; the entire family worked on the project. Father and son (shown in 1919; center) collaborated on Crow Island School, Winnetka, Illinois, 1940 (bottom).

The second lesson was that competition is for an architect, especially a European, a way of life. Competitive by nature, Eero was twelve when he won his first "international competition," a matchstick design contest sponsored by a Swedish match company. Soon afterward, his father received word that he had won second prize for the Chicago Tribune Tower competition.

With the $20,000 prize money, Eliel Saarinen decided to invest his future in the United States. In 1923, he brought his thirteen-year-old son, his daughter, Pipsan (Eva-Lisa), and wife, Loja, to Chicago. The project that proved to be Eliel Saarinen's major American commission was the complex of forty-odd buildings at Cranbrook School in Bloomfield Hills, the result of a Maecenas-like gesture by Detroit News Publisher George G. Booth, who commissioned the elder Saarinen to take over his rolling country estate outside Detroit and develop it into one of the finest educational institutions in the United States (Figure 13·6).

In the highly creative Saarinen family, building was an absorbing passion that involved them all. Cranbrook's School for Girls (1931), for instance, was designed by Eliel, decorated by Pipsan, and boasted rugs and curtains designed by Loja and furniture by Eero. To this island of Scandinavian modern came the greats and near greats of the day. Carl Milles, the sculptor, was in residence for twenty-one years; Le Corbusier stopped by to announce that American skyscrapers were too small. Frank Lloyd Wright, who thought (not without reason) that he detected more than a hint of Wright in Eliel Saarinen's later work, dubbed Eliel "the best of the eclectics." Eliel fired right back, calling Wright "Frank Lloyd Wrong."

Eero Saarinen had grown up under a drafting table, but his earliest leanings were toward sculpture. At the age of nineteen he set off for Paris, later studied sculpture at Cranbrook. But architecture proved to be too strong a calling (although later emphasis on molded, sculpturesque shapes in reinforced concrete suggests that the impulse toward sculpture did not go underground forever).

Eero Saarinen was a brilliant student at Yale, and, as might be expected, a top prize winner. It was a time in architectural education that Saarinen refers to now as the "Kerensky period: A small revolution was brewing, but a bigger one was yet to come." When Saarinen, after a fellowship tour of Europe, returned to Cranbrook as an instructor, he found there an immensely stimulating group that gave the school its golden age. All within a year or so in age were designer Charles Eames, Florence Schuster (later head of the modern-furniture firm, Knoll Associates), Chicago architect Harry Weese, Philadelphia city planner Edmund Bacon, sculptor-welder Harry Bertoia, Ralph Rapson, now chairman of Minnesota's architecture department, and Lilly Swann, a Cranbrook student and sculptress, who, in 1939, became Eero Saarinen's first wife. In the same year Eliel Saarinen formed the firm of Saarinen, Swanson & Saarinen. The new name hardly disturbed the family clan spirit at all; J. Robert F. Swanson was Pipsan's husband.

For a future architect, all this added up to an unparalleled education. Eero Saarinen worked on the plans for his father's first major commission after Cranbrook School, the Kleinhans Music Hall in Buffalo, thus getting a grounding that stood him in good stead when in 1940 he carried the main responsibility for the Berkshire Festival Opera Shed, a structure in wood designed entirely in terms of acoustics. In 1940 also the two Saarinens and Swanson teamed up with the firm of Perkins, Wheeler & Will to design the Crow Island School in Winnetka, Illinois, and Lilly Saarinen was called in to do the ceramic sculpture. Crow Island is still considered one of the trail-blazing designs that have opened the way for schools conceived in terms of function rather than as monolithic, factorylike buildings (Figure 13·8).

Designer Charles Eames, an instructor at Cranbrook at the time, recalls his first experience working with Eero Saarinen. A national competition had been declared for a new Smithsonian Museum of Art for Washington, D.C., and the office decided to submit an entry. "Eero thought the whole thing out carefully," Eames remembers, "and then told us that the first thing to do would be one hundred studies of each element that went into the building. We would then pick the best and never let our standards fall below that. Then we would make one hundred studies of the combinations of each element—the placing of the sinks in the ladies' room, for instance. Then one hundred studies of the combinations of the combinations. Then the first stage of the competition was over. And guess what? We started all over again to make one hundred studies of the elements, etc. When the whole thing was finished, Eero was almost in tears, because it was so simple a child could have thought it up. And then, of course, he won the competition."

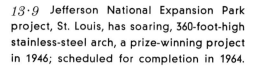
13·9 Jefferson National Expansion Park project, St. Louis, has soaring, 360-foot-high stainless-steel arch, a prize-winning project in 1946; scheduled for completion in 1964.

The curriculum at Cranbrook carried over the Scandinavian respect for craftwork. Students made their own kilns, did ceramics, weaving, painting as part of an elaborate apprentice system. Part of it was, of course, furniture. Saarinen and Eames decided to team up for the Museum of Modern Art's 1940 Organic Design Competition. For beginners they scored a remarkable success: Their molded-plywood furniture took two of the seven top awards and launched Eames into furniture design in a big way. His "Potato Chip" chair was one of the most famous of the 1940s, and nearly twenty years later, in 1959, was ranged second only to the Olivetti typewriter as the best example of modern design. Saarinen independently has continued to design furniture on the side. His "Womb" chair in the 1950s became a fixture in most modern houses. Saarinen's recent "Pedestal" chair, designed, as Saarinen says, "to clear up the slum of legs in the United States home," has already won acceptance as a note of modern elegance.

Growing up the son of a world-famous architect was no easy problem for Eero Saarinen. He had first to win recognition in his own right. The opportunity offered itself, as inevitably in the Saarinen family it must, with yet another competition, this time for the St. Louis Jefferson National Ex-

pansion Memorial. The elder Saarinen on his own submitted a formal, monumental design. However, Eero's entry was the winner, an audacious, 590-foot stainless-steel arch in the form of a reverse catenary curve that looked like a huge, glistening croquet wicket—an idea he had conceived while bending a wire-and-wool pipe cleaner (Figure 13·9). Hailed by the jury as "a work of genius which will rank among the nation's greatest monuments," it remains one of Saarinen's favorite projects.

The commission that put Eero Saarinen into the forefront of the second generation of modern architects was the 100-million-dollar General Motors Technical Center, a twenty-five-building complex spread out over 320 acres in Warren, Michigan, which has become as much heralded in the 1960s as Rockefeller Center was in the 1930s. For General Motors Technical Center and the Air Force Academy, designed by Skidmore, Owings & Merrill, are the two outstanding examples of large-scale planning which rely for their philosophy and design on the example of Mies van der Rohe. Together they best demonstrate what a large complex can become when the full design and technological resources of modern architecture are used.

In a sense, Saarinen inherited General Motors Technical Center from his father. Eliel Saarinen had been approached in 1945 at a time when General Motors was impressed with the elder Saarinen's work at Cranbrook. The project was postponed until after the Second World War, and Eliel Saarinen died in 1950. Thus, at the age of forty, Eero Saarinen found himself confronted with an opportunity of vast proportions. No longer did the precise brickwork of Cranbrook seem appropriate. The new star in the horizons for younger architects was Mies van der Rohe, and, to Saarinen, Mies's precision-designed buildings with their "skin-and-bones" construction and acceptance of twentieth-century technology seemed best suited to a corporation which prides itself on its exalted industrial products. Reinforcing Mies's influence was the example of Albert Kahn (1869–1942), a German-born architect whose automobile factories in and around Detroit had brought American factory building to its highest level (Figure 13·10).

General Motors wanted a vast research center which would provide a campus type of setting as an inducement to young engineers and technicians. This Saarinen provided by creating an industrial park within which the buildings could be com-

13·10–12 General Motors Technical Center, Warren, Michigan (1950–1956), provides campus environment for research workers. Designed around a 22-acre lake, the project challenged Saarinen to create a permanent structure with a unified concept. The basic construction vocabulary derives from Mies van der Rohe (Figure 13·1) and is carried through with great precision and imaginative use of color. Esthetic problems such as exhaust stacks for Dynamometer Building (above), where engines are tested, were successfully resolved. Equally dramatic is Styling Division staircase (below); terrazzo slabs with white marble aggregate are suspended on pencil-thin rods of stainless steel held under tension.

13·13 Sharply pitched roofs of Concordia Senior College buildings (1955–1958) dramatize the flat 187-acre campus in Fort Wayne, Indiana. Saarinen designed a special diamond-shaped brick for the chapel facade (right), repeating the motif in a grille for the building seen at the left.

posed in orderly sequence, using water as a focal point. ("The reflections give you twice as much for your money.") To give these low-rise structures individuality, Saarinen experimented with the brick kilns at Cranbrook, developed a whole series of glazes, from deep crimson, tangerine orange, and lemon yellow to sky blue, tobacco gray, and chartreuse, which gave back to architecture a color matched only by Italian polychromed Gothic churches and Assyrian palaces.

"When you do a job like this," he frankly admitted, "your mind goes back to Versailles, the Tivoli Gardens, San Marco, the way Italians used pavéments. And you think, 'Boy! Let's do that!'" But, as Saarinen quickly realized, the over-all scale of General Motors is no longer to be gauged by the footfalls of the pedestrian, as is Venice's San Marco, but more likely by a car, preferably a convertible, moving at 30 miles per hour.

The entrance lobbies thus become something like deceleration chambers, areas of pause for the motorist leaving his car and about to enter the long, gleaming corridors of a supermodern laboratory. In accord with this new time sequence, the modular façades of brick, greenish glass, and gray porcelain-enamel panels became repetitive units, to be seen as

they flash by. Only inside does the human scale become dominant, where the interiors are based on an over-all module of 5 feet.

Some of General Motors' most brilliant solutions are the result of improvisation. The decision not to build a central skyscraper deprived the complex of its strong vertical accent. To compensate for this lack, Saarinen introduced immense jets of water, creating a 115-foot-long wall of water and a water ballet, designed by sculptor Alexander Calder, with twenty-one jets which produced a mobile fountain sculpture. He set up a 132-foot stainless-steel water tower rising from the rippling lake. Picking up and emphasizing this accent is the broad expanse of the Design Auditorium, a 188-foot-diameter sphere rising 65 feet and covered with aluminum, which was conceived on the principle of an inverted pressure vessel. Using steel sheets only $\frac{3}{8}$-inch thick, it had a ratio of thinness to diameter one-thirtieth that of an eggshell. For GM designers it provides also a vast and shadowless area in which to display new cars.

Such prototype structures as General Motors Technical Center play a vital role in the development of the technology. Perhaps General Motors' two primary contributions to the advancement of the building arts are its porcelain enamel panels— a sandwich of porcelain-finished steel skin with an interior of heavy Kraft paper honeycomb—and use of neoprene gaskets (similar to those used in bus and car windows) to "zipper in" the glass. To the architects involved, this pioneering, of course, adds great zest to the game of architecture. To the public it also provides the well-made look that is the proud characteristic of America, in tune with its economy and the natural beauty-plus of American machine production.

After General Motors, it might have been predicted that Saarinen would continue to capitalize on this success, repeat it in minor and major ways. But Saarinen is convinced that architecture must be practiced as an art. He also feels that twentieth-century architecture is fast working its way into a stylistic straitjacket. "Strict functionalism was a necessary purgative," he says, adding, "Now is the time to examine the presuppositions."

Testing "the presuppositions" is precisely what Saarinen has proceeded to do. His office had expanded into a first-rate design team during the maturing years of General Motors. A second wife, Aline Bernstein Louchheim, a *New York Times* art critic, brought a cosmopolitan outlook into the somewhat ingrown world of Saarinen's office.

It proved an immensely stimulating place to work, and soon the staff found itself absorbed on the design of the United States Embassy in London, which after the usual weeks of being *en charette*, had proved the first-place winning design in a nationwide competition. Much of Saarinen's preliminary design work is done by thrashing out problems in long hours of discussion, often with Kevin Roche, the Irish-born architect who worked with E. Maxwell Fry in London and later studied with Mies van der Rohe in Chicago. How, Saarinen would ask, can we make an embassy that is both modern and a good neighbor to existing structures? How to infuse a sense of dignity, permanence, and restraint into architecture that would both declare itself as modern and still be governmental in character? How to gain back for modern architecture some of the richness that was long considered architecture's birthright?

Saarinen began by making an on-the-spot inspection of Grosvenor Square, the famed "Eisenhower Platz" of the Second World War. He found a London square that was traditional but overlaid with an ersatz of neo-Georgian. What scale remained was a generally kept cornice and roof line. This Saarinen decided to follow. The lower floor was given increased height and dignity; the floors above are office floors and proceed regularly to the parapet line of the roof. The result, Saarinen once said jokingly, had a "Toulouse-Lautrec look," short legs and long torso, but the traditional Portland stone, which will weather black (from soot) and white (from rain and wind) is an inspired choice for the façade facing. The final result, for all the care that went into its detailing, is less than exciting.

A commission to design the Milwaukee County Memorial Center (Figure 13·14) presented Saarinen with a totally different problem, that of dramatizing a relatively small building which would rest on the summit of a 40-foot bluff and serve as a kind of gateway view of the city and lake. The requirement in terms of space was primarily for veterans' meeting rooms and an art gallery. Saarinen went about solving his problem by raising the second-floor level so that it has an interior plaza, thus in effect framing the view over the lake. He then set the rooms as dramatically flaring cantilevers that carry out 30 feet into space from their triangular piers.

After the boxiness of the Milwaukee Memorial

13·14 Milwaukee County War Memorial Center (1955–1957) explores possibilities of reinforced concrete poured in rectangular forms. The boldly cantilevered structure situated on a 40-foot bluff overlooks city and lake.

13·15–18 David S. Ingalls Rink, Yale University (1956–1958), with soaring curves and clearly expressed balance of tension and load, has been compared both to an upturned Viking ship and an Oriental barn. Form is derived from the 355-foot-long central curved spine of reinforced concrete, from which steel cables hang to support the wood-decked roof covering the rink.

Center, Saarinen's design of the Kresge Auditorium and Chapel for Massachusetts Institute of Technology came as a surprise. At first glance nothing could be less Miesian than this billowing, triangular dome (Figure 13·3), but Saarinen insists, "We felt very strongly guided by Mies van der Rohe's principles of architecture—of a consistent structure and a forthright expression of that structure." Saarinen was attracted by Mies's concept of creating universal space (in this case the area enclosed under the dome) and then hanging within the functional elements (an auditorium seating 1,238). In looking in the direction of concrete-shell construction (the auditorium is only $3\frac{1}{4}$ inches thick at its apogee), Saarinen was taking a bold step. "A thin-shell concrete structure," he explained, "seemed appropriate to express the spirit of this advanced school of technology." But in many ways Saarinen's first experience with concrete-shell structures failed to resolve a conflict between architecture and engineering. The one-eighth of a sphere chosen by Saarinen is not a "natural" solution in terms of concrete-shell construction. The tremendous lateral tensions within the shell require massive underground abutments to contain them. Even as construction began, it was found neces-

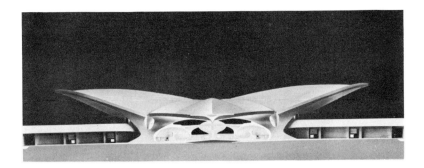

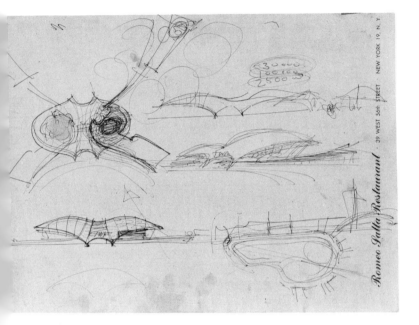

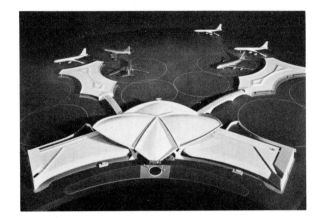

13·19–22 TWA terminal, New York International Airport (1956–1961), is composed of great interlocking vaults suggesting a bird poised for flight. The terminal was originally conceived on a restaurant menu.

sary to reinforce the open, cutaway areas. Retaining straps have now been placed at the three points where the shell and ground supports meet.

Saarinen's Trans World Airline Terminal at Idlewild International Airport, New York, is a further exploration of concrete forms, here dramatized more in terms of their great plastic values than as pure shell construction (Figure 13·19). Indeed the great wings of this structure are held up by main force, rather than their strength's being a function of form, as in true shell structures.

But sculptural the TWA terminal certainly is. This great, vaulted structure seems poised as if for flight, the most expressive structure since Erich Mendelsohn's Einstein Tower of the early 1920s. Four interacting vaults are locked at the center and supported on four Y-shaped columns. Bands of light separate the four vaults, emphasizing the sense of airiness and lightness. Within, the same plastic form world is consistently adhered to, down to the shapes of signs, telephone booths, railings, and even air-conditioning exhausts. The effect is to introduce elements of surprise and drama, billowing curves, and a plastic flow of space that, apart from the work of Frank Lloyd Wright, have been absent for decades from architecture. By

contrast to the clear, cool, and impersonal discipline of the cube, Saarinen seemed hovering on the verge of a "new" art nouveau.

By far the most successful of Saarinen's experimental roofs is the one on his Yale Hockey Rink, dominated by a monolithic 355-foot-long curved spine of concrete from which steel cables are hung in catenary curves. The effect has been compared to an up-ended Viking boat and an oriental barn, and Saarinen has frankly stated, "We have not hesitated to dramatize and emphasize." (Figure 13·18.)

Saarinen in his quest of new engineering solutions has by no means ignored the Miesian direction inaugurated with General Motors Technical Center. His checkerboard plan for the International Business Machines plant at Rochester, Minnesota, actually pushes the concept of the thin curtain wall even further by using a sandwich panel now only $\frac{5}{16}$ inch thick. Saarinen has been equally bold in stressing component parts of the Miesian esthetic. In the six-story Bell Telephone Laboratories in

13·23 Morse and Stiles Colleges, Yale University (1958–1961), combine open crescent (left) with interior courts, terraces, and paths reminiscent of Italian hill towns. The buildings will be masculine in texture, with bubble-stone walls made by forcing concrete under pressure into the rock-filled forms.

13·24 Facade detail, United States Embassy, Oslo (1959), showing staggered precast panels of reinforced concrete mixed with green Norwegian granite.

Holmdel, New Jersey, he has made the reflectivity of the glass the dominant feature by using a glass-curtain-wall façade which becomes in effect a one-way mirror. In the John Deere Tractor Company, Saarinen recessed the glass to bring the steel structure into high relief to create an "iron building."

In college architecture, Saarinen has been equally flexible. For Vassar he created a semicircular structure with narrow bay windows that serves to complete an oval in the campus plan. For the University of Chicago he has related glass, steel, and concrete to prevailing Gothic silhouettes. At Yale, Saarinen has designed the Morse College and Ezra Stiles College as a unified complex incorporating open courts and passageway which he feels are "not unlike a small Italian hill-town street." The rough-textured façade, made of fieldstone placed in wooden forms and set by cement pumped in under pressure, creates a rugged, masculine surface which recalls the effects of *art brut*.

Perhaps the most successful of all Saarinen's buildings since General Motors Technical Center is the Dulles International Airport Terminal in Washington, D.C. (Figure 13·23). In accord with the best principles of modern design, Saarinen took as his point of departure the larger problem of airport organization, which had hitherto been solved by erecting a long terminal (or, as at Idlewild, a series of terminals). But as innumerable visits to airports had convinced Saarinen, this plan inflicts on the air passenger an endless promenade from entrance to ticket booth to the ends of the long fingers where the planes are finally boarded.

Saarinen's concept reverses this. The Dulles airport functions as a series of docks from which buses (called "mobile lounges") pick up the passenger a few paces from the entrance, then transport him directly to the plane. The airport building thus can be highly concentrated. To cover it, Saarinen devised a 600-foot-long structure which combines the best features of both his TWA terminal and the Yale Hockey Rink. The great, plastic columns spaced at 40-foot intervals are actually towering pylons supporting a cable-suspended roof that slopes from 65 feet at the entrance to 40 feet on the airport side. The suspended roof curves upwards to form an aerodynamic shape, a splendid symbol for the age of flight.

"Architecture," Saarinen points out, "is not just to fulfill man's need for shelter. It is also to fulfill man's belief in the nobility of his existence on earth. Our architecture is too humble. It should be prouder, much richer and larger than we see it today. I would like to do my part in expanding that richness."

13·25–26 Dulles International Airport, Washington, D.C. (1957–1962). Forty-foot pylons support a curving, cable-suspended roof that suggests the edge of a flying wing (above) and recalls Le Corbusier's Supreme Court facade at Chandigarh and Ronchamp Chapel.

14 : **MINORU YAMASAKI**

Limited by space, a frog in a well cannot understand what is an ocean.
Limited by time, an insect in summer cannot understand what is ice.

TAOIST SAYING

Technology seemed to the founders of modern architecture a marvelous jinni who could somehow be mastered and turned to man's account. In fact, as architects are becoming increasingly aware, the jinni has turned out to be more master than slave.

One of the men who feels this most strongly is the Seattle-born architect Minoru Yamasaki. "Our technology today has brought chaos," he points out. "We have speed, traffic, fear, congestion, and restlessness. We need a place to put our lives in balance. Architecture is a good place for this. When people go into good buildings, there should be serenity and delight." [1]

Such an order is to be found in the work of Mies van der Rohe,* the architect who for Yamasaki

* See Chap. 6.

and most of his generation is the presiding genius of design. Yamasaki, for one, freely confesses, "Mies showed us that buildings built by machines can be as beautiful as hand-made buildings of the past, and for this Mies is to be thanked." But—and it is a big "but"—Yamasaki is equally firm in saying, "I dread the thought of our cities becoming endless streets in flush glass, steel, and porcelain-enamel modules, no matter how beautifully executed. With every passing day architects are beginning to realize that monotony and dullness can be the only result of this formula architecture. Our life gives promise of being spent in look-alike houses, look-alike automobiles, and look-alike buildings."

In protest against this pursuit of architecture through formula, Yamasaki has taken his place in the vanguard of younger architects who are seek-

SERENITY AND DELIGHT

14·2–3 Lambert-St. Louis Airport (1956) evokes the sensation of flight with its thin interlocking vaults (opposite page, bottom), at night revealed against the sky.

ing to bring back to architecture its whole range of tactile delights, textural richness, dramatic elements of visual surprise, and fanciful silhouettes. This excitement, induced by the exuberant use of new materials and the machine's repetitive pattern, can get out of hand, producing a kind of up-to-date carpenter's Gothic. But in structures ranging from airports and skyscrapers to campus buildings and exhibition offices, Yamasaki has in general steered shy of this danger and created buildings as gay and graceful as any on the current scene. "If Yamasaki is not already the best younger American architect," Mexico's Felix Candela * has said, "then he soon will be."

Much of Yamasaki's early life hinged on the fact that he was born, on December 1, 1912, the nisei son of a Japanese immigrant father who had arrived in Seattle, Washington, in 1908. The family pattern of frugality, strictness, and inner solidarity did not differ greatly from that of many immigrant families there. His father was a stock-room clerk in a shoe store; Minoru worked in the summers in the Alaska canneries for 50 dollars a month.

His decision to be an architect grew from his awe and delight in the plans for the proposed United States Embassy in Tokyo which a traveling Japanese uncle showed the family. Minoru re-

* See Chap. 23.

ceived his degree in architecture from the University of Washington in 1934, then headed east for more study (New York University, 1935–1936) and a series of part-time jobs, including wrapping dishes for a Japanese importer, finally landing a full-time job with Githens & Keally, where he helped Francis Keally prepare a prizewinning entry for the new Oregon State Capitol.

Yamasaki moved quickly through the big back drafting rooms of the large architectural firms, first with Shreve, Lamb & Harmon (who had designed the Empire State Building), then with Harrison. Fouilhoux & Abramovitz. Finally in 1945 Yamasaki was made the top designer of the Smith, Hinchman & Grylls Detroit office with its gargantuan staff of 600 draftsmen. In 1949 Yamasaki joined with two other architects in Detroit to form Leinweber, Yamasaki & Hellmuth, with a large housing project in St. Louis to start the new firm rolling.

Yamasaki by this time could be considered a tasteful, even clever designer, an extraordinarily hard worker, and a sound team member in design conferences. The structure that suddenly put him in the limelight was the Lambert–St. Louis Airport Terminal (Figure 14·2), in which Yamasaki took a giant stride into concrete-vault construction. The daring venture is perhaps more successful from the ground than from the air, but it was promptly hailed and awarded an American Institute of Architects first award. It should have cured Yamasaki of any lingering traces of inferiority. Actually the massive load of overwork induced, in 1954, a nearly fatal ulcer attack. Recuperation was slow, but it brought an important realization to Yamasaki: "Everyone has a complex," he says. "It took the ulcer to show me what mine was—that I was Japanese." [2]

Offered the commission to design the new United States Consulate in Kobe, Japan, Yamasaki seized the opportunity to design a modern building against the traditional background of his ancestral homeland and at the same time profited by his visits there to explore his own cultural inheritance. The combination produced a superb government building in which Yamasaki was able to make use of modern technology, integrated with formal elements of traditional Japanese landscaping, to create an exciting new synthesis.

Yamasaki was haunted by the beauty of Japanese architecture, with the dramatic transitions between dark passages opening into the blinding light of courtyards, the exquisite detailing, the sensitivity to materials, their transitions and juxtapositions. Yamasaki found he was transported "to fairyland, a delightful, peaceful dream" when he dined in a restaurant by the modern Japanese architect Sutemi Horiguchi, where the panels of the shoji screen, "with impossibly thin mullions" opened at the bottom only, to reveal outside a shallow garden with slender green bamboo stalks and dark stones against a silvery weathered fence. Only reluctantly did he realize, "The scale, structure and discipline of Japanese architecture are all inappropriate for the demands of our time. The discipline of total simplicity would be impossible for us." [3] But Yamasaki nevertheless retained what he feels is the essence, "the ability to create an environment in which the inhabitants can find utter peace and quiet pleasure."

"The two visits to Japan and the return trip around the world changed my life—maybe saved it," Yamasaki now believes. He became intoxicated with the rushing fountains of Italy, the exuberant palaces, and the Venetian skyline. "Great architecture," he discovered, "makes you want to touch it." Like the Taoist frog out of the well and the insect transported to another climate, Yamasaki found the Bauhaus blinders falling from his eyes. He was, in fact, back where his Beaux-Arts forefathers had taken their point of departure.

The significant thing about the experience for Yamasaki was his realization that what made these monuments symbols of their age was that each embodies a clear cultural concept, carried out in terms of the most advanced structural knowledge of the times. Rather than turning him into

14·4 American Concrete Institute, Detroit, Michigan (1958), is a successful exhibition dramatizing concrete, used here in both the folded-slab roof and concrete grilles.

14·5 Reynolds Metals Company, Detroit, Michigan (1959), uses aluminum in the anodized grille and space-truss skylights.

an eclectic, content to copy an arch here and a dome there, Yamasaki's intense experience of forms from the past made him resolve to evoke a similar serenity and delight using the technology of today.

"In order to vary our horizons and to express the personality of our society, it is very important that we use all legitimate forms in architecture," Yamasaki once explained to a jury. "I feel, however, that those legitimate forms should necessarily arise from a valid structural reason, rather than from an impulsive emotional reason, such as sculpture might have. Consequently, I wonder about Le Corbusier's Ronchamp Chapel, for instance. . . . If we did an office building in a manner like Ronchamp, I think we would really be in trouble." [4]

By making structure the discipline and departure point for his return to elements of serenity and delight, Yamasaki was, of course, stating a central axiom of modern architecture. Having put himself thus firmly on the side of the angels, it remained to see what happened when he spread his wings. The opportunity to build the McGregor Memorial for the campus of Detroit's new downtown Wayne University gave Yamasaki just the chance he needed to put his new feelings about architecture into practice.

The McGregor Memorial was planned as a conference building, one that could serve, in Yamasaki's words, as "a communication point between the campus and the community." Yamasaki also saw it as acting as the gateway to rapidly expanding Wayne University, and as a pace setter for the future buildings. And he frankly admits, "We believed this a real opportunity to explore richness in modern architecture." For once a board of trustees was sympathetic, raising their initial estimate from $800,000 to $1,272,000, thus making possible the sculpture garden and pools Yamasaki felt would give added importance to the setting (Figure 14·6).

The finished building gains its impact primarily through two sources: the folded concrete slabs which Yamasaki emphasized by projecting them on the façade and again in the interior and, secondly, through the dramatic skylight which rises above the flat roof and provides the central meeting room with its delightful overhead pattern and ever-changing light (Figure 14·8). Yamasaki has not hesitated to dramatize. The crisscross pattern of the roof, peaked skylight, teak doors, even the red carpet, in contrast to the classic Mies van der

Rohe "Barcelona" chairs, are all cases in point. And there was no question but that there was an eager audience for just this quality of exuberance. On dedication day, Yamasaki was cheered in a standing ovation; the American Institute of Architects followed suit by granting its highest award.

Architects in general, however, are distrustful of the individual jewel. It was up to Yamasaki to take his crusade for serenity and beauty into the broader marketplace. "Beauty through structural clarity and fidelity to technology, becomes culture" became Yamasaki's watchword. [5]

His American Concrete Institute (Figure 14·4) exemplified the multiple uses of concrete in a structure. The pleated roof, cantilevered out from the bearing walls of the central corridor and made to project a good 5 feet beyond, makes this an eye catcher even on a heavily trafficked street.

In the Detroit Reynolds Metals Company Building, Yamasaki reverted to the raised podium, a good architectural device since the days of the Greeks, and again he supplied a reflecting pool (Figure 14·5). For the façade, Yamasaki really let technology go to work for him. His solution was a completely enclosing sun screen of gold-anodized aluminum, but though it has the Tiffany finish, each element is actually a cross section of ordinary aluminum tubing. To allow the structure to come through visually, he interrupted the screen between second and third floor to announce the division of stories. Although the screen weighs some 22 tons, it is far from giving any sense of weight. Indeed, if

14·7 U.S. Science Building for the Century 21 Exposition, Seattle (1962) creates an interior court with pools and fountains surrounded by exhibition halls.

anything, its gossamer pattern tends to be lost at a distance.

As the head of his own firm Yamasaki has designed, for downtown Detroit, his first skyscraper (Figure 14·7); for the Detroit Museum of Fine Arts, a soaring series of glass-and-concrete domes that echo the famed London Crystal Palace and possibly even Brighton Pavilion. For the CBS offices in St. Louis he has designed a four-story structure in thin, repetitive barrel vaults. For the Menlo Park, California, branch of Parke, Davis & Co., he turned a combined warehouse and administration building into an elegant structure of interlocking barrel vaults that looks from above like a tufted cushion, yet manages to span 24,000 square feet with only six interior columns.

In Dhahran, Saudi Arabia, Yamasaki has designed a civil air terminal for the United States Army Corps of Engineers that calls for spanning the large area with precast concrete slabs supported every 40 feet by narrow columns. The bents are deliberately shaped as segments of a Moorish arch, and the walls have a lacy design, giving the building a touch of The Arabian Nights. In India, Yamasaki designed the United States Pavilion for the World Agricultural Fair of 1959–1960 as a forest of 40-foot domes perched on single columns, like toadstools. Now, in Birmingham, outside Detroit, Yamasaki's staff of sixty-five includes eighteen designers, a number disproportionately high for the size of the staff, but indicative of the focus of interest in the office. A most striking originality is likely to remain Yamasaki's hallmark for a long time to come. As a person, Yamasaki is still fighting an uphill battle; because of his race, he was forbidden to build a house in the suburb where he keeps his office. But he points out, "Only in America can people like myself get anywhere or try to do the thing they want to do." In architecture, he feels himself a highly indigenous American coping with essential American architectural problems. "Most of the great architecture of the past," he points out, "was built for monumental purposes—to impress and awe the masses. Today buildings are for all of us. Our democratic ideals need buildings which give us, instead of a sense of awe, a sense of happiness, peace, security." [6]

154

15·1 Philip C. Johnson's New Harmony Shrine, Indiana (1960), evokes a baroque feeling with its 50-foot-high canopy of shingled parabolic curves. Haystack forms shelter Jacques Lipchitz' bronze "Holy Ghost Descending."

15·2 Johnson's own "Glass House" (below), New Canaan, Connecticut (1949), is an elegant pavilion reminiscent of modern abstract compositions.

15 : **PHILIP C. JOHNSON :**
THE RETURN OF ELEGANCE

We cannot not know history

In a more leisured age, every gentleman knew something of the practice and theory of architecture. Thomas Jefferson adapted the forms of Palladio's La Rotonda in Italy to create Monticello and later used Palladio's principles in designing the University of Virginia. The great eighteenth-century English connoisseur Richard Boyle, Earl of Burlington, was equally an amateur when he translated Palladio's *Four Books* on architecture, and then went on to carry Palladio's principles into practice.

Today Philip C. Johnson has followed in this same tradition, but in Johnson's case the crystallizing influence was that of Ludwig Mies van der Rohe. Johnson began as a taste maker at the age of twenty-six, when he became Director of the Museum of Modern Art's prestigious department of architecture and design. He became a critic with his biography of Mies van der Rohe, and, finally, at the age of thirty-six, a practicing architect in his own right. This varied career has presented Johnson with unique problems. He has had to triumph over today's built-in distrust of the dilettante, as well as the accumulated resentments roused by his astringent critical quips. But he has managed to do this in a style which, like his architecture, recalls the elegance and refinement of the eighteenth century. Refinement and elegance are rare qualities in twentieth-century life. To have added them to architecture is Philip Johnson's by no means insignificant accomplishment.

Johnson's oblique approach to his career is, of course, a luxury denied to all but the few who, like Johnson, have considerable independent means. He was born on July 8, 1906, the only son in a family of three children in Cleveland, Ohio, where his father was one of the city's most prosperous lawyers and adviser to the Aluminum Company of America (ALCOA). Johnson was early headed for Harvard (a classmate and fellow Clevelandite was James B. Rorimer, later director of New York's Metropolitan Museum of Art), where with a strong leaning toward the classics and philosophy he read Greek for pleasure and planned his thesis on Aristotle. What Johnson today calls his "conversion of Saul" took place in 1928. He had casually picked

up an issue of *Creative Arts* and found himself reading an article on modern architecture by a young Wesleyan instructor named Henry-Russell Hitchcock. Here was a whole new and exciting world of form and a roster of then all-but-unknown names—Le Corbusier, Walter Gropius, Mies van der Rohe. On the spot, Johnson decided, "This is my field," dashed for the nearest bookstore, and treated himself to a handsome German portfolio, *Architecture in the Newest Age*.

The next summer Johnson took off for Europe, bringing along his own Cord, and set out to find the new architecture with a fellow student, John McAndrew. The 1929 trip ended abruptly at the Mozart Opera in Prague when Johnson received word that the stock market had crashed. The next summer was far more successful. In Paris, Johnson met the young Wellesley art instructor who was soon to become the first director of the Museum of Modern Art, Alfred Barr, Jr., and his bride. The newlyweds arranged a meeting with Henry-Russell Hitchcock, and Johnson proposed what turned out to be an epoch-making tour of Euro-

15·5 Wiley house, New Canaan, Connecticut (1953), is, in Johnson's words, "one more attempt to reconcile the perhaps irreconcilable": elegant pavilions and the need for privacy. Family areas are beneath the glassed-in living spaces above.

pean modern architecture. First Johnson and Hitchcock went to visit Hitchcock's idol, J. J. P. Oud, in Holland, then on to Berlin, where Mendelsohn, Walter Gropius, and Ludwig Mies van der Rohe were all practicing, then to Austria ("disappointing"), Czechoslovakia ("fascinating"), and up to Scandinavia.

Most important of all for Johnson was the meeting with Mies van der Rohe. Johnson had been impressed with his work from the moment he opened his first German portfolio. In Berlin he commissioned Mies to design a bachelor's apartment in New York, thus beginning both a friendship and an apprenticeship that were to last nearly thirty years. More fateful for the future of architecture, however, was the decision by Hitchcock and Johnson, with the firm encouragement of Alfred Barr, Jr., to pull together their summer's findings into an architectural exhibition that would introduce the new architecture to the United States.

Today the 1932 exhibition of modern architecture at the Museum of Modern Art * ranks with the Armory Show of 1913 as a great landmark in ending the cultural isolation of the United States from the vital new movements then sweeping Europe. Philip Johnson, working without salary and without title, volunteered to round up the necessary $10,000, commissioned models from the architects, including the Villa Savoye from Le Corbusier and the Tugendhat house from Mies van der Rohe. When the exhibition opened on February 10, 1932, it boasted a handsome cross section of cleanly executed works with ribbon windows rampant, flat roofs, and white stucco panels, including a sketch of Le Corbusier's Swiss Pavilion, with its monumental *pilotis,* and an early newspaper plant by Alvar Aalto. To round out the exhibition, Johnson

* The catalogue was later expanded into *The International Style: Architecture since 1922,* published by The Museum of Modern Art in 1932.

and Hitchcock invited Howe and Lescaze from Philadelphia and Raymond Hood from Manhattan and Frank Lloyd Wright.

The two organizers, Johnson and Hitchcock, for all their youthfulness, did not hesitate to lay down dicta. "The man who first made the world aware that a new style was being born was Le Corbusier," they declared.[1] J. J. P. Oud, Walter Gropius, and (out of deference to Johnson) Mies van der Rohe were hailed as the most vital figures. Frank Lloyd Wright was given credit as a "forerunner," but he was relegated to "a place apart" as the "last of the great 19th century Romantics." [2] It was a slight Frank Lloyd Wright never forgave or forgot.*

Perhaps the boldest move was the decision to label this new architecture the "International Style," a term suggested by Alfred Barr. The result was to give the architects a sense of international solidarity, a kind of self-generating tradition. The task of defining this ". . . single body of discipline, fixed enough to integrate contemporary style as a reality and yet elastic enough to permit individual interpretation and to encourage general growth" fell to Henry-Russell Hitchcock.

"There is, first, a new conception of architecture as volume rather than as mass," Hitchcock wrote. "Secondly, regularity rather than axial symmetry serves as the chief means of ordering design . . . third, proscribing arbitrary applied decoration marks the productions of the international style." [3] Hitchcock's codification can be said to have held for nearly twenty years, or until the completion of Le Corbusier's Chapel at Ronchamp.

* It was the belated realization that Wright's great legacy is his superb play of spaces, a concept of dynamic flow as opposed to the static concept of volume, which caused Henry-Russell Hitchcock later to stage the 1940 exhibition of Frank Lloyd Wright's work at the Museum of Modern Art, from which grew Hitchcock's masterful monograph on Wright, *In the Nature of Materials.*

15·4 "Glass House" is set among trees that by night function as walls. At left is living area, subdivided by low, kitchen storage cabinets. Pivotal cylinder (center) contains bath and fireplace. At right is sleeping area.

For Johnson, the 1932 International Style Exhibition served as a platform from which he launched forth on a twenty-two-year-long career as critic and taste maker. As the director of the department of architecture and design at the Museum of Modern Art, he soon had the monumental task of making explicit the whole range of commitments to new form inspired by the revolution in esthetics, from Cezanne through cubism to Mondrian in modern art, and its architectural counterpart from the Dutch de Stijl movement to the Bauhaus and Le Corbusier. For American designers Johnson's 1934 Machine Art Exhibition thus became a milestone which established the existence of a new machine esthetic. It also established new standards of exhibition techniques. For, in effect, Johnson was running a kind of top-level seminar for nearly every mature architect and designer in the United States. As a means of propagating modern architecture and design, the role played by the Museum of Modern Art is of incalculable importance in nearly every aspect of contemporary design, from furniture and "good-design" pots and pans to advertising layouts and typography.*

In 1940, Philip Johnson made an announcement that electrified his colleagues. For a man

* The design of the museum's own building, carried out by Edward D. Stone and Philip Goodwin between 1937 and 1939, took place with Johnson officially on the sidelines, his place having been filled by John McAndrew.

passionately involved with modern art and architecture, merely preaching and propagandizing was not enough; at the age of thirty-four he had decided to become a practitioner. Johnson's arrival at Harvard's Graduate School of Design in the role of student was equally electrifying. His hotel suite in Cambridge soon became the setting for endless design discussions, just as the small house Johnson built for himself on Ash Street as his thesis project became the most discussed small house in Cambridge.

By comparison with Johnson's later houses, this first student work of 1942–1943 is relatively modest. The house itself is a long rectangle disciplined in the manner of Mies van der Rohe, with glass façade running from floor to ceiling along the front, and opening onto a paved court surrounded by a tall wall, an absolute requisite for privacy. The combed-plywood walls had a temporary look, but the formal arrangement of the Mies van der Rohe glittering chromium ''Barcelona'' chairs, and taut detailing gave it distinction in Cambridge.

Out of Harvard, Johnson immediately entered the United States Army as a private, managed to exist there with heroic anonymity, and was still in the same grade when he was mustered out in 1944. Back at the Museum of Modern Art, he plunged into work on a series of projects that involved redesigning the members' penthouse, followed by an added wing to the main façade. By now Johnson was design-

ing in a style almost indistinguishable from that of Mies van der Rohe. In addition he was engaged in eight- and nine-hour sessions in German with Mies in preparation for his monograph, *Mies van der Rohe*,[4] published first in 1947, an event that put him in a double relationship of follower and biographer of Mies.

Johnson could not have better stated his understanding of Mies than he did in his own celebrated "Glass House" (Figure 15·4), a cube of steel framing completely surrounded by open glass, built on the crest of a hill in the rolling countryside of New Canaan, Connecticut. Here at last was the pure prism that had haunted architects since the beginning of the century, carried through with an elegant combination of austerity and richness.

The interior was laid out with the precision of a Malevitch painting, with the circular bathroom and fireplace placed with consummate skill off center within the rectangle. The red brick floor and cylinder were waxed to bring out a cold purple overtone; the steel was painted dark grey, while the steps and railing were of white granite. "People call this house sterile, but it isn't. Look at my wallpaper," Johnson would exclaim, sweeping his arm to encompass the carefully thinned trees bordering the lawn. "When it's snowing, I turn on the lights outside, and the snow coming down makes you seem to go up—like a great celestial elevator!"[5]

The "Glass House" earned him the nickname of Mies van der Johnson. But the building of Mies's Farnsworth house (Figure 6·13) the next year showed that master and disciple were actually more

at a remove from each other than critics had thought. Johnson's house has obvious affinities with painting on the rectangular canvas. The extension of the interior planning into the outer landscape makes this careful composing and balance of forms even more evident with the blue-tiled swimming pool (echoing the circular brick bathroom of the interior), the Lipchitz sculpture, and Frederick Kiesler gazebo, each placed with great care. Johnson dislikes putting a building on stilts: "What you get is a waste basket of trash." Mies's glass house, by contrast, is asymmetrical, with its series of floating planes caught as if by magnetism by the upright I-columns. The relation to the site is expressed primarily by the 4-foot elevation of the house above the ground. In effect, there is none, except for the reciprocity of man-made object and untouched nature.

Johnson himself has been forced to admit that his bachelor's pavilion was of limited application to the multirequirements of modern family living in the mid-twentieth century. He attempted just one more glass cage, the Wiley house (Figure 15·5), in which the glass pavilion was placed above a low-lying fieldstone podium which contains the family quarters, with two kitchens to service the upper and lower areas. With a cry that might well have broken from the throat of G. B. Shaw's Professor Higgins, Johnson exclaimed, "Why can't people learn to live in the windowless spheres of Ledoux or the pure glass prisms of Mies van der Rohe? No! They need a place for Junior to practice the piano while Mother plays bridge with her neighbors; they need a representational Victorian parlor where they never meet except to entertain. What kind of form I ask you can an artist bring forth with these crowded commitments to consider? Frank Lloyd Wright does not succeed, brilliant as are his attempts; the children still play on the balconies of his living room. Open planning indeed! Le Corbusier—no better. . . . Unfortunately, we can't yet, *en famille* at least, sleep in the public area."[6]

Faced with the realities of this *condition humaine*, Johnson, in effect, decided to invert the glass house, making the exterior solid and interior glass. His precedent, as the Rockefeller guest house in Manhattan plainly demonstrates, is actually as old as Greece and Rome, namely the classic house built around the open inner court, or atrium. The effect was not only logical but pleasing, although in the Rockefeller house the presence of the

15·7–8 Boissonnas house, New Canaan, Connecticut (1957), is based on a checkerboard pattern. Pergolas define exterior areas, relate them to the interior space.

pool does require a rather unnerving walk, on irregular steppingstones over the water, to reach the bedrooms. The Richard Davis house in Minnesota put this scheme to particularly good effect. Here the need for expansive wall space was particularly urgent to act as gallery space for the Davises' extensive collection of drawings and sculpture. Johnson provided it by enclosing the living area but placing an open fountain court in the center.

The most elaborate arrangement of space Johnson has so far attempted is in the Boissonnas house (Figure 15·7). Here, on a landscaped knoll, Johnson has created a point-and-counterpoint system of inner and outer spaces on a checkerboard pattern, which not only formally expands the space sense of the house but becomes richly suggestive of both Italian pergolas and the accumulative compositional effect of such great Japanese structures as the Katsura Palace.

Oddly enough, one of the most significant buildings in Johnson's development is one of the smallest, his own small, brick-enclosed guest house placed near the "Glass House." In remodeling the interior of this structure (Figure 15·6), Johnson finally gave full play to his great love for baroque spaces such as those created by Robert Adam and John Soane at the end of the eighteenth century. Neoclassic leanings had been long implicit in Johnson's work (e.g., the four axially placed doors of the "Glass House"). These tendencies now broke into the open with baldachins and canopies existing for no other purpose than to emphasize space and light in the most elegant manner possible. "True, I wanted people to believe—and they do—that the baldachins are structural," Johnson has confessed. "The fact that they are not seems outside the argument."[7]

The rule that structure, where it exists, must be expressed is perhaps the strongest law of modern architecture. To create false structure is reprehensible beyond belief. This Johnson was far too knowledgeable even to propose on a grand scale. But the canopies of the guest house, repeated in the Port Chester synagogue, pointed as clearly as the Poussin painting that stands in the "Glass House" to Johnson's new, classicizing direction. It was only a matter of time before Johnson would begin to exploit the drama and delight of arcades, pavilions, and even porticoes.

It was at this crucial point that Johnson, in

15·9 Temple Kneseth Tifereth Israel, Port Chester, New York (1954), dramatizes interior space with a tentlike ceiling suspended from roof beams lightly attached to vertical columns. Staggered windows are filled with panes of brilliant multicolored glass.

1954, invited several of his closest friends in the architectural profession to come for the week end, to spend two days thrashing out just where architecture stood and where it was most likely headed. "We had a wonderful time tearing each other's work apart," Johnson recalls gleefully. In the light of later events the group that attended was a weighty one indeed, including as it did I. M. Pei, Paul Rudolph, Harry Weese, John M. Johansen, Eero Saarinen, and Gordon Bunshaft. The fact that so many key men could talk in a common architectural vocabulary at the same level of presuppositions is in itself a remarkable tribute to the discipline they all acknowledged at the time, one that unhesitatingly recognized Mies van der Rohe as their elder statesman.

In retrospect, too, the meeting proved to be something of a turning point. Pei had just finished the Denver Mile High Building, but wondered if the influence of Mies was not merely "skin deep." Saarinen, with the General Motors Technical Center to his credit, seemed firmly in the Mies camp, but his plans for Concordia College, with its peaked wood roofs recalling a Swedish village, were then known, and his M.I.T. Auditorium pointed toward his later bold experiments with shell structure. Johnson himself argued, "I believe we should stand on the shoulders of the last generation and push ahead. I once defined architecture as the organization for pleasure of interior space. I think there are values in history that Modern has thumbed its nose at and that Modern has lost. What's wrong with marble and silk? We're all now expanding the grammar we learned from Mies—we're coming out from the shackles."

All the architects present were, in fact, to design future buildings each highly expressive of Mies van der Rohe's own "skin-and-bones" philosophy. All still believe in expressing the technology of their period with the greatest economy and attention to detail. But a crack in the almost monolithic solidarity of the most talented members of the second generation of modern architecture had become apparent. Ironically, the building which more than any other accelerated the departure from Mies van der Rohe's classic modernism is the Seagram Building,* a building on which Philip Johnson was to act as co-architect. As it stands, Seagram's may well mark the end of an epoch that stretches from the early days of Sullivan to the end of the 1950s. For by triumphantly demonstrating his principles to perfection, Mies left his followers no place to turn but to lesser buildings in the same manner.

The completion of Seagram's also effectively marked the end of Johnson's nearly thirty years of apprenticeship to Mies van der Rohe. Fundamentally, all styles rest on temperament, and there is an almost mute yet awesome simplicity about Mies, who can declare that "God is in the details," which is lacking in Johnson's more mercurial personality. If the massive solemnity of the great bronze shaft of Seagram's can be taken as expressive of Mies, to a lesser extent the glitter, tautness, and high-style elegance of Seagram's

* See Chap. 6.

$4,500,000 restaurant, The Four Seasons (Figure 15·11), can serve to represent Johnson's delight in movement, light, and textural richness.

Johnson's discovery of a more personal idiom with strong baroque overtones can be seen in his Port Chester synagogue (Figure 15·9), which represents only a tentative move in the direction of baroque space sensations. So does the Munson-Williams-Proctor Museum in Utica, New York (Figure 15·10), a museum that is axially oriented and arranged around a center court, canopied with glass bubbles. It is far more compartmented than Mies's concept of a museum as exemplified in the Houston Museum's Cullinan Hall. True, the great bronze girders above the roof directly recall Mies's Crown Hall at the Illinois Institute of Technology. But, as Johnson himself was the first to recognize, the interior concept of a great room is far closer to Frank Lloyd Wright's Unity Temple.

"It has always seemed proper in the history of architecture for a young man to understand, even to imitate, the greatest genius of an older generation," Johnson told a meeting of Yale architectural students, as the 1960s began. "Mies is such a genius! But I grow old! And bored! My direction is clear: eclectic traditionalism. This is not academic revivalism. There are no classic orders or Gothic finials. I try to pick up what I like throughout history. We cannot *not* know history." [8]

Just what Johnson will make out of his "eclectic traditionalism" remains largely to be seen. But enough of his post-Mies work has been built to indicate that it will be rich in evocative new forms. He has turned for inspiration to such areas as Hindu stupas and Norwegian stave churches for his New Harmony Shrine (Figure 14·14) and his Nuclear Reactor Building in Israel (Figure 14·17), to the master plan for Jefferson's University of Virginia for his St. Thomas University in Houston, to the colonnades of Adam and Soane for his Lincoln Center Theater of the Dance with finely molded columns in reinforced concrete. The Muses may well chuckle that the most pure of the modern purists should now flaunt the standard of tradition. "How could the shrine at New Harmony exist without Bramante," he demands, "or the Lincoln Square colonnaded plaza without St. Peter's? Or even the Fort Worth Museum without the Loggia dei Lanzi, and the Lincoln Square theater without Vitruvius or Schinkel?

"*Vive* the new traditionalism!" [9]

15·10 Design of Munson-Williams-Proctor Institute, Ithaca, New York (1960; opposite), uses Wrightian concept of central room.

15·11 New York's Four Seasons Restaurant (1959) has vibrant space effects.

15·12 St. Thomas University, Houston, Texas (1959), gains unity with colonnades.

We always advocate study of the ancients. But what does that mean other than: Concentrate upon the real world and seek to express it? For that is what the ancients did in their day. GOETHE (TO ECKERMANN)

16·1 Concept of Frederick Kiesler's "Endless House" project (1959; here shown in model) dates back to 1923, with Kiesler's experiments in enclosed forms. Floors melt into ceilings in egg shapes reminiscent of Hieronymus Bosch.

16·2 Bernard Maybeck's First Church of Christ Scientist, Berkeley, California (1910), is a highly original structure combining elements of Gothic tracery (windows) and the deep overhangs of Japanese architecture. Akin to Wright, Maybeck strongly influenced West Coast design.

16 : **THE SECOND GENERATION** :

THE EXPANDING TRADITION

In ascertaining the future influence of the founding greats of modern architecture, no architect presents a more puzzling enigma than Frank Lloyd Wright. In his own time he stood out like a lonely genius, a figure towering above his contemporaries. His own longevity, however, created a myth of Olympian proportions that in many ways obscures Wright's own quick perception of the new problems, the shifting patterns of culture, and evolving technology. Wright, particularly Wright in his mature middle years, was all that Goethe attributed to the ancients, a man who concentrated on the real world and sought to express it.

But Wright's influence on those closest to him would only seem to underline the adage "In the shadow of the oak, little grows." For all the breadth of his principles and sweep of his philosophy, his direct followers, including his own son, Lloyd Wright, number barely a handful.* Among them

* Louis Sullivan presents a parallel case. With the exception of Frank Lloyd Wright, his only faithful disciple was the little-known George G. Elmslie (1871–1952).

might be numbered Paul Schweicker (born in 1903), who worked early in the manner of Wright, only to develop his own forms. Bruce Goff (born in 1904), a lifelong admirer of Wright who now keeps his office in Wright's Price Tower in Bartlesville, Oklahoma, designs with an extravagance that seems like Wrightian principles gone wild. Alden Dow (born in 1904) has worked with great sensitivity within the forms evolved by Wright, without, however, infusing them with the sense of germinal potential that even Wright's most casual work possesses. Perhaps the most successful of Wright's own pupils is the Puerto Rico-based architect Henry Klumb (born in 1905), who significantly was in his youth one of the rebels from Wright's Taliesin.

Wright's career thus presents the curious course of a great river that flows with ever-mounting power during the early years, only to be diverted, and, like the great rivers that flow into the Sahara, disappear from sight, to continue their flow beneath the sands. What makes this the more puz-

16·3 D. R. Gamble house, Pasadena, California (1908), was designed by Henry and Charles Greene, combining shingle style and Japanese post-and-lintel structure.

zling is the increasing evidence that Wright was far less an isolated phenomenon than he at one time appeared. The great broad-eaved shingled bungalows, such as the W. G. Low house (1887) designed by the firm of McKim, Mead & White in Bristol, Rhode Island, indicate a direction of development very similar to Wright's prairie houses of a decade later. In California, the work of Bernard Maybeck (1862–1957), eclectic though it is, also points, in such works as his First Church of Christ Scientist (Figure 16·2), to an emerging native American style. The most vigorous of all of Wright's contemporaries working in a similar vein were the Greene brothers (Charles, born in 1868, and Henry, born in 1870), who combined features of the shingle style with the post-and-lintel structural system expressive of Japanese architecture to create, in such residences as the Gamble house (Figure 16·3), an indigenous California style.

Along the Pacific Coast today, it is this tradition of Maybeck and the Greene brothers, germane to Wright but not lineally descended, that has proved the more vigorous root, one that has brought forth some of America's handsomest regional architecture. Its principal exponents are Pietro Belluschi, famed for his early Pacific Northwest houses, and the native-born Californian William Wurster (1895), dean of San Francisco Bay Area architects. As might be expected of an outright admirer of Alvar Aalto, Wurster retains the timber vernacular, exploiting to the utmost the richness of redwood, natural texture, and dramatic sites (Figure 16·4).

Farther south, in the Los Angeles area, the immensely sophisticated interpreter of the Greene brothers is Richard J. Neutra,* whose work clearly demonstrates his firsthand acquaintance with Frank Lloyd Wright as well as with such founding figures of modern architecture as Erich Mendelsohn and Adolf Loos. Perhaps because flexibility is such a salient characteristic of Neutra's work (it impresses on sight by its excellence, rather than by its pronounced personal signature), Neutra has

* See Chap. 8.

16·4 Center for the Advanced Study of the Behavioral Sciences, Stanford University, is the work of William Wurster (Wurster, Bernadi & Emmons). Redwood, deep eaves, and sensitive use of site reflect the influence of Maybeck and Alvar Aalto.

16·5–6 Rich possibilities of wood construction are used by Pietro Belluschi in his Gearhardt, Oregon, house (1941) and Central Lutheran Church, Portland (1951). Both have regional flavor, are uncompromisingly modern in their clear use of structure.

16·7–9 Peaked roofs, long anathema to modern architects, have been rediscovered by younger designers such as Edward L. Barnes, whose 1955 Fresh Air Fund Camp cabin (center) is both functional and imaginative. More elaborate exploitation of form is seen in the 1958 Miller house, Chappaqua, New York; here units are grouped around an entrance court (bottom) and cantilevered over a lake site. Such configurations recall Japanese architecture and the structures by Neutra and Breuer.

proved eminently assimilable. Harwell Hamilton Harris (born in 1903), Gregory Ain (born in 1908), and Raphael Soriano (born in 1907) have all worked with Neutra and all continued to design freely while retaining much of Neutra's crisp line and careful detailing. Whitney Smith (born in 1911) and his partner Wayne Williams (born in 1919), as well as A. Quincy Jones (born in 1913) and Thornton Ladd (born in 1924), have all utilized Neutra's strength in articulating and expressing structure to produce work which, if it lacks the tautness of the followers of Mies van der Rohe, is perhaps as clear and gracious an expression of American mid-century living habits and abode as is to be found.

The influence of another major architect, Finland's Eliel Saarinen, who practiced outside Detroit from the early 1920s until after the end of the Second World War, might be dismissed as negligible, apart from his own major work, Cranbrook School, and the fact that he sired an even more famous son, Eero Saarinen.* However, the cluster of outstanding design talents that ranged themselves about the elder Saarinen at Cranbrook in the mid-1940s is an exceptional list. There were the Chicago architect Harry Weese (born in 1915), Ralph Rapson (born in 1914) and now head of the University of Minnesota department of architecture, Philadelphia city planner Edmund Bacon, sculptor Harry Bertoia, designer Florence Knoll, and probably the most brilliant all-round American designer of today, Charles Eames (born in 1907).

It would overly stretch coincidence to see a com-

* See Chap. 13.

16·10–11 Studio and summer house, Barrington, Illinois (1958), by Harry Weese. Bedrooms are located beneath eaves, are connected by interior catwalk.

mon Scandinavian quality in their work. Instead, the influence of the elder Saarinen on these designers seems to have taken the form of a kind of inoculation against latter-day hero worship. All his students are anti-academy, even to the point of being accused of eclecticism. Bacon cheerfully combines new with old in his Philadelphia townscapes; Harry Weese, who attended both Harvard and M.I.T., and worked with Skidmore, Owings & Merrill as well, has asserted the right of a house to have once again a peaked roof (Figure 16·10), pointing out, "After all that is the way a child draws it." Perhaps the most daring feat of all was the house Charles Eames designed, using prefabricated steel and standard elements ordered from standard manufacturers' catalogues (Figure 16·21). It was a case-study house that could have become the *reductio ad absurdum* of all that modern architecture stands for, but it is saved by Eames's own great skill, fantasy, and imagination.

Of all the systems of modern architecture, the one that has proved the most serviceable is the Bauhaus tradition as introduced at Harvard by Walter Gropius and continued by Marcel Breuer. With a consistency that at first verges on monotony and finally becomes overwhelmingly impressive, the note "studied at Harvard under Gropius and Breuer" appears in the biographies of second-generation leaders in architecture. As the architect and critic Peter Blake has pointed out, "Few other schools of great architecture have produced so many excellent apprentices in so short a time."

It may be that the very lateness of the arrival of an authoritative spokesman for modern architecture (Gropius came to the United States in 1937) created a pent-up hunger and demand. Perhaps Gropius's emphasis on method rather than form, and the firsthand example of Breuer's own adaptation of Bauhaus traditions to a new setting, would have inspired students in any part of the world. In any case, the results were spectacular and immediate.

Eliot Noyes (born in 1910), who graduated just as Gropius began teaching, became a highly original designer (for International Business Machines), an educator (he conducted the New York Museum of Modern Art's modern-design competitions which introduced the early Eames and Saarinen furniture), and an architect who has proved that the main lines of the Bauhaus tradition can find native roots and flourish almost overnight. His own work in shell concrete and residential architecture (Fig-

16·12 Prefabricated Techbuilt house, Weston, Massachusetts (1954), by Carl Koch is built with flexible partitions. Most successful mass-produced house to date, it includes some twenty-two different models.

ures 16·19 and 16·20) indicates what prolific avenues modern architecture has opened. Only a year younger than Noyes, Carl Koch (born in 1911) has taken up another facet of the Bauhaus's early concern, the need for mass-produced shelter, and with the Techbuilt house has produced one of the truly workable and flexible prefabricated structures (Figure 16·12).

Edward Larrabee Barnes (born 1915) is another prize student who has demonstrated that Breuer's discipline can proliferate solutions that broaden the tradition of modern architecture at the same time that they enrich it (Figure 16·7). Many of Gropius's students have also proved that a common discipline is also a common meeting ground for cooperative efforts. Both in individual structures, such as apartment houses, as well as in city planning projects, Gropius's students have proved effective and powerful design teams. And yet this has not inhibited their individual adventuresomeness.

Hugh Stubbins (born in 1917), a member of several team-designed projects, is also the designer of Berlin's Congress Hall (Figure 16·13), one of the most venturesome of reinforced-concrete structures. Canton-born Ieoh Ming Pei (born in 1917), an instructor in the Harvard Graduate School of Design, has pioneered Gropius's principles of city planning in what still remains the most difficult field in architecture, that of urban renewal. Often in

16·14–16 Denver's Courthouse Square development includes two buildings by I. M. Pei—the Denver Hilton Hotel (left) and May-D & F department store with hyperbolic-paraboloid entrance canopy (opposite page, bottom). Nearby is Pei's Mile High Center (opposite page, top), with its plaza and fountains.

16·13 Congress Hall, Berlin (1957), by Hugh Stubbins and engineer Fred Severud, uses shell structure symbolically. (left)

16·17–18 "Air Foam House" project by John M. Johansen will be built by spraying concrete on armatures of pipe, rod, and metal mesh. Plexiglas will be used for windows.

association with the real estate developer William A. Zeckendorf, I. M. Pei is responsible for one of the best skyscraper complexes, Denver's Mile High Transportation Center (Figure 16·15), and one of the best-coordinated urban groupings, Denver's Courthouse Square (Figures 16·14 and 16·16). Highly gifted as both a designer and planner, I. M. Pei has developed the master plan for whole areas in Washington, D.C., Chicago, and Philadelphia.

A polarity often asserts itself by its opposite ends, and the Gropius approach has produced brilliant rebels of the order of Paul Rudolph and Victor Lundy.* But it is most effectively measured by the degree to which its force reaches out to the very border of conflicting ideologies. John Johansen (born in 1916), in his project for an "Air Foam House" (Figure 16·17) orbits on the very fringe of Gropius's gravitational field. The project for an "Endless House" (Figure 16·1) by the brilliant Viennese architect–sculptor–stage designer Frederick Kiesler (born in 1897), by contrast, clearly breaks with the Bauhaus's orientation

* See Chap. 17.

around machine production in favor of an all out spatial sequence akin to sculpture.

Frederick Kiesler has been derided as "the greatest nonbuilding architect of our time." But, though his work has been largely restricted to designing for the stage (including "staging" Peggy Guggenheim's Art of This Century Gallery and Manhattan's World House Art Gallery), Kiesler's basic concepts of a form that would express an endless flow of space actually date back to 1923, only a few years after the founding of the Bauhaus itself in Weimar, Germany. The working model of Kiesler's "Endless House" rather suggests a sculpture by Jean (Hans) Arp executed by France's late Germaine Richier. But surrealist overtone aside, Kiesler's vigorous conceptualizing (given more concrete form in the Museum for the Dead Sea Scrolls in Jerusalem designed with Armand F. Bartos) is a tart reminder that the broad mainstreams of modern architecture are likely to be even further enriched by lines of development present in embryo from the outset, but retarded by lack of opportunity, or structural materials, from demonstrating their relevance to our time.

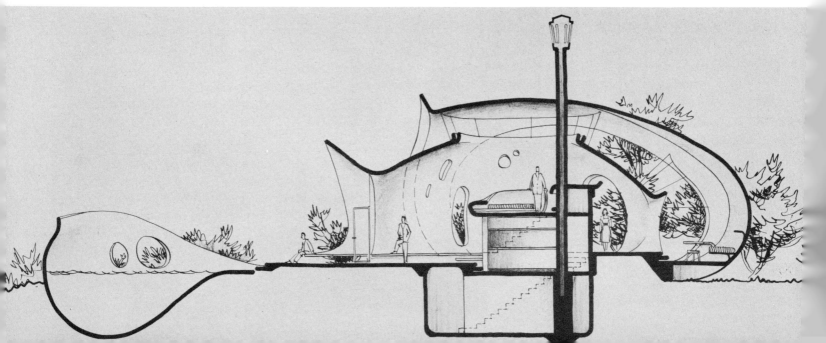

16·19–20 Eliot Noyes's own house, New Canaan, Connecticut (1956), was designed as an open rectangle bounded on two sides by fieldstone walls; enclosed is grass-covered interior court. Living quarters (above) are placed in front, with sleeping area for the family (including four children) in the rear, linked by an open passageway.

16·21 Case-study house, designed by Charles and Ray Eames in Santa Monica, California (1949), was constructed entirely of factory-produced elements such as steel-frame windows and corrugated roofing. Collection of well-designed objects blends with Eames-designed leather chair of Edwardian proportions (foreground).

17·1 Rudolph's Mary Cooper Jewett Arts Center, Wellesley College (1958)

17·2 Paul Rudolph's Sarasota High School addition, Sarasota, Florida (1959)

17·3 Lundy's Warm Mineral Springs Inn, Venice, Florida (1958). Design combines seventy-five hyperbolic paraboloid shells on columns to create clusters of "white palms" covering nineteen guest rooms. Glass clerestories seal area between shells.

17·4 Lundy's St. Paul's Lutheran Church, Sarasota, Florida (1959). Deep overhangs provide additional space when congregation increases during the tourist season.

Among the now-maturing younger generation of American architects, two new talents in particular have captured the imagination of their contemporaries, Paul Rudolph (born in 1918) and Victor Lundy (born in 1923). Both studied at Harvard with Walter Gropius, both began their respective practices in Sarasota, Florida, after the Second World War, both have been consistent prize winners. Each in his own way has brashly contradicted his elders, and yet won their respect through pure talent in design. Rudolph and Lundy are names to watch.

Lundy still views his Harvard experience with mixed feelings. "I never really learned anything until I went into Gropius's masters' class," he recalls. "In my case, I think Harvard almost ruined me. I want my buildings to be exuberant, not safe, lovely cubular things. Creative architecture comes out of the individual, not out of group design."[1]

Rudolph, for his part, came to a remarkably similar conclusion: "Gropius's greatest contribution was to introduce you to the International Style of the 1920s and 1930s and then to release you. Gropius may be wrong in believing that architecture is a cooperative art. Architects were not meant to design together; it's either all his work, or mine."

The direction that each of them took, however, in their revolt from the Bauhaus differs in a significant way. Rudolph is an immensely sophisticated architect, and his early Florida houses showed a concern for structure that made each one a thesis in design. Rudolph was obviously searching for lightness, a tense, lithe quality, plus a clear articulation of structure. Materials were used sparingly. Tension members were expressed as exposed cables, a design element that may even owe something to Rudolph's wartime acquaintance with ships' rigging. At least one structure, the Sanderling Beach Club, looks literally like the flying bridge of a fast cruiser (Figure 17·7).

The buildings, however, were almost too clever. This fact Rudolph himself confessed in later years, admitting that he had come perilously close to becoming a "structural exhibitionist" in the Healey house (Figure 17·8). This guest house, which employs a catenary curved roof held in tension by steel rods, is altogether too showy a structural sys-

17·5 Paul Rudolph

It is a bad plan that admits

of no modifications.

PUBLILIUS SYRUS

17·6 Victor Lundy

17·7–8 Rudolph's Sanderling Beach Club and the Healey guest house, in Florida.

tem to span 22 feet. "It should have been used on a 200-foot span," Rudolph acknowledges, "but I couldn't wait."

Such taut design was no drawback, however, to Rudolph's professional career. At the age of thirty-five he was named "The Outstanding Young Architect" at the São Paulo Bienal. In 1958 he was appointed chairman of Yale University's department of architecture and received the Brunner Memorial Prize awarded by the National Institute of Arts and Letters to the man "who shows promise of widening the horizons of architecture as an art."

Paul Rudolph's arrival at Yale sparked what has come to be called the "Yale Renaissance." Through Rudolph, top architects such as Skidmore, Owings & Merrill's Gordon Bunshaft, Eero Saarinen, and Philip C. Johnson were brought to the attention of the Yale Corporation and given campus commissions. Rudolph's lectures, as well as

those of the brilliant young architectural historian Vincent Scully, brought an atmosphere of wit, sharp criticism, and exuberance into what had been, on the whole, a rather staid department. "Modern architecture," Rudolph pointed out, "has a range of expression today from *A* to *B*. We are building isolated buildings with no regard to the space between them, monotonous and endless streets, too many goldfish bowls, too few caves. . . . We need desperately to relearn the art of disposing of buildings to create different kinds of space. We must realize that the motorcar has rendered the traditional solutions invalid. . . . The unique element in architecture is, to quote [William Marinus] Dudok, 'this serious and beautiful game of space.' This has nothing whatsoever to do with the allotment of so many square feet to this and that function, important as that may be, but with the creation of living, breathing, dynamic spaces of infinite variety, capable of helping man forget something of his troubles." [2]

Rudolph soon received the commissions that offered him the opportunity to practice as well as preach. His first major challenge was the 3-million-dollar Mary Cooper Jewett Arts Center at Wellesley College (Figure 17·1), a complex that suffers, if anything, from too many ideas, too many brilliant solutions. Rudolph wanted to design a building that would be "mine, down to the last detail" (in contradistinction to Gropius's principle of team design). He also wanted to introduce his own concept of urban design on a campus setting. "Marcel Breuer's dormitory for Sarah Lawrence College," Rudolph pointed out, "is in itself a jewel. But it has no relation to its surroundings." Rudolph's solution was to design a complex that would both relate to the existing brick and stone college Gothic and create, as well, through its disposition at the foot of Norumbega Hill (until then used as a parking lot), an open plaza which Rudolph calls "a great open room to facilitate the casual encounter."

To integrate his Arts Center with the campus architecture, Rudolph conscientiously adhered to the regular 15-foot bay used throughout the older buildings. Faced with the competing flamboyance of neo-Gothic gables, dormers, and pinnacles, Rudolph used peaked glass skylights to give his own buildings a skyline, remarking, "One doubts that a poem ever got written to a flat-topped building silhouetted against the setting sun." Rudolph noticed that most of Wellesley's buildings are situated

17·9 Greeley Forestry Laboratory (Rudolph, 1959), Yale, exploits reinforced concrete both in its Y-shaped columns and its terminal sun louvers.

on the knuckle of a hill. Although Rudolph had purposely picked a low-lying site (in order to create a grand stairway entrance to the plaza area on Norumbega Hill), he nonetheless felt at a disadvantage.

His solution was ingenious. He carried the upper story of the Arts Center forward to create a kind of loggia, and then advanced the sun screens even further to give his structure the soaring effect gained by the older buildings through their hilltop sites. This elaborate sun screen, which Rudolph refers to as "man-made ivy," is a highly enriching device, reading at a distance like a great banner and, at close range, like an open screen. But it is a device that passed over into a mannerism with its first use. Why, one may ask, is a sun screen needed on the north side of the building? And is projecting a sun screen well beyond the façade valid? The effect seems to be almost giddy-making, perilously close to neo-Victorian.

Rudolph's next major project, the Greeley Forestry Laboratory at Yale, seems austere by comparison, but it is packed with rigorously carried through design concepts. The column is made expressive by dividing the capital into a Y shape (in fact, even the return of a capital to a column is noteworthy). The terminal sun breaker too has an air of authority, being both functional (it shuts out the western sun) and a highly dramatic device for announcing the termination of the building, a problem that must be solved if a low, horizontal building is not going to appear like an endless loaf of sliced bread (Figure 17·9).

What may well prove the most significant of

Rudolph's building is his Sarasota High School (Figure 17·2), a building in which the orchestration of both structure and space is more ambitious, complex, and, happily, far more successful. In siting his school, Rudolph created a podium of landscaped earth, a dramatic effect in hill-less Florida. "Most school buildings today are one-story structures running all over the lot," Rudolph has observed, "This school means to stand up and be counted." In approaching the problem of organizing the spaces, Rudolph made use of a concept first introduced by Louis Kahn in his Yale Art Museum, the distinction between "servant spaces" and "master spaces."* The former Kahn would reserve for mechanical equipment. Rudolph took this concept and incorporated it into the roof, where each column is capped with a concrete duct to house air conduits and electrical cables. The repetition of these concrete ducts gives the roof its rhythm and silhouette.

Within the building, Rudolph has separated structural elements, dramatizing each in its own right. Catwalks connect across the opening portico, walls stop short of floors in order to let the light penetrate deep into the structure of the building. The roof slabs overlap, thus giving access to air and light. This separation and articulation of structural elements results in an extraordinary play of spaces, one against the other, with a view now of the bright blue Florida sky above, or unexpectedly downward. It is also reminiscent of early work by Rudolph Schindler and Richard Neutra † on the

* See Chap. 18.
† See Chap. 8.

17·10 Temple Street Garage project, New Haven, Connecticut, is Rudolph's solution to the problem of finding an "architecture of parking."

17·11 Lundy's Fellowship Hall, Venice-Nokomis Presbyterian Church, Venice, Florida (1957), is made of laminated wood. Its simple lines are Gothic in feeling.

West Coast in the late 1920s, which suggests the fascinating possibility that the influence of Frank Lloyd Wright's work, which becomes mannerism when copied too closely, may now be influencing the second and third generation through the medium of such men as Neutra.

Certainly Rudolph's most recent houses, which incorporate as many as twelve different levels within the structure, is highly Wrightian in its programing, and yet reminiscent of some of the architecture of the 1920s, an area Rudolph, for one, thinks well worth reinvestigating. Innovations of Rudolph's that have attracted more attention, however, are his massive slab sun screens, carried like a great blanket down from the roof in the Sarasota High School, and his exploitation of mechanical spaces. It is this last which Rudolph believes in the long run may be the most significant. "Why," he asks, "shouldn't duct work be a veritable tree inside, or a vine climbing over the façade? If we are to spend up to 60 per cent of our building budget on mechanical equipment, we should derive more than physical comfort from it. Visual exploitation of it may become the sculpture of our time."

If Rudolph's play of space and structure is immensely sophisticated, the laminated-wood and reinforced-concrete structure of Victor Lundy are of the essence of romance. Rudolph's revolt against the monotony of modern architecture still remains within the larger context of what most modern architects are thinking; Lundy has reached back to the ribbed arches of Gothic cathedrals for inspiration. Implied in Lundy's lively roofs and exotic concrete parasols is a radical departure from most tenets of modern design.

Lundy dates his disillusionment with aging modern from his meeting in Paris with Le Corbusier.*

* See Chap. 4.

"It was in that dark little bathroom of an office," Lundy recalls, "and Le Corbusier was sitting there with a spotlight playing on the sculpture of a big hand. And suddenly I wondered why was I there. We had nothing to say to each other." Lundy went to see Le Corbusier's now ruined Villa Savoye, and then on to Le Corbusier's Salvation Army Hospital in Paris: "It was terrible inside, long, narrow, dungeonlike dormitories. The people who were supposed to be in them were all sitting outside, and suddenly I knew why. Le Corbusier's architecture had nothing to do with human beings. It was totally repulsive."

Lundy tore up his scheduled tour of modern buildings and, spent the rest of his eighteen months in Europe sketching the monuments of Europe's great past, from Notre Dame in Paris to the temples at Luxor. Soon after he returned to the United States, he decided to move with his wife and two children to Sarasota, Florida, determined to create architecture that was both expressive and, as he puts it, "for people." In the scramble for commissions, Lundy experimented with laminated wood, at first using local southern pine, and then going farther afield to procure Douglas fir and redwood from the Pacific Coast. His reputation, both locally and nationally, was made by his first structure, the Bee Ridge Presbyterian Church, which cost only $50,000 and yet was a poetic shelter, easily expandable, a solution to Florida's seasonal congregations.

"Do you think," the nineteenth-century art and architecture historian John Ruskin asked over a century ago, "that by any splendor of architecture —any height of stories—you can atone to the mind for the loss of the aspect of the roof?" In 1853, Ruskin was speaking of thatched English cottages. But his argument was telling. Louis Sullivan felt called upon to crown his early skyscrapers with massive, floriated lids. Frank Lloyd Wright made the roof the dominating motif of his domestic architecture. But in the 1920s, modern architects banned the roof, replacing it with the flat roof garden. Rudolph has reacted against this by bringing back the pointed, playful silhouette. Lundy went even further and made the roof the whole essence of his buildings.

As shown in the Pacific Northwest churches of Pietro Belluschi, laminated wood takes on almost Gothic expressiveness when used in church architecture. Lundy's highly successful churches exploit this fact. Using cross ribbing to give his

roofs added strength (Florida is hurricane country), Lundy achieves a draped, flowing pattern of intersecting structural curves that is one of the loveliest forms evolved in wood in this century. Lundy also exploits the inherent drama of laminated roofs by carrying the outer eaves almost to the ground, and then allowing them to soar as high as 60 feet over the narthex.

These mighty roofs, of which St. Paul's Lutheran Church (Figure 17·4) is an outstanding example surpassed only by the plan for the First Unitarian Church of Fairfield County in Westport, Connecticut (Figure 17·12), are highly expressive of Lundy's whole approach to church architecture: "The design of the place of worship is a crystallization, a concentration in one ultimate statement of the forces at work in the creation of any great work of art. A church must look like a church, inside and out, and when it does, it becomes a symbol."

Lundy's designs for commercial enterprises have proved equally successful. His furniture showroom in Sarasota, Florida, is a most spectacular flower-shaped display case which is meant to catch the eye of motorists speeding by at 60 miles per hour on the throughway bound for Miami. The Warm Mineral Springs Inn is equally a traffic stopper. And yet, while working in hyperbolic paraboloids (some seventy-five in all are employed), Lundy has made them appropriate to the setting, where they seem like a man-made forest against the black Florida pines, yet symbolic of the nearby splashing fountains of Warm Mineral Springs spa. "There is nothing contrived about my architecture," Lundy maintains. "It is bold and naked. If it doesn't succeed, then everybody knows about it." [3]

Unquestionably Lundy's great roofs with their enclosed spaces do succeed, just as Rudolph's intricate articulation of structure and play of spaces makes for a highly exciting orchestration. Lundy's approach is both structural and highly romantic; Rudolph's forms excel in their rigorous composition, exploitation of mechanical areas, and search for dramatic space sequences. Both approaches are valid; both point to a future architecture richer and more varied than the past.

"Form follows function" has been repeated, sometimes fervently, sometimes piously, ever since Sullivan. But functionalism as a central concept has changed over the years almost beyond recognition. In the latest works of Mies van der Rohe, it has in effect been replaced by a concept of universal space, vast areas whose functions are defined by the furniture within them, much as a stage can become a palace one night, a clerk's office the next. Le Corbusier, in his monumental government structures such as Chandigarh's Supreme Court, is so absorbed in exploiting the space sequences of the building that the judges complain of being ill housed. Even the new world of the vast shell coverings of men like Pier Luigi Nervi answer more to the statical requirements of reinforced concrete than to any interior function.

Does this mean that functionalism is dead? Far from it. What has died, and rightly so, is the rather narrow, mechanistic concept of functionalism as a made-to-order space container—something like the automobile hood enclosing an engine. For architecture is not packaging; it is the creation of space for man. The revival of functionalism rests on the expanded vision of what man is, an all too human creature whose emotional needs are bound up in the spaces within which he lives. As the great psychoanalyst Sigmund Freud has pointed out, "There is no very evident use in beauty; the necessity of it for cultural purposes is not apparent, and yet civilization could not do without it."[1]

The man who has made the most stimulating redefinition of the relationship between this higher view of functionalism and architectural space is the Philadelphia architect Louis Isadore Kahn,* an impassioned teacher and, profoundly poetic personality, whose reputation is based on only a handful of completed buildings.

As Gropius says, "In this disintegrating world of men reduced to partial beings, Lou Kahn stands up as a total man."[2] To follow Louis Kahn in his

* Not to be confused with German-born Albert Kahn (1869–1942), whose automobile assembly plants in Detroit set standards in mass production of factories; nor with Ely Jacques Kahn, senior partner of Manhattan's Kahn & Jacobs.

thinking is an exciting odyssey into the realm of the spirit. Born in 1901 on the island of Osel, Estonia, Kahn passed his youth in Philadelphia, where the Kahn family emigrated. He showed such talent in both painting and music that he could have made a career in either. But at the age of sixteen he turned down two scholarships to the Pennsylvania Academy of Fine Arts for architecture. Kahn's training at the University of Pennsylvania took place in the heyday of the Beaux-Arts system, one that placed great emphasis on draftsmanship, at which Kahn excelled.

Today Kahn seems to be like one of the younger-generation rebels; indeed, for many he is the acknowledged leader. In fact, he is of the same generation as Wallace K. Harrison and Edward D. Stone, and like them he made his grand tour of the architectural monuments of Europe. But whereas most Beaux-Arts–trained Americans tended to idealize

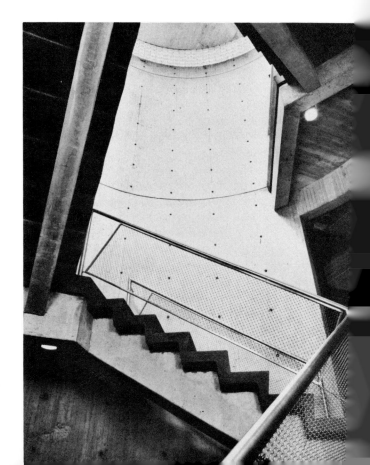

THE ESTHETIC OF SPACE

Architecture is the thoughtful making of spaces

18·2–4 Yale Art Gallery, New Haven, Connecticut (1953), reveals the vigorous quality of Kahn's work in reinforced concrete. Stairway (opposite page) bears undisguised marks of the wood framework into which concrete was poured. Exterior (right) is restrained, with bands of concrete projecting from the brick facade to indicate floor levels; within, exposed ceiling (above) is formed of joined tetrahedrons and serves as space for light conduits. The great strength of this structural system allowed Kahn to do away with interior supports, thus making for flexible planning.

18·5 AFL-CIO Medical Center, Philadelphia (1954), boldly exposes its structural elements on the interior. Hexagonal areas in trusses carry mechanical equipment.

Renaissance styles, for Kahn it was the great restored medieval city of Carcassonne that captured his imagination, and it has served him ever since as a poetic reference point.

Kahn's early professional work in synagogues and psychiatric hospitals was marked by an extraordinarily acute sense of textures, the play of light and shadow, the ingenious use of economic structures, and carefully thought-out planning. His mature work can be said to date from the Yale Art Gallery (Figure 18·2), a building designed in association with Douglas Orr and dedicated in 1953. It is a building whose revolutionary impact is likely to dawn only slowly on the visitor. It is faced with brick to the south, a severe plane ornamented only by the extruded concrete floor slabs. On the north, the wall becomes pure panels of fixed glass between pairs of columns, with a bridgelike approach from the small paved plaza.

It is only on the interior that one becomes aware of being in a highly ordered sequence of spaces and novel structural systems. "The fabric of the building is more than just spanning elements," Kahn believes. "Without closing anything off, without offending, it should be ready to do anything, give you light, give you air. The structure must do this." Kahn's answer was a honeycomb ceiling of exposed concrete tetrahedrons (four-sided "triangles") which is one of the strongest structural systems known. It also provides open spaces for lighting and air conditioning, accepted in the Yale Art Gallery as a natural part of the building and not something to conceal behind a false ceiling (Figure 18·3).

Kahn's love of structure has earned him the name of being "The Bucky Fuller of esthetics."* But Kahn's delight in columns, spaced with great art and precision, ornamented only by the marks left by the wood molds, clearly relates him to another great master in reinforced concrete, France's late Auguste Perret.†

* See Chap. 25.
† See Chap. 3.

"It was a great architectural event, centuries ago, when the walls parted and the columns *became*," Kahn says. "The column is the greatest event in architecture, for at that moment rhythm enters into architecture, the play of shadow and light, of infinite mystery. The wall is open. The column becomes the giver of light." To Kahn the great columns of the Egyptian temples at Luxor, the early Greek temple of Paestum, or the great piers at Chartres do more than support. They are the devices which give order to the realms of spaces. It is the desire to have space emerge in its most evocative power that is the heart and soul of Kahn's architecture. The power of space to move or imprison men, Kahn feels, is almost beyond calculation. Far from its being function which creates space, he believes it is space which initiates life, or as he puts it, "Form evokes function."

Kahn once illustrated his belief lightheartedly by saying, "You can take a bath under an 8-foot ceiling and come out clean. But imagine what it is like to bathe under a 150-foot ceiling as the Romans did in the Baths of Caracalla!" It is the extra dimension that space can give to man's inner life and the quickening of his spirit that concern Kahn. He defines architecture as "the thoughtful making of spaces," and points out, "Merely to put a package of walls and a roof around a process, whether it is a manufacturing plant or a family's life, is not doing anything for it. That isn't efficiency. A building should add something to the process it harbors, and make it better, *more* efficient, more rewarding." [3]

Kahn's desire to attain a release of greater spaces has led him to make an important distinction between what he calls "master spaces" and "servant spaces," a concept which he first built into a structure with the Jewish Community Center Bath House in Trenton, New Jersey. By using reinforced concrete (or concrete blocks), Kahn realized that today the columns can be hollow. These "hollow stones," as Kahn calls them, provide perfect subsidiary areas for servant areas. In the Trenton Bath House, for instance, they contain the ticket booth, entrance to the chlorinating plant, toilets, closets. The major spaces then become free and unencumbered.

"All the forms of the Renaissance," Kahn points out, "whether domes, vaults, columns, are just as valid today as they ever were. The difference is that now you don't expect a dome to talk back; the echo must be deadened. It must also be temperature-

18·6 Alfred Newton Richards Medical Research Building, University of Pennsylvania

controlled. It must be an area where night becomes day. All of these services now are required. The dome today becomes alive because of its demands. We must have servant areas which serve these great spaces. The finding of such service areas is now added to the economic needs of the building. I have learned to respect mechanical equipment because it is the great destroyer of space.''

The division of spaces into master and servant areas is the organizing principle behind Kahn's Medical Laboratory for the University of Pennsylvania, one of the most important trend-setting structures of the early 1960s (Figure 18·6). Observing how scientists work and the variety of experiments and devices used, Kahn said, ''No space you can devise can satisfy these requirements.'' But Kahn was equally certain that the usual solution—a corridor with toilets, services, and animal rooms on one side and, opening off the other side, rooms where scientists work—was far from ideal. ''I thought what they should have was a corner for thought, in a word, a studio instead of slices of space. A studio *wants* to be a place free for every man to decide for himself. There should be no circulation through it. It should be more like a table on which you work.''

Kahn's second observation also derives from functional considerations: ''I decided that you should never come in contact with the air you throw away. Protoplasm shies away from its own excreta. These research men will be infecting animals with germs. They will be working with isotopes and noxious gases. My solution was to create three great stacks of studios and attach to them tall service towers which would include animal quarters, mains to carry water, gas and vacuum lines, as well as ducts to breathe in the air from 'nostrils' placed low in the building and exhaust it out through stacks high above the roof.''

The building that resulted, despite its cramped site, clearly expresses these functions. The close proximity of dormitories across a narrow lane makes all of Kahn's concern with exhausting air eminently sensible. The levels of studio-laboratories, dramatized by their projecting reinforced-concrete cantilevered floors, seem indeed spaces for free decisions. But the most thrilling aspect of all is the emergence of a new form from strictly functional requirements. These great exhaust stacks rising 25 feet above the roof recall not only medieval· watch towers but great chimneys. They can be understood at a glance. The interior spaces are equally self-

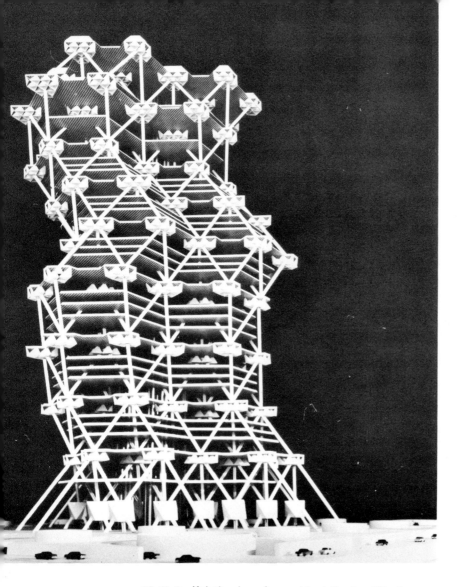

18·7–9 Kahn's plans for an ideal Center City (opposite page) with parking "harbors," massive 700-square-foot central plaza elevated above traffic (below), and tetrahedron structure (above) for municipal offices.

declarative, while the servant areas are densely packed service cores. The web trusses providing support for each floor are plainly and unabashedly exposed, functioning as both supports and passageways through which mechanical equipment can be threaded to outlets in the laboratories.

"A building is like a human," Kahn insists. "An architect almost has the opportunity of creating life. The way the knuckles and joints come together make each hand interesting and beautiful. In a building these details should not be put in a mitten and hidden. Space is architectural when the evidence of how it is made is seen and comprehended." [4]

Perhaps the most spectacular example of Kahn's bare-knuckle approach to architecture is his design for a municipal administration building (Figure 18·7) which would employ a tetrahedral system similar to that employed by Buckminster Fuller for his octet trusses. Each leg (or column) of this gigantic Tinkertoy construction would measure 66 feet and be joined by a "knuckle" some 11 feet in depth and containing atmosphere control and mechanical services. Sheathed in glass, this structure could develop great chambers and subdivisions. Towering above the skyline, self-braced against the wind and elements, it might have become a symbol for Philadelphia as inspiring as the Eiffel Tower for Paris. But as has happened too often in the past, the architect's native city shows little interest in carrying out the artist's most daring schemes.

For Louis Kahn most certainly is an artist, but one who accepts the limitations of his profession. "A sculptor," he once pointed out, "can start with square wheels, if this helps him express his emotion. Giotto could draw birds that can't fly, because he did not have to answer to gravity. An architect has to start with round wheels. There are limits. An

architect must make clear statements. If it's a stunt, then it's not architecture."

Still within these limits, Kahn has evoked one of the most poetic images of the city to emerge in this century (Figure 18·9). The controlling vision may well harken back to Kahn's student enthusiasm for the great French walled city of Carcassonne, but the controlling metaphor is that of the river. Kahn himself would probably go even further and declare that he is only developing the will to being of the city, its own inherent "principle of order." For Kahn, Carcassonne's "principle of order" was self-defense, a fact which makes its walls, towers, and crenelation as organically a part of the city as its streets, market places, cathedrals, and palaces.

The "principle of order" of today's cities, Kahn believes, is movement. Today's streets, he feels, "want" to be buildings. They can no longer be treated as simple paths; they are now becoming complex structures, with layers of roofing and immensely complicated "innards" composed of gas mains, sewer pipes, and electrical conduits. Their function too is changing and not necessarily for the better. "The mixture of bus movement and car movement," Kahn points out, "makes the street only as good as the bus. There must be an architecture of stopping, now pitifully called a garage. It should be part of the street in the same way that the walls of Carcassonne are part of the city. The image should be clear between stopping and movement."

Kahn's own poetic image is that of the harbor with docks becoming a multistory garage below, topped by a roof garden surrounded by even taller apartment or office stories. With these redoubts in place, Kahn surveys a master city plan in which expressways would approach the city like great waterways, unimpeded in their flow. Branching off

from these would be side canals, leading to temporary unloading areas. The civic center itself would be a great elevated island beneath which the black macadam roads would flow. Above this tide, Kahn would build a modern Venice, dotting it with fanciful structures, oval arenas, truncated pyramids (department stores), and, climaxing them all, his towering municipal building.

"Why," he demands, "should the city hall today be a place for collecting taxes, where the mayor really does not want to be. The city hall should be in a position where patriotism can exist. But its 'existence will' has been changed. In much the same way a school is a realm of spaces where it is good to learn. An architect may find such a realm is a pantheon, with siminar spaces attached and some form of garden. One should recall the original existence will of a school. It was a man under a tree around whom others gathered. This man became the institution, but the institution has almost fatally destroyed the concept from which it sprang."

This brooding sense of form as space willing itself into existence is extraordinarily transcendental for an age that prides itself on its scientific rationalism. But Kahn, in searching for the human roots from which institutions emerged, whether churches, markets, arenas, or parliaments, is boldly reaffirming that architecture exists not for itself but for man's needs. In this sense functionalism takes on an almost Platonic sense of harmony with man's own innate nature.

"The continual renewal of architecture comes from changing concepts of space," says Kahn, and he is certain the new forms will be both recognized and welcomed. "Form," Kahn points out, "is much closer to everybody's liking than any design can be. Beauty comes from acceptance, from need."

19 : **KENZO TANGE** : THE MEETING OF

19·1 Tange's house, Tokyo (1953), combines modernity with tradition. Tange has simplified complex joints, raised structure 8 feet, replaced shojis with glass.

EAST AND WEST

We must make something new of tradition

The architecture of Japan has charmed architects from Frank Lloyd Wright to Walter Gropius. With such a rich heritage to draw upon—buildings exotic yet eminently rational, modular in rhythm and yet the result of handcrafts, of consummate harmony between indoor and outdoor living—modern Japanese architects might have been expected to lead the world.

The difficulty, of course, has been that what Westerners most admire, the thatched Ise shrines from the dim Nara period (710–794 A.D.), the massive Shosho-in storage houses built for the eighth-century Empress Komyo, and the floating quality and elegance of the Katsura Palace, are all essentially anachronistic in the mid-twentieth century, contemporary neither in materials, techniques, nor function.

As a result Japanese architects until very recently have looked abroad rather than into their own culture. This cult of the West resulted first in the wholesale importation of Beaux-Arts designs, heavily encrusted with classic orders which had nothing whatsoever to do with Japan but which did present a reassuring façade of Westernized respectability. Following in the train of this Westernization came a reaction paralleling the modern movement in Europe and the United States. As early as 1920, Sutemi Horiguichi, then a young architect of thirty-five, together with Togo Murano, who had studied in Holland with Dudok, and Mamoru Yamada formed a group called Bunriha ("Secessionist"). Increasingly young architects traveled abroad, attracted by the activity of the Western schools then forging a new International Style. Kameki Tsuchiura and Arata Endo studied with Frank Lloyd Wright at Taliesin; Bunsharo Yamaguchi, Owao Yamawaki, and Shuchu Kurato went to the Bauhaus; Kunio Maekawa and Junzo Sakakura were among the earliest foreign students to work in Le Corbusier's atelier in Paris.

Much of the architecture created by these returning young Japanese architects was sound, if not striking, work in the prevailing International Style. Today such structures as Horiguichi's Oshima Observatory or Mamoru Yamada's Bauhausian Tokyo Communications Hospital have a peculiarly dated look. Yet these early shoots might have taken vigorous root in time. But one of the earliest victims of Japan's zenophobic nationalism in the late 1930s and early 1940s was modern architecture, a phenomenon repeated in both Nazi Germany and Fascist Italy. Perhaps nothing short of the dreadful Armageddon that destroyed the center of nearly every Japanese city and left some 3,500,000 homeless could have altogether obliterated the deeply intrenched feudal basis of Japan's society.

It is a profoundly symbolic act of poetic justice that the first clear statement of Japan's new postwar architecture should be made in Hiroshima, and on the very spot blasted by the first atomic bomb. The Hiroshima Peace Center (Figure 19·3) is an exciting affirmation that the seedlings of modern architecture planted by the earlier generation had survived the devastation. The buildings, composed of a museum, assembly hall, library, and shrine, are placed deftly within an open plaza. The reinforced-concrete vocabulary, as well as the placing of the structure on stilts, reflect Le Corbusier's influence. But the low, massive vault of the central memorial obviously stems from other sources of inspiration. In fact, it is remarkably similar to the ancient clay Haniwa houses found in the burial mounds of Japan's early emperors. This combination of symbols evocative of Japan's past and modern structural materials marks the emergence of a brilliant new talent in Japan, that of Kenzo Tange, an architect determined "to make something new of tradition." [1]

Born in September, 1913, in Imaharu, on Shikoku Island, Tange dates his commitment to architecture from his schoolboy days when he first ran across pictures of Le Corbusier's ill-fated projects for the Palace of the League of Nations and the Palace of the Soviets. Apparently architecture was in the air, for at least three of his classmates made a similar decision. Tange went to the Imperial University in Tokyo, and soon after graduating in 1938, joined the office of Kunio Maekawa, a former pupil of Le Corbusier's. The goal of Maekawa and the young architects gathered around him was to combine the discipline of the Bauhaus with the plasticity

of Le Corbusier in the cultural sphere of Japanese architecture. Later Tange was to note ruefully, "He did most of his fighting on paper. Very little ever got built. But for us he embodied modern architecture."[2]

With Japan's war machine grinding into high gear, priorities went to arms and war industries. The best that modern architects could do was to keep their spirit alive through competitions. Tange, who returned for a graduate degree at the Imperial University between 1942 and 1945, was extraordinarily successful in these *concours*, winning three straight first prizes. Only one, a small wooden structure, the Kishi Memorial Building, erected for a national athletic organization, was built, although, as Tange now adds with a smile, "This was perhaps fortunate."

Apart from his small temporary exhibition structure at Kobe (1949), Tange was almost unknown when he won the national competition for the Hiroshima Peace Center. And though this commission made him overnight a major figure, Tange in many ways found it a frustrating project. The Library, for instance, was handed to a local contractor to design, a blow that one of Tange's fellow architects compared to the plight of a composer allowed to complete only two of the three movements of his first symphony. By way of compensation,

Tange was allowed to build his first shell structure, a small Children's Library (1951–1952) in the Hiroshima Peace Park. Taking as his theme "The Shade of a Tree," Tange designed a softly unfolding shell which curves outward like a great, unfolding flower to create beneath it a delightfully enclosed space (by means of hung glass walls), providing a pleasant, sunlit atmosphere.

The Hiroshima Peace Center announced the three major themes which have occupied Tange ever since: the civic center, shell structures, and the reconciliation between historical evocation and modern technology.

Working with one of Japan's leading structural engineers, Yoshikatsu Tsuboi, Tange has erected a series of massive shells throughout Japan. The large Convention Hall at Ehime, for instance, takes the form of a tilted shell, hung within with an almost vegetablelike profusion of sound and light diffusers. An even bolder structure is the Shizuoka Convention Hall (Figure 19·5), in which Tange experimented with the saddle-shaped hyperbolic paraboloid so successfully used by Mexico's Felix Candela and others. Tange, however, has added a dimension of his own. It is the nature of the hyperbolic-paraboloid form that it rests on two points. This structural fact Tange seized upon and emphasized by making these two compression

19·3 Hiroshima Peace Center (1949–1953) is Tange's three-building group commemorating the city's A-bomb victims, with library (background) and vaulted shrine structure suggesting prehistoric Haniwa clay houses. Associate architects: Asada and Otani.

189

points, where the shell touches the ground, into magnificent, oversized waterspouts.

Tange's work has not been restricted solely to shells, however. Working with the structural engineer Fugaku Yokoyama, Tange designed the Tosho-Insatsu Printing Plant in Hara, where he employed a daring steel-truss cantilever that spans 291 feet from twin central posts and is perhaps the best example of factory architecture built since the war. Working in the rectangular, post-and-lintel tradition, Tange has been equally successful. His elegant Tsuda College Library, which uses deep overhangs and clear-glass façade to enclose a two-story structure connected by a series of long, walk-like stairs (a Tange trademark), was hailed as one of Japan's best examples of modern architecture. So successful was this structure that the highly respected Japanese critic Shinji Koike wrote, "Kenzo Tange, by thus standing most exactly at the center of the crossroads where the tradition of Japanese architecture and the contemporary architecture of the world meet, is the creative artist who is daringly in the lead of modern Japanese architects today." [3]

The crossroads as Koike describes it is more a goal than a fact. No one is more aware of the deep contradictions involved in such a synthesis than Tange himself, and his major structures reflect the balance shifting now toward the massive concrete forms associated principally with France's Le Corbusier, now toward a rather forced straining after historical evocation in the use of heavy post-and-lintel elements in concrete that recall earlier prototypes in wood. The most highly praised single building by Tange, and certainly the most important, is the Tokyo City Hall (Figure 19·4), designed in 1952 and completed in 1957.* It is a powerful, even monumental, slab structure that recalls Le Corbusier's gigantic apartment houses. Vertical and horizontal slabs (a variant of Le Corbusier's sun breakers) are installed to provide sun control for the setback glass, and the structure rests on Le Corbusier's familiar stiltlike *pilotis*. Tange's personal design sense appears, however, in the use of ramps and stairs which actually lead into the reception room and which Tange feels act to engage the visitor in the time sequence of the structure. The searchlights, embedded in sculpturesque hoods that seem to flow organically from the pavement, are another

Tange touch, one, incidentally, that heralds the arrival of night illumination as a permanent, built-in embellishment of modern architecture.

In many countries the pioneer is plagued by resistance to modern architecture, and Tange has been no exception. With the Tokyo City Hall, Tange found chauffeurs unwilling to trust the car elevator, and he had to add a special ramp leading to the underground garage. The basement at first collected water, which bred mosquitoes. Civil servants, accustomed to barricading themselves behind shabby filing cabinets, complained of feeling like goldfish, and even protested against air conditioning, which they efficiently sabotaged by opening the windows. In a moment of despair, Tange cried, "The modernity I strove for has been totally nullified."

This is a feeling all architects have experienced, but in Tange's case it provided a spur to delve even deeper into Japanese culture for roots on which to graft modern architecture. "To make something new means to make something creative," he decided. "This must spring from the depth of the feelings of contemporary people."

19·4 Tokyo City Hall (1952–1957) threads ramps through a balconied building that recalls Mies's detail and Le Corbusier's apartments. Front: searchlight mounting.

---

* It won the first *Grand Prix* in architecture to be awarded by the leading French architectural review, *L'Architecture d'aujourd'hui,* in 1959.

19·5 Shizuoka Convention Hall (1953–1954) uses hyperbolic-paraboloid system to span 375 feet. Structural engineer: Tsuboi.

The route Tange's investigation followed is difficult to retrace for those not intimately bound up in the traumatic conflicts underlying the surface of Japanese cultural life. Tange took a radical position: "Tradition cannot continue to live of its own force, and cannot be considered in itself a creative energy. To be transformed into something creative, tradition must be denied, and in a sense, destroyed. Instead of being apotheosized, it must be desecrated."

This destruction of tradition in order to release new energies is a recurring pattern in art, as movements from cubism to abstract expressionism testify. In spite of the over-all iron discipline that seems to rule Japanese visual forms, and Japanese society itself, Tange believes he has found traces of just such iconoclastic energy. The great aristocratic tradition of Japan—and the one best known to the West—centers on the concept of "floating space," a form world where structure is strictly ordered, modular, and almost weightless, where space seems to penetrate and interpenetrate between interiors and exteriors and proportion is highly elaborated and refined. But on a deeper level, Tange found evidences of a coexisting subculture, consistently denigrated but tenaciously surviving in rural teahouses and farmhouses.

The aristocratic style is called *yayoi;* its opposite is known as *jomon,* and derives, in all probability, from the prehistoric pit house, half buried in the earth and covered with thatch. It was toward the primordial style of *jomon* that Tange resolved to direct his work, creating a style that would emphasize weight, mass, and sense of enclosed volumes. Once Tange had sensed this dichotomy, he was able to apply it even to his already built shell struc-

tures. By his reckoning, the Ehime Convention Hall would be space-encompassing and, hence, *jomon;* the Hiroshima Children's Library, which emphasizes tension and open floating space would be more akin to *yayoi.**

The building that comes closest to satisfying Tange's new ideal is the Municipal Offices at Kagawa Prefecture. Here, in the seaport town of Takamatsu on Skikoku Island, Tange has erected a nine-story office structure that rises massively above the low-lying assembly hall and auditorium. Its strong silhouette, delineated by the exaggerated reinforced-concrete joists supporting tier upon tier of balconies, gives the building a powerful rhythm, one that is quite reminiscent of massive post-and-lintel structures in wood. The rock garden designed by Tange makes an inviting open space, one that echoes the gardens of Katsura Palace, while the seats placed beneath the *pilotis* are an open welcoming gesture in a civic structure by tradition closed against the public (Figures 19·6–8).

The interpenetration of public spaces into governmental areas is the aspect of the Kagawa Prefecture that most pleases Tange. He is delighted to find out that the mayor has actually given public musical recitals in the sculpture garden. "There is a new openness to Japanese society," Tange explains. "Formerly the government was closed against citizens. Now the citizens can contact the mayor at will. This new relationship must be expressed in architecture."

It is significant that this use of architecture to create a new image of Japan's social structure should begin with the governmental centers, both in Tokyo and in the outlying regional capitals. And it is equally heartening that, in searching for new forms, architects like Tange have maintained the discipline of structure and the nature of materials at the same time that they are finding ways to give it the characteristic imprint of the society for whom it was created. Already Tange's work has given Japanese architecture the vital, life-giving sense of belonging in Japan. As such it fulfills the goal Tange has set for himself, "to reflect the mood of the people with dignity and with truth."

* Although the cultural context is completely different, Mies van der Rohe's Farnsworth house would belong to the aristocratic tradition of *yayoi;* Le Corbusier's Chapel at Ronchamp, at least the interior, would be closer to *jomon.*

19·6–8 Kenzo Tange's Kagawa Prefectural Office, Japan (1955–1958). Tange's most ambitious attempt to "make something new of tradition," the building translates post-and-lintel vocabulary of wood construction into reinforced concrete. Entrance hall (above) contrasts the rock-slab desk with ceramic murals of two Zen symbols signifying harmony. Rock garden and bridge (below) were planned as strong contrast.

20·1–3 Brasilia, capital of Brazil (1956–1962), represents a massive national effort to create a new city in a wilderness savannah and to realize a more than century-old idea. The principal governmental buildings are all the work of Oscar Niemeyer, whose inventiveness and almost Renaissance love of geometric form is everywhere visible, from the marble-sheathed concrete of the President's Chapel (upper left) to the domed Senate. Saucer-shaped House of Deputies is offset by the vertical accent of the twin-office skyscraper (right) on the Plaza of the Three Powers, which includes the Supreme Court with its tapered columns (right, below). As a newborn city Brasilia is rivaled only by Chandigarh in India's Punjab.

20·4 Church of St. Francis, Pampulha, Brazil (1943; above). One of the finest of contemporary chapels, it marked the emergence of Brazilian modern architecture. The roof, baroque in feeling, is supported by multiple barrel vaults without columns. Tile murals are by Portinari.

20·5 Palace of the Dawn, Brasilia (1960; below), was the first structure completed in the new Brazilian capital and is Niemeyer's most poetic. The flaring columns have become the symbol for Brasilia.

20 : **OSCAR NIEMEYER** :
BUILDER OF BRASÍLIA

The prewar tourist always delighted in the echoes of Portugal in Brazil. The narrow Rua Ovidor in Rio de Janeiro with its outdoor flower market, the rectangular *praças* opening on baroque churches, all hauntingly recalled their Portuguese prototypes. But during the past thirty years Brazil has undergone revolutions in nearly every sector of its culture, from politics to architecture. The once slumbering Valley of Tea in São Paulo is now a roaring, traffic-choked boulevard with throughways propelling the visitors past gigantic office buildings. The bay shore of Rio is carved out with superhighways and dotted with modern museums and airports. In the interior, whole new capital cities have sprung into being. And now crowning them all is Brasília, a new national capital carved out of wilderness savannah in the miraculously short time of four years, a symbol that Brazil, the "land of tomorrow where tomorrow never comes," is at last catching up with her destiny.

The figure who represents Brazil's new awakening in the 1930s is the gaucho dictator Getulio Vargas, who rode into power on the wave of protest of the poor, the needy, the disenfranchised. The world he destroyed was an oligarchy of Brazil's oldest families, one that prided itself on its republican tradition and responsible elite. Its defeat has its parallels in Germany and Italy—wherever national fascism came to power. But although Vargas's dictatorship acquired the bootjack trimmings and bullying techniques of fascism, he still expressed the national aspiration for a glowing future for Brazil in the forefront of the new world nations.

In architecture, too, the battle for modernity partook of the metaphor of revolution. The year 1930, which saw Vargas's gaucho supporters ride their cow ponies into Rio de Janeiro, also initiated the heroic decade in the younger architects' battle for modern architecture. Their recognized leader was Lucio Costa, a saturnine figure, quiet in manner but unbelievably tenacious. Appointed head of the National School of Fine Arts in Rio, he promptly began a thorough overhaul of the curriculum to bring it in line with the latest teachings of the Bauhaus and Le Corbusier. It was a bold and sweeping reform, but, in revolutionary language, "premature." Within a year the "counterrevolutionists" had capitalized on a classroom incident, and used it to topple Costa from his position of power.

The first significant break-through for Brazilian modern architecture occurred in 1935 when the Minister of Education, Gustavo Campenéma, decided to ignore the competition winners for the new University City and the Ministry of Education and Health building and gave the commissions instead to Lucio Costa (whose project had previously been disqualified). Costa seized the opportunity, forming a group around him composed of Carlos Leao, Jorge Moreira, and Alfonso Reidy, soon joined now by Ernani Vasconcellos and a young unknown named Oscar Niemeyer.

The Costa team had their plans ready for the new ministry building in May, 1936. To criticize them, as well as help on the University City project, Costa then suggested that France's Le Corbusier * be invited to come to Brazil. Le Corbusier had passed through Rio and São Paulo in 1929 and had packed auditoriums at his lectures. His *Esprit nouveau* articles, along with his book, *Vers une architecture,* had become the bible of the young moderns. And so it was with rising excitement that the four pioneer moderns awaited the arrival of Le Corbusier in July, 1936.

Le Corbusier proved a dynamo in action, burst-

* See Chap. 4.

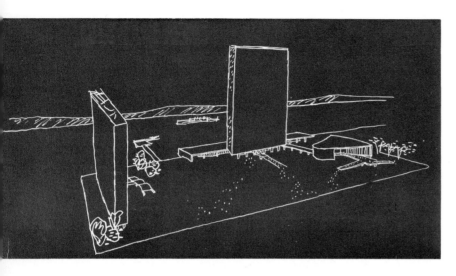

20·7–8 Many architects find Niemeyer's scheme for Secretariat and Assembly (above) with central plaza superior to the design developed largely by Le Corbusier (Figure 10·7). Niemeyer's Ministry of Education and Health, Rio (right), was the prototype for the UN.

ing with ideas that he had conceived over his long years of frustration. First he flew back and forth over the city, sketching its outline and profile. Then he dramatically shifted the position of the new ministry to a site beside the lovely bay (it was later moved inland again). The building was to be raised on stilts to allow pedestrian space to flow through and under the building. To protect the great slab walls, a system of sun breakers was devised. Noting the handsome blue tiles (*azulêjos*) on the traditional Portuguese buildings, Le Corbusier suggested that they too be incorporated into the building to ornament the stark, concrete walls. The Brazilian painter Francisco Portinari was called in to decorate them. The new ministry was also to have roof gardens, another Corbusier trademark. Another young painter and landscape architect, Roberto Burle Marx, was summoned. To decorate the great blank wall of the auditorium, which was later to serve as the prototype for the United Nations Assembly (as indeed the whole Ministry of Education and Health foreshadows the later UN scheme), Le Corbusier suggested his old friend and early patron, the cubist sculptor, Jacques Lipchitz.*

*The resulting sculpture proved one of the great disappointments of Lipchitz's career. The preliminary sketch model was cast without increasing its dimensions. As a result, the present sculpture has only one twenty-seventh of its planned volume, and appears distressingly like a small fly on a blank wall.

Turning then to the University City project, Le Corbusier sketched literally a whole catalogue of the individual forms that had been for so long germinating in his mind, including the Palace of the Soviets with its roof suspended from a great steel and concrete parabolic arch, and his concept of an "endless museum." These buildings, supplemented by the six public lectures he gave in Rio during the first two weeks of August, suddenly brought home to the young architects and students the whole range of Le Corbusier's form world, engendering an excitement that makes Le Corbusier even today the most important architectural influence in Brazil.

On Oscar Niemeyer, Le Corbusier's impact was even more remarkable. The young Brazilian was a born draftsman then working in the office of Lucio Costa. But by nature Niemeyer was one of innumerable playboys who passed their time playing *futbol*, fishing and lounging on the white sands of Copacabana. But the day Oscar Niemeyer met Le Corbusier he became a changed man. When at the end of three weeks Le Corbusier departed for Paris, Niemeyer had become his most fervent disciple. In short order he also proved himself the most talented. When Le Corbusier's fixed sun breakers proved ineffective in keeping out the bright tropical sun, Niemeyer designed the first movable sun breaker. The *pilotis* (stilts), which Le Corbusier had designed to be 13 feet high, were extended

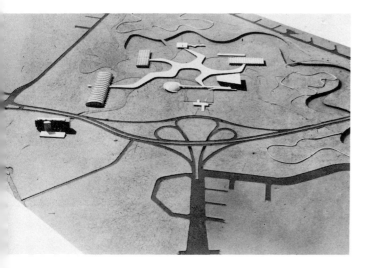

20·9–10 Niemeyer's plan for Ibirapuéra Park (1953; above) and the Brazilian Pavilion for the 1939 New York World's Fair (right) designed with Lucio Costa. Soaring ramps and covered walkways used as functional sculpture have always fascinated Niemeyer.

to a full 32 feet, giving the Ministry (Figure 20·8) its lofty, soaring effect. When Lucio Costa resigned as active leader of the group designing the Ministry of Education in 1939, Oscar Niemeyer, the young unknown who had had to beg for a job without pay three years previously, had so grown in stature that he was automatically made the new leader of the design team. It was a high honor, and resulted in a spectacular achievement. Even today, nearly twenty years later, Rio de Janeiro's Ministry of Education and Health is one of the most significant milestones of modern architecture in the world.

The state of the building and construction arts in Brazil is still abysmally low, but Niemeyer in his buildings leading up to Brasília has managed to create a new kind of organized space out of curving ramps, powerful and sculpturesque columns, and undulating walls. Indeed, many of Niemeyer's buildings seem like the triumph of pure draftsmanship over technologically backward methods of execution. In the great Renaissance tradition, his structures often stand out as beautiful objects in space or great stagelike backgrounds. Concrete, in obedience to Niemeyer's pencil, has been forced to swirl, gyrate, and leap through space in rhythmic, almost dancelike movements of great power and beauty.

This triumph of draftsmanship over materials has been achieved at a price. Maintenance is almost

unheard of in Brazil's public buildings (although Brazilian homes are waxed and polished to near perfection). As a result, Niemeyer's buildings have often aged very poorly; tilework, once it is broken, is rarely replaced, and frequently concrete becomes discolored. Often, too, the pure theatrical qualities of Niemeyer's space conceptions have acted as powerful deterrents to effective and full use of the structures. The interior of his exhibition halls in São Paulo (Figure 20·10) have a breathtaking sequence of ramps, which become almost sculpture in motion when crowded with visitors, but they are also space-devouring out of all proportion to their functional use.

And yet the poetry of Niemeyer's pencil has yielded inspired results. One of the first to recognize Niemeyer's great talent for spectacular design was Lucio Costa himself, who felt that Niemeyer's contributions to the Brazilian Pavilion for the 1939 New York World's Fair had become so central to the design that he handsomely credited Niemeyer as co-architect (Figure 20·9). Even more important in the development of Niemeyer were the structures he designed for the lake resort of Pampulha, a few miles on the outskirts of Belo Horizonte.

"For five years after Le Corbusier's visit we followed him faithfully," Niemeyer has explained. "It was with Pampulha that we began to act more freely, and Brazilian architecture began to develop

20·11 Secondary School Auditorium (1954), a fanciful building designed for the lake resort of Pampulha near Belo Horizonte, Brazil, resembles airplane wing.

20·12 Model for a modern-art museum (1955) in Caracas is one of Niemeyer's most imaginative projects. Designed in inverted-pyramid form, museum will be placed on the edge of a mountain top, with the entrance through specially built ramps.

on its own.''[1] These buildings, which Niemeyer correctly identifies as the beginning of a modern Brazilian architecture, are, like the Brazilians themselves, rather lighthearted—a yacht club, a dance hall, and a gambling casino. The best known of them all, and deservedly so, is the small barrel-vaulted chapel dedicated to St. Francis of Assisi (Figure 20·4).

This structure was meant to be a neighborhood church, and Niemeyer designed it to enclose intimate spaces. But for its size, it is surprisingly open on the interior. Niemeyer used concrete vaults to cover the nave and sacristy, eliminating interior columns altogether. The result, on the exterior, is a curving line that is remarkably similar to the spirit of the colonial baroque churches with which Brazil is so richly endowed. Pampulha was also a striking example of the collaboration of the arts. Portinari was again called in to create scenes from the life of St. Francis for the exterior tiles ; Roberto Burle Marx took over the landscaping. But as spectacular as the final results were—it is surely one of the finest chapels of modern architecture—it brought forth cries of outrage from the conservative Roman Catholic hierarchy, and in fact went unsanctified for some sixteen years after its completion.

Niemeyer's inventiveness has shown no signs of weakening with time. Many of his commissions, of course, are for straightforward office and apartment buildings. But his design for the Museum of Modern Art in Caracas (Figure 20·12), a spectacularly inverted pyramid perched precipitously on the edge of a mountain, is an extraordinarily original concept. Even Le Corbusier, who is apt to see little of merit in the work of his fellow architects, has not troubled to conceal his admiration for Niemeyer's highly poetic architectural achievement, and after seeing Niemeyer's *Works in Progress*,[2] promptly sat down and wrote Niemeyer: "It is remarkable! And I am happy to be able to tell you how much I admire your inventiveness, your flexibility [*souplesse*] and your spirit of architecture. Truly you know how to give full freedom to all the discoveries of modern architecture. Bravo!"

Le Corbusier's praise is highly prized by Niemeyer, who still carries Le Corbusier's letter in his wallet, and who has repeatedly labeled Le Corbusier "the master . . . the greatest architect in the world." (Niemeyer also admires Mies van der Rohe, but for an exuberant Brazilian, Mies seems too strict a disciplinarian.) Many of Niemeyer's projects consciously reflect Le Corbusier's forms, with two differences: Niemeyer exploits curved façades and emphasizes scale. His enormous Quintandinha Apartment House at Petropolis, Rio's hot-weather resort capital in the mountains, called for a massive curved façade some thirty-three stories tall, 1,380 feet long, with space for 5,700 families. It has been called "perhaps the boldest single building project in our time." But it is not likely to be built.

The inflationary world of Brazil requires quick and cheap buildings; Niemeyer has endlessly fretted at quick-profit projects which, he feels, fetter his own creative surge: "They're always changing my plans for economy's sake," he has complained. Added to this are the gross social inequities of

20·13 Niemeyer's house, Canoa, Rio de Janeiro (1953), consists of a free-form concrete-slab roof (echoed in the outdoor swimming pool). Areas are defined by free-standing partitions. Glass walls leave a magnificent view unobstructed.

Brazil, graphically exemplified in the shantytown clusters of buildings hugging Rio's domelike rock outcroppings. In protest, Niemeyer at times has openly espoused the Communist Party line, and, though deeply troubled, still continues his adherence.

The turning point in Niemeyer's career came with Brasília, the new Brazilian capital city now situated on the upland plateau of Goías, some six hundred miles northwest of Rio de Janeiro. The commission to design the governmental buildings came with dramatic unexpectedness. Juscelino Kubitschek, the newly elected president of Brazil, casually told Niemeyer that he wanted him to design them. Niemeyer realized that he held within his grasp one of the great architectural projects of his time and reacted with a vigor that astonished even his closest friends.

A great new inland capital that would exploit the vast interior of Brazil's great land mass and move people inland from the hot semitropical coast where they had huddled for centuries has been a part of Brazil's dream of destiny for well over a hundred years. As far back as 1823, José Bonifacio, "the Patriarch" of Brazil's independence movement, had proposed it, and even given the city its name. The dream had been reaffirmed with the first republican constitution in 1891 and had been repeated in each subsequent constitution. But it remained for President Juscelino Kubitschek, a former governor of an inland state himself, to make it a reality. A government corporation soon had seventy construction companies as subcontractors with a working force of 40,000. An international competition was held to decide the master city plan. It was won by Niemeyer's first master, Lucio Costa, who jotted down his ideas on two post cards and casually dropped them in a mailbox.

Lucio Costa's plan is indeed extraordinarily simple. "Founding a city in the wilderness is a deliberate act of possession," he declared, and celebrated this fact by making the sign of a great cross, the traditional gesture of possession of both *conquistadores* and *bandeirantes* in the New World (Figure 20·14). But Brasília is also the first true capital of the air age. The site itself had been picked by aerial topography survey conducted by the United States firm of Donald J. Belcher & Associates. Later the first cement was to be flown in by plane. And as if in response to this fact, Costa later bent the cross axis to give Brasília the form of the airplane (Figure 20·15). In accordance with

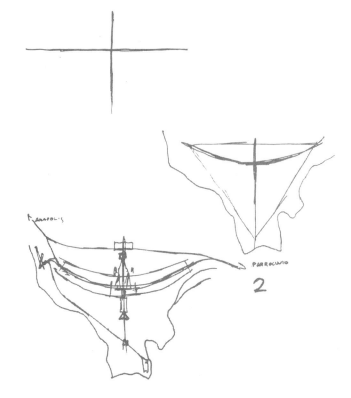

20·14 Lucio Costa's first sketches for Brasília.

this image, the Plaza of the Three Powers is in the nose, or cockpit; then a series of huge ministries and *institutos*, each ten stories tall, lines up along the mall until the "wings" are reached. These two great sweeping wings, measuring 7½ miles in span, carry the superblocks, each containing 3,000 inhabitants with their own church and shopping area, modeled on Le Corbusier's Unité d'Habitation, and the sumptuous embassies that are yet to be built.

The fuselage of the plane is a 5-mile-long axis, which includes playing fields, a zoo, and a botanical garden. In the tail is the railroad station. Surrounding the capital site on three sides is a 24-mile-long lake created by damming up a local river. The airport, already the longest jet strip in Brazil (8,800 feet), is on the outskirts, as are twin cemeteries, situated at the wing tips so that Brazil's elaborate funeral processions will never tie up the center of the city. Finally, at the heart of the axis is a series of monumental superimposed cloverleafs. Here will be the entertainment center, a Brazilian reinvocation of Rio's Cinelandia, Manhattan's Times Square, and London's Piccadilly rolled into one.

20·15 Air view of Brasília shows swept-back cross axis of the residential areas. Long row of ministries (upper right) leads to distant Plaza of the Three Powers.

Such a site has the great advantage of simplicity of conception, clear axes, and monumental open malls. And it was with this bare skeleton that Niemeyer was faced. He knew it called for great daring and even greater speed, for the fate of such projects is ever uncertain once the initiating sponsor is removed from power, and by the Brazilian constitution President Kubitschek was forbidden to succeed himself. In fact, speed of design is Niemeyer's virtue almost to the point of fault (he has designed a skyscraper in a single evening).

Before Brasília, Niemeyer has confessed, "I regarded architecture as an exercise to be practised in a sporting spirit. And that resulted in negligence, made easy by my indiscipline and bohemian attitude, so that I accepted projects and executed them in a hurry, confident of my capacity for easy improvisation." With Brasília, however, Niemeyer launched into a much more disciplined esthetic. "My interest is in compact, simple, and geometric solutions," he has explained. "Problems of architectural hierarchy and character; unity and harmony among buildings, expressed not by secondary elements but by structure itself entirely integrated within the original plastic concepts."

The meaning of this new esthetic of geometric structure for Niemeyer is best understood by looking at the first of his governmental buildings for Brasília, the presidential residence known as The Palace of the Dawn (Palácio de Aurora) situated on the lake front about three miles from the capitol proper. This is basically a three-story structure (the third story lies partially below ground) erected on a column-and-slab system, with the interior hollowed out to become two stories high, with an interior mezzanine overlooking the reception hall. "My objective," says Niemeyer, "was to build not just a large residence, but a true palace, with fitting nobility and monumental effect. I sought to achieve this through the very structure—its fundamental supports: the columns, which rise sinuously from the earth." (Figure 20·5.)

Niemeyer's columns, shaped like great curving sails of marble-veneered concrete, have already become almost the trademark of Brasília. The fact that they are only semifunctional in character (the weight of the veranda roof is largely supported by columns behind the glass façade) militates against it very little. It is the resulting qualities of lightness and grace that caused even Frank Lloyd Wright to exclaim when he first saw them, ''Ah, there's architecture.''

The greatest challenge of Brasília, however, was the great Plaza of the Three Powers (Figure 20·2), a gigantic equilateral triangle of raised earth measuring 3,000 feet on each side and held by massive masonry retaining walls. Here all of Niemeyer's bold play of forms was called for. And his solution is in many ways even more dramatic than the Caracas Museum. For the House of Deputies he created an immense saucer, swelling outward until it terminates on the interior in the public gallery. By contrast he created the Senate as an

20·16 Apartment house, Berlin (1959). Massive V-shaped columns and detached elevator structure are Niemeyer trademarks.

inward-turning dome in reinforced concrete. Against these two pure, contrasting geometric forms, Niemeyer then set the twin skyscrapers, twenty-eight stories tall, and the only buildings at Brasília to employ a steel-skeleton framework.

The two structures at the remaining angles of the Plaza of the Three Powers are the executive offices of the President, the Palace of the Plateau, and the Supreme Court (Figures 20·1–3). Both are monumental in scale, and are faced with the same columns first employed on the Palace of the Dawn. As variation, however, Niemeyer has set the two similar structures at right angles to each other. He has further varied the façade by turning the columns a full 90 degrees so that they act as ribs.

The final edifice among Brasília's key governmental buildings is the cathedral, the most daring of Niemeyer's structures, and the one which will in all probability be built last. This extraordinary structure, which is approached by tunnel, is in the shape of a huge cone, with great concrete ribs opening up to form a funnel terminating 130 feet above the ground and enclosing an area 230 feet in diameter capable of holding 4,000 communicants. Slightly apart, and also approached by underground tunnel, is the egg-shaped baptistry, a form that recalls the sculpture of Jean Arp.

Having accepted such fantasy, the visitor to Brasília is inevitably let down by the long, harshly military formations of the long lines of ten-story ministries. Even the huge housing blocks, each for 3,000 inhabitants, may prove to have been built on dubious sociological premises. The vast distances between living areas divide, rather than unite, the city. How explain the absence of garages in a town patently laid out for an automobile economy? Function raises problem upon problem for Niemeyer's great public structures—how, for instance, to control the acoustic echoes of the two houses of legislation? But the delight of these sculptured forms in space is overwhelmingly welcome in an age which has begun to turn out structures which equate the jail with the school, the clinic with the morgue. The play of plane and curve in such structures as Niemeyer's perhaps overly small Presidential Chapel (Figure 20·1) is rich compensation for functional problems that in time will prove not too difficult to solve. Brasília has been born under the protection of the angels—baroque angels, it is true—but still its conception now grown to living reality is one of the wonders of modern architecture today.

O Sleepless as the river under thee,
Vaulting the sea, the prairies' dreaming sod,
Unto us lowliest sometime sweep, descend
And of the curveship lend a myth to God.

HART CRANE, "TO BROOKLYN BRIDGE"

PART THREE Structures in Space

Who can resist the majestic power of bridges? They have been enshrined in children's jingles and celebrated by poets as symbols almost godlike in their vault through space. The Pons Augustus in Rimini declares the glory of Roman engineering as triumphantly as the great aqueducts; the An-Chi Bridge at Chao Chou, Hopei, China, tells us much of the Sui Dynasty, just as London Bridge (forever falling down) evokes the densely packed medieval city, or St. Bénézet's Pont d'Avignon (*"l'on y danse"*) expresses the power of the medieval monastic orders. For though architecture is concerned with creating man's spaces, its skeleton, tendon and bone, derive from structure. And the bridge is precisely such a structural system, displayed in space in all its logic, purity, and grace.

A sure sign that a great new structural principle has been born is the evolution of a new bridge system. Such was the case with John A. Roebling's Brooklyn Bridge (1869–1883), when its powerful piers and spidery suspension cables declared the strength of steel in tension. Its descendants are San Francisco's dramatic Golden Gate Bridge and the Hudson's regal George Washington Bridge. But a bridge can be a roof as well as road or floor. Hints of such uses of steel in tension appear again and again in Frank Lloyd Wright's projects, in Matthew Nowicki's North Carolina State Fair Building, and in Eero Saarinen's Yale Hockey Rink. R. Buckminster Fuller tells us that with present alloys it would be possible to erect a dome spanning a distance of two miles; the shelter enclosed beneath would cover all the monuments of classic Rome under one massive tent.

As man learned the lesson of the spider, so he has now solved the riddle of the egg, namely, that strength can evolve from form. (A simple crease in a sheet of paper makes it a rigid member.) The mathematical system which allows us to predict the behavior of shells dates back to 1821, when a French mathematician, Augustin Louis Cauchy, derived the basic differential equations for the theory of elasticity. In 1833 two other Frenchmen, Lamé and Clapeyron, applied it to membrane structures. In this century the German optical manufacturer Carl Zeiss discovered that equations for optics applied to reinforced-concrete structure, and used them to vault the Zeiss Works in 1924.

But man needs symbolic structures more than a formula to comprehend new principles. For the world of steel-skeleton structures, such a symbol was Paris's Eiffel Tower, erected in 1889 by the bridge builder Gustave Eiffel (1832–1923). For the world of concrete shells, the great symbols were the massive airship hangars erected at Orly, France, in 1916 by the French engineer Eugène Freyssinet and the thin ribbons of concrete spanning Alpine gorges designed by the Swiss engineer Robert Maillart. The visions of Etienne-Louis Boullée and the surrealist bubble-and-egg fantasies of Hieronymus Bosch are now equally within the grasp of modern man. The circular Sputniks and Explorers orbiting in space declare the sphere to be the new form of the space age. Man in his age-long conquest of space has triumphed by creating a microcosmos of the very earth.

21·1–3 The pioneering achievement of Swiss engineer Robert Maillart is shown in the first mushroom column, developed for the Lagerhaus-Gesellschaft, Zurich (1910; right), in the girder-flat bridge across the Arve River (1937; above), and in Maillart's final work, Cement Industries Hall, Zurich (1939; top), a thin shell structure.

The creators of the new architecture are the engineers
HENRY VAN DE VELDE

THE VAULT THROUGH SPACE

The emergence of a new material does not automatically bring with it the knowledge of the efficient and purposeful manner in which it should be used. The Greeks carried the massive post-and-lintel construction of wood beams and columns into stone without ever realizing that this was an anachronism. Today steel, which is vastly stronger in tension than in compression, still follows the rectangular grid carried over from wood construction. Concrete has had to go through an equally long exploratory period before its true merits were exploited. The big technological break-through came with the engineers, and men such as Italy's Pier Luigi Nervi, Spain's Torroja, and Mexico's Candela all acknowledge their debt of gratitude to the heroic pioneer of concrete structures, the Swiss bridge builder Robert Maillart.

Maillart was born in Bern on February 6, 1872, studied civil engineering at Zurich's Ecole Polytechnique, and immediately after graduation in 1894 began practice. The new horizon opening up to engineers at the turn of the century was the little-discovered world of concrete, and Maillart promptly made it his domain. The standard practice of engineers at the outset of Maillart's career was to use concrete much as it had been evolved by the French engineer François Hennebique,* a man with whom Maillart actually collaborated in 1907 in building a sanatorium in Davos. Recalling the state of concrete engineering at the time, Maillart once wrote, "It was laid as if it were steel or wood, girders spanned from wall to wall and from column to column. . . . The slab was considered as a structural element only by the machine engineer in the construction of boilers; the structural engineer had done nothing about it."[1]

Maillart realized that the secret of reinforced concrete is that steel rods and bulk concrete both expand and contract at the same coefficient, thus creating a monolithic material. This, of course, had been known for some time, but in Maillart's mind it set off a chain reaction of experiments. In his workshop he experimented with laying the rein-

*See Chap. 3.

forcing rods in a crisscross fashion, thus making the slab so strong that it could be used without supporting beams. He also discovered that bending the rods through the junction between the top of the column and the slab made an extraordinarily strong connection. The form that resulted was today's mushroom column, actually a flow of stresses from column to the slab. By 1910, Maillart was able to put his research to work with the Lagerhaus-Gesellschaft in Zurich (Figure 21·3), creating the first beamless concrete ceiling in Europe and the first mushroom column.

The economies Maillart realized by being able to build with a beamless slab also stood him in good stead in his bridges. In his first famous structure,

21·5 **Cement Industries Hall, front view**

21·6-7 Salginatobel Bridge (left), an audacious 269-foot span over a ravine near Schiers, canton Grisons, Switzerland (1930)—the longest and most spectacular bridge built by Maillart. Below is the curving Schwandbach Bridge (1933) erected near Bern.

the Tavanasa Bridge, in Grisons, designed in 1905 when he was thirty years old, Maillart had integrated the arch into the roadway, much as he absorbed the beam into the ceiling. To gain added lightness, he then carved out the spandrel area where the concrete would merely have functioned as bulk. The Tavanasa Bridge, to be sure, still echoed the crowned arch of masonry construction. Maillart's system at that time called for hinging the arch at either end and at the center. It was a system that could give breathtaking results, as his Salginatobel Bridge (Figure 21·6), high in the Alps near Schiers, proves. There the span is 269 feet, the longest Maillart ever attempted.

Maillart's study of methods of vaulting concrete through space remained in constant evolution. Working always under the greatest pressure to economize (he survived by underbidding his rivals), Maillart, in 1924 when he was fifty-two years old, evolved an even more effective system, one that paved the way for a whole new chapter in spanning great distances in reinforced concrete. This new system, known as ribbed-arch construction, is clearly shown in the 111-foot span of the Schwandbach Bridge (Figure 21·7), where a ribbon arch less than 8 inches thick rises to touch the roadbed, which significantly is now flat and treated in the manner of a rigid, horizontal beam without any hint of the center crown he had earlier carried over from masonry construction. This bridge is a tour de force in more ways than one. By adding stiffeners, Maillart was able to curve the roadbed of the bridge to meet a difficult site problem, something almost inconceivable with masonry or even steel suspension bridges.

"Reinforced concrete does not grow like wood. It is not rolled like steel and has no joints as masonry," Maillart wrote.[2] The essential characteristic of this new material, Maillart believed, was its ability to give a beautiful and fluid continuity to structure. "The engineer should then free himself from the forms dictated by the tradition of the older building materials," Maillart urged, "so that in complete freedom and by conceiving the problem as a whole, it would be possible to use the material to its ultimate. Perhaps then we would also arrive at a new style as in the automobile and aircraft construction, as beautiful, and in the same way determined by the nature of the material."[3]

Some of the directions that this approach might take is suggested by Maillart's latest work. The bridge over the River Arve (Figure 21·2) built between 1936 and 1937 indicates the highly evocative forms derived from purely functional considerations. The lower supports are tapered in at the waist, suggesting archaic sculpture; in actuality the tapering expresses the concentration within of reinforcing rods which give the supports the function of an elastic joint.

Overtones of a new, evolving esthetic of reinforced-concrete shell construction are also demonstrated by the spectacular thin-shell pavilion Maillart designed for the cement industry at the Swiss National Exhibition in Zurich in 1939 (Figure 21·5), and finished the year before he died. A display structure destined from its inception to be destroyed for testing purposes, it is Maillart's only pure shell structure and was admittedly inspired by the airship hangars that the French engineer Eugène Freyssinet had erected at Orly, France in 1916. But in its soaring shape, which rises like a membrane of concrete only 2⅜ inches thick, it heralds a new day in structure.

22 : **EDUARDO TORROJA** :

Each material has its own message for the creative artist

FRANK LLOYD WRIGHT

Great creative engineers are almost invariably found in countries of advanced technology, and in the twentieth century it is no surprise to find structures of great daring and originality in France, Germany, Switzerland, and the United States. By contrast, the presence of a brilliant engineer, Eduardo Torroja, in Spain is an exceptional example of one man's creative response to challenge.

In any list of key reinforced-concrete buildings of the twentieth century, at least three, and perhaps more, of the structures designed by Eduardo Torroja y Miret would rank at the top of the list: the pioneering market at Algeciras, the Madrid Hippodrome at Zarzuela, and the Fronton de Recoletos. Torroja's contribution, moreover, does not end there. An all-round engineer, he has built subways, dams, aqueducts, airplane hangars, all of great refinement and high esthetic value. His Las Corts football stadium, for instance, is one of the most dramatic modern structures in Europe. His Esla Bridge arch was in its time the longest reinforced-concrete span in the world. And his churches and chapels are among the most delightful new buildings in the new world of shell construction.

It may well be that despite such considerable accomplishments, Torroja's reputation is not more widespread because he has chosen to work primarily in Spain. Unlike Pier Luigi Nervi, the only contemporary engineer in Europe whose works are of equal importance to Torroja's, he has never been invited outside Spain to take part in a major international building such as the UNESCO Headquarters in Paris.

Within Spain, however, Torroja is founder and director of Madrid's Technical Institute of Concrete Construction, one of the three most important testing and research stations in the world. He has the rare distinction of having even won acceptance from Spain's architects, notoriously unwilling to admit other professions to their midst, who have made Torroja an honorary member of Madrid's College of Architects. In Mexico, Spanish-born architect Felix Candela has hailed Torroja as a "leading master in the art of shell structure."

Even Frank Lloyd Wright doffed his pork-pie hat in salute and said of Torroja: "He has expressed the principles of organic construction better than any engineer I know."

As a Spaniard, Torroja had two deep wellsprings to draw on in approaching his career. In architecture, Spain is a treasure chest of great feats of building, with ancient monuments dating back into prehistory with the dolmens and cyclopean caves of Tarragona. The great engineering tradition of Rome is a living reality with the existence of the still-functioning Roman aqueducts. The delicately balanced columns of the Alhambra at Granada and the buttressed splendors of the medieval cathedrals all had their lessons for a young man who found delight in structure.

Torroja was born in 1900, the son of a Catalan mathematics professor at the University of Madrid, and Torroja even considered making mathematics his own career. What decided him on engineering was a desire to move out of the realm of pure theory. As Torroja puts it today, "I believe that you can do many things which you can't prove mathematically."

Spain's Civil War cast a long shadow over Torroja's career, as it did over every Spanish architect and engineer. Building came to a halt. Projects under way had to be suspended. Many structures already built were victims of bombing and artillery fire. Torroja's Fronton de Recoletos, an indoor court for the Spanish game of *pelota,* was so badly damaged by bombing that it collapsed.

In one sense the Fronton de Recoletos is a special structure, developed to fit the exacting needs of *pelota,* with its high frontal, lateral, and rebound walls, as well as its 160-foot-long playing pitch. To solve the problem, Torroja and the architect S. Zuazo worked out an ingenious system. Two barrel vaults were laid so that glass skylights inserted in the shell would let in north light; these extended the entire length of the hall. The topmost shell, which illuminates the courts, is a segment of a circle with a radius of curvature of 40 feet. The second vault, which lets light into the upper balcony,

THE ART OF STRUCTURE

22·1 Algeciras market, Spain (1933), was a pioneering shell structure by Eduardo Torroja. Reinforcing rods along the channels of stress support a span of 156 feet with a shell only 3½ inches at the crown; the shell thickens to 18 inches as it meets the supporting columns. Octagonal hoop is secured by turnbuckles.

22·2 Alloz Aqueduct (1939) appears supported by giant scissors of reinforced concrete.

has a parellel horizontal radial center, but the radius of curvature is only 21 feet long.

Torroja is fond of distinguishing between architecture and engineering by pointing to the two forms that sum up their philosophies: the column and the arch. The column, brought from rough tree trunk to the final tapered symmetry of the Parthenon, represents thousands of years of master design. But, for Torroja, the arch will always be the more inspiring. "Like a crossbow, the arch in stone will always be connected with the idea of powerful stress, of a leap to dominate distance," he has written in his *Philosophy of Structures*. "Therefore, an arch, always of monumental character, was predestined to proclaim the honors of victory." [3]

The arch in stone is, of course, first cousin to the cantilever in reinforced concrete or steel. It is a dominant theme in Torroja's work, whether in his aqueducts (Figure 22·2) or airplane hangars. Probably its best expression, apart from the Madrid Hippodrome, is Las Corts Football Stadium (Figure 22·5), a swooping 83-foot cantilever that seems poised with airy grace over the stands to shelter the soccer fans beneath. The monumental foundations that support this huge span are reinforced concrete, but for the actual roof Torroja chose a steel-truss cantilever framework which allowed him to shape the gull-wing form that seems poised in space. The final touch is the upsweep at the most extended edge, a curve that makes the roof seem to soar.

As Spain slowly dragged itself out of the rubble and chaos of the Civil War, Torroja's institute gained increasing acceptance. The Spanish government has awarded it a grant which pays 30 per cent of its running expenses; the Spanish cement industry accounts for another 40 per cent. The remainder is easily made up by the flood of projects that come from all over Europe, models to be tested, aggregates to be examined, and an endless search for better cements.

With the institute at last on a solid financial footing, Torroja was able to go ahead with an old dream, build up the whole institute from scratch, making it into a showpiece of reinforced concrete (Figure 22·10). Perhaps the most impressive, and fanciful, element is the ribbed pergola that greets the visitor on arrival (Figure 22·13). The pergola ribs—which emerge from the side of the wall like waterspouts, flare upward, and then trail off into space like jets of water swept by a high wind—

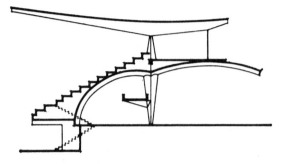

22·3 Madrid Hippodrome, section

are unforgettable; in fact, they have given the name of "Costillares" (ribs) to the institute.

One of the most unexpected elements at Costillares is the coal silo, a pure white dodecahedron (Figure 22·11) set adjacent to the institute's boiler plant. Made of equal and identical sections, it was economical to build and ingeniously designed to fulfill its purpose (Figure 22·12). Its beauty lies in its pure geometric form, with its cleanly cut surfaces and sharp edges. The coal silo seems almost to be the mascot of Costillares; seen with its changing play of light and shadows it is also an object of pure esthetic delight.

As a young man, Torroja plunged enthusiastically into the difficult curriculum of civil engineering courses at the University of Madrid. After graduation, he, like Pier Luigi Nervi, set himself to learning the realities of engineering by working for one of Madrid's major contractors, headed by Eugenio Ribera, the man who in the early 1930s was doing the major pioneering concrete work in Spain. Torroja himself, a quiet, short, soft-spoken man with the mien of a philosopher, soon found he was ill equipped for the brass-lunged histrionics and sharp bargaining that are part of construction contracts. After five years, Torroja decided to try "a more tranquil life." With his friend José Maria Aguirre, today head of Spain's largest construction firm, Agroman, S.A., Torroja in 1934 founded an experimental institute to try out his own theories as to the exciting new possibilities inherent in reinforced concrete.

The beginning was modest, so modest in fact, that for years the institute ran at a loss and was kept afloat only by Torroja and Aguirre, who put part of their own fees toward meeting operating expenses. But Torroja had had early confirmation that he was on the right track. He had landed a contract to build a marketplace for the city of

22·7–8 Pont de Suert Church (1952) is constructed with brick vaulting and expressive campanile (above). Torroja used the ogival vaults of the church sacristy in erecting the simple wayfarer's mountain shrine (below).

22·6 Xerallo Chapel (1952; above) on rock outcropping in the Pyrenees, is built of interlocking triangles with peaked roof.

Algeciras. To span the 156-foot diameter, he had devised a concrete shell with reinforcings that almost exactly matched the areas where the stresses theoretically would be at a maximum (Figure 22·1). As a result he was able to throw a covering of concrete over the area which measured as thin as 3½ inches, thickening to a width of approximately 18 inches near each of the eight supporting columns.

An even more important opportunity for the two young innovators, Torroja and Aguirre, was the competition for a new Madrid Hippodrome, to be situated on the city's outskirts at Zarzuela Torroja later confessed, "I tried to make the plans look as conventional as possible. Otherwise no one would have considered them."[1] In the final plan, nothing could have been less conventional, or more sound.

For most of the three months allowed the competitors, Torroja concerned himself with working through the technical details called for in the specifications. The final solution did not come until one o'clock one morning, when in a matter of minutes, or even seconds, Torroja found his final solution. From this sudden flash of insight, Torroja drew a fundamental conclusion: "To me it seems clear that the imagination can operate successfully only in conjunction with the basic principles that a long experience of technical creative work leaves in the unfathomable depths of our personality, so that these may later subconsciously condition our intuitive thought. But those basic principles are not enough in themselves to create, critically and deductively, a new form. For this to emerge, a spark of imagination is required."[2]

In confronting the problems of a race track he was in effect resolving the same problems faced by the master builders of the medieval cathedrals. In fact Torroja's final solution (Figure 22·3) can be read in terms of church architecture. The flaring vault at right corresponds to half the nave. The arch under the bleachers is equivalent to the flying buttress. But as satisfying as the final solution for the understructure is, the vaults over the Madrid Hippodrome are its true glory, a feat of engineering that architects and engineers alike have hailed as one of the most daring and esthetically pleasing structures to be raised in reinforced concrete in this century (Figure 22·4).

The secret of the great arches that seem suspended in air as if by magic lies in their form, great elliptical shells constructed as overhanging

22·9 Main portal of Torroja's church at Pont de Suert was built by Catalan bricklayers. Arches suggest the Romanesque.

hyperboloidal sectors needing no supporting ribs. Their strength is thus a function of their form. Balanced at the fulcrum point, they require only a thin tie rod, barely visible, to maintain stability even in high winds. The form also proved to be extraordinarily strong. In preconstruction tests, one unit of the shell was loaded with sandbags to three times the maximum required load without signs of failure. During Spain's Civil War the soaring, 73-foot shells withstood an even more arduous trial by shellfire. Situated between the firing lines, the Hippodrome roof received twenty-nine direct hits and still remained sound.

"The possible shapes of reinforced-concrete structures are, at present, far more limited by financial considerations, due to the cost of frame work, than by strictly technical considerations," Torroja points out. Torroja in his Pyrenees churches has been able to overcome this in part by designing vaults that can be constructed of bricks, or by using Spain's inexpensive hand labor. Another impediment to the more rapid expansion of shell structures is the immense difficulties of calculating them mathematically. For as Torroja explains, "The structure of concrete cannot be figured mathematically. It is much stronger than the mathematician can prove. And you can't wait for the mathematician. You have to go ahead and try what you know by intuition."[4]

Like Mexico's brilliant Spanish-born architect Felix Candela,* Torroja prefers to test structures in model phase and calculate the mathematics of the structure later. Behind Torroja's further exploration of shell forms is a sense of immense opportunities to be exploited. "For the first time in the history of art," he has written, "the structure has acquired an independent personality, so that its own intimate esthetic quality can be appreciated." Combined with this is Torroja's grasp of the poetic quality to be found in the pure expression of mathematics: "Every mathematical curve has a nature of its own, the accuracy of law, the expression of an idea, the evidence of a virtue."[5]

*See Chap. 23.

The architect of the future, Torroja is convinced, must be a "structural architect." "What is important," he has warned, "in this evolutionary process, is to develop form without confusing values, without allowing oneself to be swept away by the purely romantic glamor of technical forms, without evaluating their origin, and hence, their proper field of applicability." The final solution for Torroja is thus the fusion of engineering and architecture as an integrated whole that alone can produce a great architecture, exploiting to the limit the new resources of a technological age. And in describing it Torroja finds himself approximating the organic philosophy that Frank Lloyd Wright so valiantly defended. "I mean a natural, logical design," Torroja states, "capable of expressing by itself all that it is, and the reasons why it is so, where form and function are not independent, or even a marriage of convenience, but a fusion such that they become two aspects of a single thing."

22·10 Technical Institute of Concrete Construction at Costillares is world's largest concrete research station as well as a showplace for director Torroja's architecture.

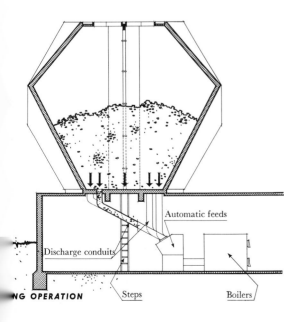

Discharge conduits

Automatic feeds

...NG OPERATION · Steps · Boilers

23·1 Soaring hyperbolic paraboloids of his Church of San Antonio de las Huertas provide setting for Candela.

23·2 Dominican chapel of Nuestra Senora de la Soledad (1957), in Coyoacán, Mexico, is a thin shell resting on masonry supports.

Only the fantastic can be exact. The mathematical stems
from the same roots as poetry, from the imaginative gift

ORTEGA Y GASSET

23 : **FELIX CANDELA** : THE WORLD OF SHELLS

Anyone who has ever ridden in the molded metal body of an automobile, used a spoon, or examined the curving surfaces of a leaf has observed the principle of shell construction. The clam shell, the lobster, the crab, and the egg demonstrate one of nature's basic ways of utilizing form to gain strength. In fact, it would seem that nature abhors the right angle. The question then arises: Why have architects persisted in ignoring so basic a natural law? The answer seems to be as old as human history:

Primitive man, building his mud hut, or the early nomad putting up his tent, probably did have and use an intuitive understanding of shell construction, but man's most accessible building material—wood—comes in straight planks and beams. It is thus most easily used in rectangles. A child in kindergarten can build with blocks; making a snow igloo takes a bit more doing. And so a rectilinear style has become enshrined in building, carried over into stone by the Greeks and into steel in the skyscraper.

It is only in the very recent decades that thin-shell construction has made its bid for major attention. Proliferating a whole series of exciting solutions in the structural domain, shell construction seems, for the moment at least, to be opening architects' eyes to a vast new world of space-spanning structures.

By definition a shell to be a true shell must be (1) curved, (2) thin, and (3) adequately supported. This involves highly complicated mathematics and, often, a willingness to experiment. As a result, the pioneering so far has been done primarily by highly gifted structural engineers, such as Italy's Pier Luigi Nervi and Spain's Eduardo Torroja, who combine imagination, a flair for mathematics, and work as practical contractors, as well. A third major figure is the Spanish-Mexican architect Felix Candela, the most articulate spokesman and skilled technician of the younger generation today.

Candela is an architect by training, a highly skilled mathematician, and a contractor all in one. Born in Madrid on January 27, 1910, he became interested in shell construction while still an undergraduate in Madrid's Escuela Superior de Arquitectura. Fascination with domes seems to come naturally to Spaniards. They are surrounded with the masterful examples of Moorish mosques; the Catalonia vault, made with hollow bricks by average masons, is one of the rare survivals of primitive shell construction still in use. But in architectural school Candela found the theory of shells bedded in a thicket of abstruse mathematics: "The mathematical barrier so cunningly laid by the German scientists who developed the method," he recalls, "restrained me for some years from seriously considering the possibility of building shells myself."[1]

The mathematical complexities of shell analysis still remain formidable. In fact, Nervi, Torroja, and Candela have all resorted to experimental models as a short cut to test new structures. The Spanish architect Antonio Gaudi had occasionally used a double-curving hyperbolic paraboloid in some of his work. In 1916 Eugène Freyssinet had put up his huge Orly airship hangar, using folded concrete sections, and managed to span 320 feet. For Candela the actual shell structure that fired his imagination was Maillart's 1939 Cement Industries Hall in Zurich (Figure 21·15): "It gave me a hint of the real behavior of such vaults."[2]

At this time he was in Mexico City, far from his native Madrid, and engaged as an architect designing traditional Mexican colonial houses. As a student he had been a crack athlete, playing on Spain's soccer team and ranking as a champion skier. During Spain's Civil War, he had fought with the Loyalists. With the triumph of Franco's forces he had fled across the border to France, where he was found by the Quakers, who sent him to Mexico in 1939 as a political refugee. Once there he set up as an architect and also formed his own construction company, Cubiertas ALA, S.A., with his brother, Antonio Candela, who, ironically, had fought the war on the side of Franco.

Spurred on by the example of Maillart's exposition shell,* Candela had by 1950 made three fledg-

* Candela had also heard Spain's Eduardo Torroja lecture, but was never formally his student.

ling flights into shell construction, enough to be noticed by Mexican architect Jorge Gonzalez Reyna, who just then had been asked to design the Cosmic Ray Pavilion for Mexico's University City, with a roof so thin that it would offer practically no resistance to cosmic rays. At Reyna's request Candela designed a reinforced concrete dome that was only ⅝ inch thick at the crown, increasing slowly until it reached a maximum of 2 inches at the springings. It still stands as the thinnest reinforced-concrete shell ever built.

In designing the Cosmic Ray Pavilion (1950–1951), Candela made use of the hyperbolic paraboloid, a double curved shell similar in form to the Western saddle. Since it is a double curve, it is extraordinarily strong. It also has another great advantage: It can be constructed with straight timber forms, a highly important factor if expensive curved-wood-form work is to be avoided. It is not, of course, a creation of Candela's. Hyperbolic paraboloids were built in the late 1920s in Italy and as early as 1910 in France. Nor has Candela restricted himself only to this one shell form. Long and short barrel vaults as well as conoids and folded slabs appear often in Candela's work. But so masterful has Candela's execution of the hyperbolic paraboloid been, and so rich and ingenious his solutions, that he, more than any other architect-engineer, deserves credit for bringing about its present overwhelming popularity.

As his own contractor, Candela has been able at first hand to watch his structures rise and can make adjustments if he feels they are necessary. "If I make a mistake, I pay," he points out.[3] Basically Candela's approach could be called intuitive. He designs with great rapidity. For instance, his most complex combination of hyperbolic paraboloids, for the Church of La Virgen Milagrosa (Figures 23·4 and 23·5), designed by Candela in collaboration with the Mexican architect Enrique de la Mora, was completed in a week. The actual structural computations, Candela says, were ". . . rather boring, lengthy and made at a later date."[4] Another outstanding example is the bandstand of the Santa Fe housing development in Mexico City (Figure 23·7). Architect Mario Pani came to Candela and told him, "I want something spectacular here." Candela showed him an office model of six hyperbolic paraboloids cantilevered from a common base. Pani said, "Go ahead," and the bandstand shell with its 40-foot span was as good as done.

Two factors have been of particular importance is Candela's concentration on reinforced-concrete shells: One is the relatively low pay scale of Mexican workers, which allows Candela to keep his concrete in a handcraft state; the other is the high cost of steel, which places a premium on concrete structures needing a minimum of reinforcement. For these conditions, shell construction is ideal. For covered walkways and for factory unloading platforms, for instance, Candela's shells cost only 50 cents per square foot, half of what a steel structure covered with corrugated asbestos or aluminum would have been.

What interests architects and businessmen alike in Candela's work is the manner in which he arranges his shell forms. Mexico City's Lederle Laboratories, for instance, has a floor of a conventional flat concrete slab (to allow a second story to be erected eventually), but the remaining area of some 61,000 square feet is covered by no less than fifty-four hyperbolic paraboloids, measuring in size from 10 by 20 feet to some 43 feet square, plus fourteen cylindrical shells and cantilevered conoids. As a final touch Candela has signed his work by erecting at the entrance gate another of his dramatic cantilevered hyperbolic paraboloids.

Candela himself is the first to admit that ". . . the paraboloid stemmed from purely functional and economic reasoning. I doubt very much that it can be the answer to any stylistic problems."[5] Nonetheless Candela has done a magnificent job in refining this saddle-shaped form in his open San Antonio de la Huertas church and his Nuestra Señora de la Soledad chapel for the Dominican seminary in Coyoacán (Figure 23·2). This last known as "El Altillo" (the little hill), is probably Candela's purest statement of the paraboloid to date. A great leaf resting weightlessly on its ashlar stone foundations, it has almost no nonstructural elements to distract from its beauty. As a pure statement of a simple structural form, it remains one of Candela's most handsome.

Los Manantiales Restaurant, designed for a small promontory in the midst of the Floating Gardens of Xochimilco, may be an even better signpost to the future architectural potentialities of the hyperbolic paraboloid (Figure 23·8). Designed with Joaquin and Fernando Alvarez Ordoñez, and built, as are most of Candela's structures, by his own company, the structure is quite strictly symmetrical, composed of eight groined vaults formed by the meeting of four double-curving hyperbolic paraboloids.

23·3 Project for a market place (opposite page) shows Candela's trademark, a combination of hyperbolic paraboloids.

The site, with its gaily decorated boats and floating gardens, suggested to Candela a flower-petal-shaped restaurant, one that would rest lightly on the silty soil. The lotus flower was, in fact, Candela's actual inspiration, and it is reflected in the final form, with its petal shapes lofting effortlessly across the 150-foot spans. Even the edge beams, required where the shell is interrupted, are here done away with (the forces are absorbed into the groins at the top of each curve). Painted white on the interior, with black-and-red accents on the window frames, it is a delightful pavilion, a touch of man-made elegance in the midst of a naturally lush setting.

What significance does the work of Candela have for the future of architecture? Unquestionably the arrival of shell construction poses the first challenge since the sweeping triumph of the International Style with its rectilinear grid compositions and heavy reliance on the esthetics of de Stijl and cubism. "It would be a tragedy," Candela has said, "if the production of cubic masses, arranged into rectangular planes of glass and accentuated with murals and plants, should win recognition as synonymous with Architecture in the minds of the new generation. . . . The 'International Style,' as epitomized in the recent erection of cubist abstractions, has nothing further developable to offer us." [6]

The fault Candela sees in the whole revolution of the International Style is that, first, it failed to get at the heart of the matter, namely, the structural system and, second, it has clung too long to functionalism as a guiding principle. What the International Style did was to reorganize the surfaces and façades of buildings, he argues, but it left the classical skeleton untouched. Furthermore, in Candela's view, the founders of the International Style completely misunderstood the nature of reinforced concrete: "Reinforced concrete skeleton frame is a structural composition almost as inconsistent as the stone lintel, being also an unimaginative copy of wood or steel structures in concrete." Their purpose, Candela suspects, was to win an easy victory of styles: "It was a classical revolution against classic art." [7]

Modern architecture to date, Candela feels, has been typified by the analytic and destructive phase; the constructive phase is just beginning. The problem now is "the search for a style or common language able to offer us something more than the aridness of mere routine." Candela sees this task falling to the men who are both architects and en-

23·4–5 Church of La Virgen Milagrosa, Mexico City (1953), was designed as an economy structure for a poor parish. Through shell construction Candela achieved startling concrete forms. Associate architect was Enrique de la Mora.

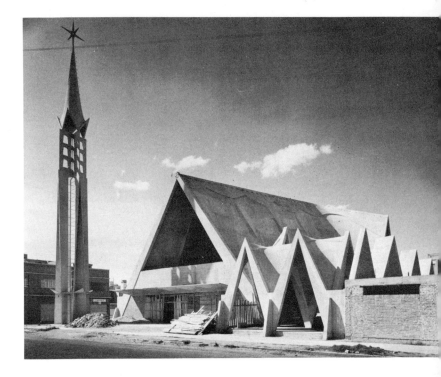

gineers, once more reunited in the title of "master builder," an area which, both Nervi and Torroja point out, is at present the no man's land of architecture. "Yet," Candela affirms, "on those numbered occasions when someone has had the courage and talent to take his stand there—such as Maillart and Nervi from one field and Nowicki and at times Wright from another—the results have been so extraordinary as to force us to consider whether it is not there, finally, that lies the hidden solution to the fundamental architectural problem of our age." [8]

That the rise of shells is a new challenge, most architects are strongly aware; certainly there is no area where there is more excitement and daring in building today. As one draftsman said, "hp no longer stands for horse-power; today it means hyperbolic paraboloid." Many architects protest strongly that such forms as the hyperbolic paraboloid are too rigidly determined, and in the end will become boring. Others, however, see the two major structural systems of the twentieth century —the steel skeleton and the thin shell—as mutually complementary, much as the Renaissance used a rectilinear façade embellished with the classic orders, yet gloriously incorporated vaults and shells into its major space-spanning structures. Perhaps we are now at a similar point.

Candela, for one, feels, "If the symptoms are to be believed, we are on the verge of a new creative epoch." If this is so, Candela continues, then ". . . architects should be pleased, especially if they manage to regain their lost role of 'master builders,' since in order to build at such a time it perhaps will not be necessary to master so much science, but to have some talent." [9]

23·7 Bandstand, Sante Fé housing project, Mexico City (1956). Candela combines six shell forms cantilevered out 40 feet.

23·8 Los Manantiales Restauraunt (1958), in the form of a lotus, seems to rest effortlessly beside Xochimilco's floating gardens.

24·1 Palazzetto dello Sport, designed by Nervi
for the 1960 Olympics. A concrete shell resting on
Y-shaped columns, it is a modern Pantheon.

24·2 Palazzetto's interior. Floral pattern of dome
(200 feet wide) is a direct expression in concrete
of the mathematics of stress and compression.

Non murato, ma veramente nato. (*Not built, but truly born.*)

GIORGIO VASARI

24 : **PIER LUIGI NERVI** :
POETRY IN CONCRETE

The single individual who has done most to revive the great tradition of Italian architecture and who, by almost universal consensus, most warrants the august title of "master builder" in Italy today, is ironically not an architect at all (though he has been several times honored as such) but an engineer and contractor: Pier Luigi Nervi. What is more, engineer Nervi belligerently insists that his swirling concrete staircases, soaring exhibition halls, stadia, sports palaces, and factories are conceived with no esthetic concerns in mind, only the truth of structure. If so—and there seems no reason to doubt his word—Nervi is that rare being, an instinctive artist, the man who would reason only in prose but can speak only in poetry.

Reinforced concrete, the material Nervi calls "the finest construction material man has found to this day," seems to have been predestined to become his medium of expression. Although Roman engineers used cement to create their massive concrete vaults, it was not until the nineteenth-century discovery that iron and concrete have an equal coefficient of expansion that a new organic material of undreamed-of possibilities was developed.

Nervi's own contribution has been decisive. His Turin Exhibition Hall, completed in 1948, is now recognized as a monumental symbol of the new age of concrete. "Not since Joseph Paxton opened his Crystal Palace in London," one critic has said, "has Europe seen an exhibition hall as magnificent. . . . This hall of Nervi's is, with Le Corbusier's Unité d'Habitation [at Marseilles], the most significant building erected in Europe since the War."[1] The Palazzo dello Sport, designed by Nervi for the 1960 Olympics, is a lesson in dome construction that even Rome, the city of domes, has hailed as a masterpiece. This Olympic amphitheater spans a space three times the dome of Hagia Sophia and more than twice the towering dome Michelangelo erected for St. Peter's.

What most strikes the mid-twentieth-century eye in Nervi's work is its organic beauty. Nervi insists that this is simply a by-product of his engineering. "In any building," he says, "esthetic perfection derives from technical perfection. Beauty does not come from decorative effects but from structural coherence." To Nervi the aim of architecture is utilitarian, "the creation of a living environment for man, as natural and necessary to him as plankton to fish or humus to vegetation." Indeed he refers to his own structures merely as "coverings" of "space limits." The organic and highly decorative designs, almost like massive lily pads, that result in his great ceilings are, he insists, the direct expression of sound engineering, "a rigid interpretation of structural necessities" and nothing more.

Nervi was born on June 21, 1891, the son of a civil servant in Sondrio, in northern Italy. Fascinated with building from childhood, he studied civil engineering at Italy's 800-year-old Bologna University. In 1913, his final year, Rome's new Risorgimento Bridge was just being completed by the French engineer François Hennebique. Nervi's professor read with delight a letter from his German colleagues proving conclusively by mathematics that it was in immediate danger of falling, in fact should have failed already. Actually, of course, it was then in full use, and still is. For Nervi it was proof that the then known theories were inadequate to explain the properties of this new material, reinforced concrete. Nervi determined to find out its true possibilities by becoming a practical constructor.

After receiving his degree, Nervi put in two years working for Bologna's National Construction Company. When the First World War interrupted his career, he joined the Italian Army's Corps of Engineers as a lieutenant and for three years built pontoon bridges and trenches; during the bloody Isonzo River campaign he served eight months under shellfire and nearly died of typhus. After the war he returned to the National Construction Company, worked for four years out of its Flor-

24·4–5· Florence Municipal Stadium (1930–
1932) vividly demonstrated the new potentialities of reinforced concrete with its
75-foot cantilevered canopy and stairways

The commission that made Nervi world-famous
was the Florence Municipal Stadium (Figure
24·5), a contract Nervi won by offering to build
a concrete structure to hold 15,000 spectators for
the fantastically low price of $2.90 a seat. The
stadium, with its 75-foot cantilevered covering,
which recalls the bridges of Maillart, and the
thematic staircases, which swirl upward in a free
semihelix (Figure 24·4), created an artistic sensation. Nervi had had his eye strictly on economy and
engineering. The flattering comments came as something of a surprise and, Nervi admits, nearly turned
his head. For the first and probably last time
in his life, he began to strive for conscious esthetic
effects. It was for Nervi a colossal failure, and he
dropped it, to return to strictly structural analyses,
convinced that in the end "functional progress
always results in esthetic progress."

It is perhaps wise that Nervi abandoned his conscious estheticism early in the game. For, contrary
to the experiences of the great Renaissance builders who plumbed the secrets of Rome's classic
ruins, Nervi is not rediscovering the great engineering secrets of the past but pioneering with a radically new material. This high adventure into the
realms of new forms demands great vision; it also,
as Nervi's career attests, often requires the invention of new techniques. "Two of my most interesting projects, the hangars built of precast cements
and the roof of the Turin Exhibition Hall," Nervi
has pointed out,[2] "would have been impossible
without a simultaneous invention of the structural
method."

Nervi's first important technical innovation grew
out of the materials scarcity in Italy during the
Ethiopian campaign. The Italian Air Force ur-
gently needed two large hangars at Orvieto. Nervi
won the nationwide design competition, primarily
because his scheme, unorthodox though it appeared,
required a minimum of steel and lumber. Nervi's
solution (Figure 24·8) was a basket weave of reinforced-concrete ribs supporting a 2-inch-thick shell
of reinforced concrete covered with asbestos. To
hold this gigantic covering aloft and compensate for
the lifting forces of the wind, he designed huge
diagonal columns (Figure 24·7) which also served
to support the sliding hangar doors. So complex
was this structure that he resorted to plastic models
to test its strength.

Even more dramatic were the four hangars Nervi
was called on to design between 1939 and 1941.
Still rigorous material shortages led to his second

ence office, crowding in a wealth of hard-earned
practical experience and achieving one notable success, the single-span concrete bridge, slim and graceful, near Pisa. In 1922, at the age of thirty-one, he
felt ready to go to Rome and set up his own office,
known first as Nervi & Nebbiosi and since 1932
as Nervi & Bartoli.

In reinforced concrete the manner of execution
is often as important as the design itself. The fact
that all Nervi's structures (with the exception of
UNESCO and Milan's Pirelli Building) were
erected by his own construction company has gone
far to give them their fine finish and economy,
and has been a vital factor in keeping costs under
control, important since most of Nervi's work has
been won on the basis of competitive bids.

24·6 Seaplane hangar, one of several designed by Nervi for the Royal Italian Air Force (1939–1941), reveals in this construction photograph the basket-weave design of precast reinforced concrete which lent such extraordinary strength. Each unit of the space trusses was prefabricated on the site, then lifted into place by large cranes. All of Nervi's hangars were unfortunately demolished in the Second World War.

24·7–8 Nervi's earliest hangars were constructed of concrete owing to acute shortage of building materials. Roof of this hangar (1935) is only 2 inches thick and covered with asbestos weatherproofing. Corner support (right) is more complicated than support in seaplane hangar (24·6).

major contribution: the use of reinforced concrete in prefabricated units. Whole sections of the roof were precast on the site, then lifted into place by huge cranes. The results were spectacular: a 30 per cent saving in steel reinforcements, a 35 per cent saving in concrete, and a 60 per cent saving in form lumber. The new assembly technique also brought a clarification and simplification of form. The new hangars (Figure 24·6) seemed to float from six supports with an airy grace and grandeur.

Such pioneering is not without its risks and its moments of agony. Nervi had to wait four years for the deformations of his first Orvieto hangars finally to cease, the sign that the stresses within this huge, 330-foot-long covering had finally achieved equilibrium. Nervi's main concern was with the soundness of the welded joints. Nervi's chance to test their strength came unexpectedly and tragically in 1944, when the retreating German Army systematically dynamited all six of the hangars, sending them crashing to earth. Nervi's son Vittorio (now working as an architect in Nervi's office) recalls his father's anguish at the time: "He wanted to crawl under those hangars and die with them." Nervi's only consolation was that examination of the rubble disclosed vast chunks of the joints still intact and uncracked, convincing proof that the joints, far from being the weakest section of the structure, were in fact the strongest.

24·9 Nervi's ketch "Nennele" (1947) had ½-inch concrete hull, proved a good sailor.

After the Second World War Nervi withdrew into intensive research. In 1946 he arrived at what he had been looking for, a mixture of fine concrete mortar strengthened by several layers of fine steel mesh and bars of small diameter that he calls *ferro-cemento* ("iron cement"). The results Nervi has been able to achieve with it are barely short of miraculous. The walls of his first experimental shed, for instance, were only $1\frac{3}{16}$ inches thick, yet by corrugating it the shed proved strong and durable. In 1948, Nervi used his *ferro-cemento* to construct his 39-foot ketch *Nennele* (Figure 24·9). The hull, built up of seven layers of fine mesh and thin longitudinal bars, was only ½ inch thick, yet proved completely watertight and seaworthy. When he heard that Eugène Freyssinet had actually constructed an airplane wing of prestressed concrete (1953), Nervi hailed it triumphantly as "flying stone." "Concrete," Nervi exclaimed, "is the ideal building material. It is a living creature which can adapt itself to any form, any need, any stress."

The revolution brought about by Nervi's precasting of the radically new *ferro-cemento*, however, dates from the Turin Exhibition Hall (1948–1949). Once again it was a national competition and Nervi was the low bidder, promising a vast structure that would span an area 240 by 309 feet (the largest area covered by concrete in the world at the time), but would cost only $500,000.

What made Nervi certain was his knowledge of the fantastic strengths of his new *ferro-cemento*. To exploit it he designed curving corrugated arches into which he could incorporate glass and yet keep these vast space-spanning members down to a thinness of only 1½ inches. The great ribs supporting the roof could be precast on the spot and then lifted into place, thus avoiding the costs of expensive form work. A light tubular scaffolding was all that was required for the workmen, one that could be easily moved after the completion of each section.

The new construction method was a test of Nervi's whole life work, and he admits, "I stayed awake nights worrying and wondering about it." As it turned out the entire structure was completed by 180 workmen in just slightly under eight months. The final results (Nervi later added two more sections) astounded Europe. Its soaring beauty and lightness were exhilarating, and yet from a functional standpoint it made an ideal sunlit exhibition hall for trade fairs and automobile shows.

24·10　Gatti wool factory, Rome (1953), employs Nervi's precast-slab ceiling. Pattern derives from the isostatic lines of stress.

Nervi has received architects' plaudits in great abundance, but in his practical work he has been forced to base his appeal primarily on efficiency and economy. Far from being a detriment, this has acted in Nervi's case as the most powerful of stimulants. In a whole series of warehouses, factories, resorts, swimming pools, boathouses, and even ballrooms, Nervi has refined, expanded, and rationalized his techniques until today even his most utilitarian buildings are works of art. His twin Salt Depots at Torona (1951) are a double parabola providing 55,000 square feet of covered space for only 100,-000 dollars, and at the same time it powerfully evokes the mystery of a church nave. His Tobacco Warehouse in Bologna (1952) is equally utilitarian, yet its huge barrel vault of prefabricated sections is a thing of beauty, with diamond-shaped skylight revealing its attractive basket-weave grid construction. "Beauty does not derive from the decorative effects, but from structural coherence," Nervi points out when such buildings are praised on esthetic grounds, then slyly adds, "In the absence of taste, economy is the best incentive for art."[3]

Concrete naturally takes on the marks of the wooden forms that mold it. Frank Lloyd Wright allowed these imprints to remain visible on the exteriors of his buildings, from his 1906 Unity Temple (Figure 2·13) to the Guggenheim Museum. Le Corbusier in his Marseilles Unité d'Habitation even exploited this drawback to achieve a purposefully brutal texture. Nervi's esthetic sense, however, has always rebelled against what he calls these wooden fetters. "Until these bonds are totally removed, the architecture of concrete structures is bound to be, even if briefly, an architecture of wooden planks."[4]

To overcome this, Nervi has developed two methods. Sometimes he forms the mesh, then sprays it with concrete (the system used in the ketch *Nennele*); other times he shapes the forms in plaster, which produces a satiny smooth surface, then creates from these the master mold in *ferrocemento*. Because prefabrication makes it possible to use repetitive units—in fact its whole justification lies in this—the result is identical components, each with the same superb uniform finish.

Nervi's striking design and his fantastic production records (his crews erected the Turin Fiat Factory, nearly 2,000 feet long and three stories tall, in 100 days) made him a logical choice as the third member of the triumvirate selected to design the Paris UNESCO Headquarters, along with Marcel Breuer and Bernard Zehrfuss. Although UNESCO was a genuinely group effort, Nervi's contribution can be clearly seen in the precise tapering of the columns in the eight-story Secretariat, with their transmittal of thrust from a rectangle at the top to an oval base on the main floor. The great Conference Hall, however, is Nervi's UNESCO masterpiece. The accordion pleats of the folded slab roof are carried down over the façade to create one of the greatest façades of modern architecture.

The UNESCO Secretariat introduced Nervi to the problem that has obsessed the twentieth century, the high-rise office building. Since then, with the distinguished Italian architect Gio Ponti, Nervi has carried through an even more ambitious scheme, the thirty-story-tall Pirelli Building in Milan, one of the most powerful and commanding reinforced-concrete skyscrapers ever to be erected in Europe. In Milan, Ponti and Nervi were unable for economic reasons to use the welded-steel framework of American office buildings. Instead they solved the problem of wind bracing by creating a boat-shaped structure, wedged in at either end and strengthened by four tapering, reinforced-concrete cores which enclose the stairways, elevators, and service conduits. The ground floor includes a 600-seat auditorium; a garage is placed in the three underground stories. The final result, towering against the Milan skyline, is as triumphant a symbol of the resurgent and prosperous new Italy as Adler & Sullivan's skyscrapers were of the booming Chicago of their day.

It is in Rome, however, that Nervi has probably created his greatest monument, the three-structure complex—two domes and a stadium—that he designed for the 1960 Rome Olympics. The smaller Palazzetto dello Sport, a dome structure that seats

24·11–12 Palazzo dello Sport, built for the 1960 Olympics, is a vastly larger structure than the Palazzetto (24·1–2). 15,000 can be seated in a column-free oval.

5,400 (Figures 24·1 and 24·2), rises effortlessly on its Y-shaped supports and opens up within like some exotic flower, hovering ethereally above the ground. Spanning 194 feet (nearly one-fourth more than Michelangelo's chain-girded dome of St. Peter's), it was enthusiastically hailed as "A Pantheon in reinforced concrete." But it was surpassed by the erection of the second and even larger dome, the Palazzo dello Sport. A massive covered arena capable of seating up to 15,000, it is rapidly becoming as great a landmark of Roman building—and Roman love of sport—as the Colosseum of classic time. The final structure, the Flaminio Stadium, while it falls short of a project Nervi proposed for Rio de Janeiro, is a magnificent feat of engineering (Figure 24·14). The oval structure, built of 7,652 precast concrete elements, seats 46,250 spectators, of which some 8,000 are beneath the cantilevered reinforced-concrete canopy. Beneath the stands are no less than five gymnasiums and an 82- by 42-foot swimming pool. Sheathed on the external lower portions with polished Roman travertine, it is a fine climax in Nervi's long career.

As Pier Luigi Nervi goes into his seventies, he is restless, wrinkled, and graying. Spare of build, he shuns extravagance of speech or action, lives quietly on the ground floor of the six-story apartment house (concrete, but faced with travertine) he built

24·13 1960 Olympic Stadium, Rome, holds over 46,000. Its diagonal supports suggest ships' ribs as they rise upward to receive the stadium's massive thrust.

in 1930. His office, on the same floor, is crowded with drafting tables, for he still scorns a desk, and the twenty-five assistants who include three of his four sons, two of them architects, one a civil engineer (the fourth is a doctor). His son Mario speaks for the others when he says, "His work is our life. We do hardly anything else and we love it."

Nervi is all too aware that building does not take place in a vacuum, that his own structures have raised many questions, both for engineering and architecture. "It is obvious that engineering and the mental make-up produced by engineering training do not suffice to create architecture. But it is just as obvious that without the realizing techniques of engineering any architectural conception is as nonexistent as an unwritten poem in the mind of the poet."[5] Although he doubts that modern architecture can repeat the technical and architectural miracle of the great Gothic cathedrals, he feels that "The architect of tomorrow will have wonderful commissions, but to realize them as true architecture he will also have to acquire—above all —a completely intuitive mastery of structure and full knowledge of construction techniques."[6]

"During the last one hundred years," he points out, "all the factors which directly or indirectly influenced construction have been harmoniously directed toward a new architecture which has no real connection with the past." For Nervi the growth of technology is thus clearly moving toward "statical truth," meaning that strictly engineering solutions tend toward one optimum structural form. Such a trend, he points out, is already visible in jet-airplane design. Even in bridges once a certain span is achieved, the form is frozen. As an example he cites the profile of an arch bridge of more than 300- or 400-foot span, which cannot differ much from the curve determined by the resultant pressures of the permanent load.

This new world of predetermined forms, dictated by mathematical formulas and the nature of materials, is a prospect from which many an architect will flinch. But Nervi's own structures, through which the filaments of steel seem as organic as nerves embedded in flesh, indicate that these new shell structures can achieve a beauty close to nature's, not made, but truly born. For all nature is involved in this same research. The architecture of the future may well prove to be as luxuriant and varied as the leaves of the forest or the shells of the sea.

24·14 Palazzo del Lavoro, Turin (1961), shows Nervi's first use of naked steel girders, here supporting 130 x 130 ft. roof panel.

25 : R. BUCKMINSTER FULLER :

DESIGNER FOR THE SPACE AGE

The regulating system of architecture almost from time immemorial can be understood in terms of Euclid's geometric axioms. Not until the world of curved shell structures emerged in this century was another kind of mathematics required, the differential equations which underlie the theory of elasticity. With R. Buckminster Fuller, however, architecture for the first time has a designer who steps forth boldly into Einstein's universe.

It was Fuller's genius to come to grips with this fact as early as 1935, when he wrote that Einstein's theory of relativity must ". . . catalyze a chain reaction ultimately altering altogether the patterning of man's everyday world. . . . This stupendous fact seems apparent. Newton's static norm must be replaced by Einstein's dynamic norm—always operative at the speed of light.[1]

What design principle could be derived from such a historically revolutionary situation? Fuller's belief was that it must be anticipatory, such was the rush of technological advance. Second, it must be total. Just as Einstein's theory that energy equals mass multiplied by the speed of light squared $(E = mc^2)$ inevitably led to nuclear fission and the H-bomb, so the revolution in metallurgy and synthetics could be projected to provide materials for solutions that can be envisioned now, and fulfilled within a time of approximately a quarter century. Underlying the urgency Buckminster Ful-

ler has brought to his task of providing prototype solutions for this new age is his belief that for the first time in history man's wealth and glory lies in his ". . . industrially organized ability to project certain and constantly improving standards of survival by the many—*without deprivation of any.*"[2]

This belief has cast Fuller in the role of a kind of superstrategist of technology, and "Bucky," as he is known affectionately to the thousands of students to whom he has lectured around the world, has made a career out of preparing for the world of the day-after-tomorrow, when whole cities will be placed under one great dome, when man will exploit the sea in underwater islands, and space platforms will hover in outer space. To this self-assigned task Fuller has brought the imagination of a fiction writer, a mechanic's knack for invention, the dogged insistence of a Yankee, and the fervor of his noncomformist New England ancestors.

Those who would follow in his transcendental flights must be prepared for hard going. His terminology alone would make a nineteenth-century German metaphysician blink. A ship is "an autonomous, far-ranging tool-complex," athletics are "an historically differentiated family of controlled physical principles," and a house is simply "an energetic environment value."

For many years, the worlds of science and architecture alike had their share of laughs out of all

25·2–3 Geodesic dome, constructed on principles evolved by R. Buckminster Fuller, is here used by the Casa Manana Theater, Fort Worth (1958), as a theater-in-the-round seating 1,832. Domes by Kaiser Aluminum Company are used as banks and factories.

25·4–5 Union dome, erected by the Union Tank Car Company in Baton Rouge, Louisiana (1958), is the largest dome ever built, measuring 384 feet in diameter and rising to 116 feet. Designed as a tank-car repair shop, it encloses a secondary dome (opposite page) as a control tower. Large dome cost less than $10 per square foot.

this, mostly at R. Buckminster Fuller's expense. In pursuit of his vision of a superrational, super-technological society, he has spent his own fortune, drawn heavily on his friends, existed by a process of "emergence through emergencies."[3] But to the vast discomfiture of his critics and scoffers Fuller has emerged triumphant. His principles of energetic-synergetic geometry come as close as any mathematics in explaining the structure of the atom. His geodesic domes have now been flown round the world, are in use (as radomes) the length of the DEW line, and as personnel shelters in both the Arctic and Antarctic. As space coverings, they are already spanning distances greater than ever before known, and Fuller confidently expects to see them grow to 2 miles in diameter.

The story of Fuller's growth, for all its tragi-comic aspects, is, in the final analysis, a stirring story of moral courage, one that makes him one of the most influential and controversial personalities of the machine age. By heritage, Fuller is a Yankee. His great aunt was Margaret Fuller, "the high priestess of transcendentalism," and co-founder with Ralph Waldo Emerson of *The Dial*, New England's foremost literary and philosophical journal. Buckminster Fuller was born July 12, 1895, the son of a well-to-do Boston merchant (tea and leather goods). He was educated at Milton Academy and summered on Bear Island in Penobscot Bay, eleven miles off the rocky Maine coast. There he got his first, and enduring, love for the sea, the ships that sail in it, their navigational lore, rigging, and construction. But as the fifth-generation Fuller to arrive in Harvard Yard, Fuller promptly disgraced himself, was twice expelled "for riotous living," the last time for good.

Fuller's next move was to plunge into practical work, first as a mechanic for a Canadian spinning mill, then as a beef lugger for Armour & Co., and finally, at the outbreak of the First World War, as a chief bosun in the United States Navy. Given a stiff course of training at the Naval Academy and commissioned an ensign, Fuller found in the Navy the discipline precision of thinking (ballistics, navigation) and a concern with strategy that have characterized his thinking ever since. As a communications officer he was in on the first conversion of radio voice signals from spark to arc, making possible the first transatlantic voice conversations. He invented a stern boom and grapple to lift capsized planes after crash landings in the sea, later experimented with a "flying bedstead" which roared over the water surface held aloft by jets of air.

Fuller's introduction to housing was brief, intensive, and disastrous. In 1917 he had married Anne Hewlett, daughter of a prominent Manhattan architect, James Monroe Hewlett. In 1922 Fuller founded the Stockade Building System to exploit the system of molded fibrous building blocks (now manufactured by Celotex), invented by his father-in-law. Before the company was bought out from under him in 1927, Fuller built and installed the machinery in four plants, and completed five factories and some 240 houses. He left convinced that the building industry was one of "methodical ignorance."

The financial failure of the Stockade Building System created a crisis in Fuller's life and began what he has called his "blind date with destiny." As every general staff has at least one man thinking of the war after the next, so Fuller, decided to become program director for the future technology, confident that eventually he would be needed. "Man backs up into his future," Fuller observed, as he decided to become a one-man conning tower. The exact task Fuller assigned himself has no name; Fuller's own term is "comprehensive designer," which he defines as "an emerging synthesis of artist, inventor, mechanic, objective economist, and evolutionary strategist."

Fuller retired into a run-down Chicago suburb and began to think. The priority task was that of shelter: "I must employ the resources of this earth so effectively that I can design a high standard of living for all. I am the anti-Malthus. I say there

25·7 Dymaxion transport unit

25·6 Dymaxion House

is enough for all, but it can only be had through design, not politics.'' Behind this emphasis on shelter lies a deep transcendental purpose for Fuller, one rooted in his own personal life. In 1922, his first child, Alexandra, had died after contracting a succession of war-aggravated epidemic diseases— influenza, spinal meningitis, and infantile paralysis. He has never ceased to feel that the solution to unnecessary suffering and death lies somehow in design; that, by utilizing an understanding of the potential of industrialization, that part of the world's population which has not the necessities of clothing, food, and housing can be provided for. What Fuller really wants is to give shelter to the world.

His first design was his most imaginative. The year was 1927, the Lindbergh year, and Fuller turned to the aeronautics industry for his structural system, a twelve-deck structure suspended from a central mast, and using lightweight metals. The whole system, including swimming pool, gymnasium, hospital, and library, would weigh only 45 tons and cost $23,000. It was to be delivered by a zeppelin (then capable of lifting 90 tons). As Fuller envisioned it, the zeppelin would first drop a bomb, perhaps in the Arctic, then lower the structure into place as a tree is planted. Temporary stays would hold the structure aloft until cement was poured around the base and then, as Fuller ebulliently wrote at the time, ''Off goes the zep to make a few more deliveries.''

Such thinking is of the essence of popular science; Captain Nemo should certainly be at the controls. And Fuller's structure was nearly as revolutionary as he thought. He called it ''4-D,'' for the fourth dimension, and it is the first clear enunciation of the concept of time as a dimension in architecture. Its use of steel and light alloys in tension is predicated on the conversion of aircraft and automobile manufacturing techniques to the problem of shelter. Even its most ridiculed aspect, air-deliverable houses, is now a reality with Fuller's own helicopter-delivered geodesic domes, and, as Fuller is fond of pointing out, one trade-fair dome has now flown nearly round the world.

The first example of what he came to call the ''Dymaxion House'' (a term coined by Chicago publicist Waldo Warren from ''dynamic and maximum efficiency'') was a more modest five-room model, first shown in 1929 in Marshall Field's Chicago store (Figure 25·6). Scorned by the American Institute of Architects,* it included air conditioning, a prototype TV screen ''for educational conning of environmental events,'' and a packaged service core. It was a ''machine for living'' with a vengeance. But when Fuller approached aluminum companies for materials, he recalls, ''They said this was very amusing, but they used aluminum only for souvenirs and dishpans.'' Five years later, in 1932, heat-treated alloys became available.

Fuller made of this rebuff another law, that technology lags some twenty to twenty-five years behind the possibilities envisioned by industry's most advanced planners. Until this built-in time lag could be overcome, Fuller devoted his time to a whole series of dymaxion designs, teaming up whenever possible with big industry, technologically his logical partner. With the American Radiator Co. he developed a full-sized bathroom made in four die-stamped components in 1931, and further refined it in 1938 in the Phelps Dodge laboratories. Features such as chemically purified and recirculated water and a ''fog gun'' for more economical showering (it used 90 per cent air, 10 per cent water) earned him a reputation as the man who wants to put ''fancy nozzles on sewer mains.'' (Recirculation and re-use of water will be of vital importance in any manned space satellite.)

From 1927 to 1932 he worked on a dymaxion transport unit, a three-wheeled, eleven-passenger, rear-end-engined automobile good for any terrain and efficient enough to run 22 to 30 miles on a gallon of gasoline. The car's resemblance to a zep-

* In May, 1928, Fuller offered the patents to the 4-D Dymaxion House to the American Institute of Architects. The offer was emphatically refused and a motion passed: ''Be it resolved that the American Institute of Architects establish itself on record as inherently opposed to any peas-in-a-pod-like reproducible designs.'' In 1959 the AIA relented to the point of making Buckminster Fuller an honorary member.

25·8

25·9 Ford rotunda (1952–1953)

pelin gondola or aircraft frame body (Figure 25·7) introduced the automobile industry to stream-lining; two of the dymaxion cars were in operation nine years later, each with over 100,000 miles. His transportation unit had proved his point, but it had used up the small family inheritance. Checked for the moment, Fuller turned back toward build-ing. The actual inspiration for form in this case was the glistening galvanized and corrugated grain bins outside Hannibal, Missouri. His traveling com-panion and new backer was the novelist Christopher Morley, who pledged a part of his profits from *Kitty Foyle* to producing what Fuller termed the "dymaxion development unit,"[4] a cylinder using the strength of metal-shell construction and a cen-tral mast. A wartime project, it saw actual use as a radar operating hut by the hundreds.

By 1946 the aircraft industry was preparing for a drastic peacetime change-over. Fuller de-cided it was the propitious time to bring about his long-dreamed-of merger of the aircraft indus-try and prefabricated shelter. Teaming up with Beech Aircraft, Inc., in Wichita, Kansas, he pro-duced his 1947 Wichita House (Figure 25·8), with single die-cast bathrooms designed to sell for $4,000.

Fuller's second major series is grouped roughly under the heading of "geodesic" structures. ("Ge-odesic" is a term Fuller took over from the navi-gator's geometry of curved surfaces used in calculating great circle routes. In Fuller's vocabu-lary it means "the most economic distance between events.") In one sense, Fuller maintains that these geodesic structures have been in evolution since he began evolving his own system of geometry in 1917. For Fuller the globe was not only the shape of the earth; it was also inherently a form of shelter, with the most volume within the least surface.

All Fuller's geodesic structures are derived from his own system of mathematics, which he calls "energetic-synergetic geometry." ("Synergy" re-fers to "the unique behavior of whole systems un-predicted by the behavior of their respective parts.") Essentially this system is concerned with finding the relationship between the maximum form (sphere) and the finest finite system (a figure con-

25·10 Trade-fair dome, Kabul, Afghanistan

25·11 Marine Corps dome (1954)

25·12 Octet truss and octahedron cantilever

25·13 Hawaiian village geodesic dome, Honolulu (1956), erected and used for a symphony performance in twenty-two hours.

structed of four triangles, namely, the tetrahedron). The tetrahedrons can be combined into octahedrons (eight-faced figures) or icosahedrons (twenty-faced figures). The result is a space-frame truss of extraordinary strength in which tension or compression is shed through linear, triangular patterns. Alexander Graham Bell, inventor of the telephone, used tetrahedron construction in erecting an 80-foot tower which weighed less than 5 tons in 1907. Fuller, however, proved that a tetrahedron-octahedron truss had capacities far beyond what had been realized. In 1953, in a University of Michigan experiment, Fuller constructed a truss of 170 slim aluminum struts, each weighing ⅓ pound, and proved that this 65-pound structure could support 6 tons, the weight of a small army tank.[5]

Such a system, since it is made up of linear elements, will never achieve the smoothly curved surfaces of reinforced-concrete shells. Fuller, in fact, was able to progress rapidly just because he separated the problems of structure proper (taken care of by his geodesic system) from surface covering, with the result that today his structures can be covered with everything from plastics and aluminum to sheet steel.

Fuller's first commercial venture into geodesic domes proved the efficiency of his new structural system. The Ford Motor Company wanted a dome over its Dearborn rotunda for the company's fiftieth anniversary celebration. But the temporary structure in place could support little weight. Time was desperately short, and Fuller's dome seemed worth a try. He received the contract on December 24, 1952, and the dome was up by May 1, 1953 (Figure 25·9). Spanning 93 feet, its structural aluminum and plastic elements weighed barely one-twentieth the tonnage of an aluminum radial-arch dome and were erected in just over three weeks. For Fuller it was a high moment; the very symbol of mass production, Ford, had come to him, because "he had the better mousetrap." Even the date, just twenty-five years after his first air-deliverable structure, coincided exactly with his time schedule.

The Ford dome made Fuller respectable. In quick order the United States Marine Corps and the Air Force came to him for help. With vertical take-off attack tactics made possible with the helicopter, the United States Marine Corps needed a semipermanent shelter, to weigh less than tents, cost less, bulk less, and require fewer man-hours to erect. With the help of his seminar program operating in technical schools and his own Geodesics, Inc., he soon had five full-sized domes, ranging from a 50-foot-diameter hangar of magnesium to a 36-foot expendable structure made of paperboard that the Marines promptly nicknamed "Kleenex houses." On January 29, 1954, at Orphan's Hill, Raleigh, North Carolina, Fuller watched as helicopters took off, carrying the domes slung beneath them, and the age of the air-deliverable structure was born. In July, 1955, the United States Marine Corps, hailing Fuller's geodesic dome as ". . . the first major basic improvement in mobile military shelters in the past 2,600 years,"[6] announced that they would henceforth be put into general use, replacing forty-seven different types of shelter, ranging from the pup tent to the Quonset hut.

The momentum of the Marine Corps success soon led to geodesic domes for radar. Again Fuller had the satisfaction of proving other experts wrong. Calculations at M.I.T. showed the structures would collapse at winds over 15 miles per hour. But a three-quarter-sphere dome on Mount Washington stood up to 182-mile-per-hour winds. One of Fuller's earliest commercial structures, a restaurant at Woods Hole on Cape Cod, Massachusetts, withstood 1954's hurricane "Carol." The Air Force was won over. Today Fuller's domes, developed by Western Electric, span the 2,000-mile-long DEW line. Other geodesic domes are in use in both the Arctic and Antarctic. "That makes me feel pretty good," says Fuller, "I'm really around the world with structures at the North and South Poles."

Fuller is reconciled to the fact that without an emergency, there is no progress. It has made his life an endless series of crash programs, hectic but challenging. An example is a telephone call he received on June 1, 1956 from the Department of Commerce. The United States badly needed to be represented in Afghanistan. To make the deadline, a pavilion would have to be flown in by DC-4 and from Karachi to Kabul, Afghanistan, by DC-3. Fuller designed an aluminum-tube geodesic structure with nylon skin that covered 8,000 square feet

25·14 Space lattice, Russell Township, Ohio (1960), with 250-foot diameter, was erected by the American Society for Metals to dramatize strength of modern alloys.

of floor space. The dome components were flown in, erected in forty-eight hours. Since then geodesic domes have been viewed in Poland, Casablanca, Milan (where Fuller won the Gran Premio in the 1954 Triennale), Istanbul, Tunis, Bombay, New Delhi, Madras, Bangkok, and Tokyo. In the 1959 United States Exhibition in Moscow, the geodesic dome took even Premier Nikita Khrushchev by storm. After seeing Fuller's dome, Khrushchev exclaimed, "I would like to have 'J. Buckingham Fuller' come to Russia and teach our engineers."

It was inevitable that such universally useful and economic space structures should find a major producer. Henry J. Kaiser was the first to exploit the geodesic dome on a large scale. The first Kaiser dome, a 145-foot structure, built in Honolulu in 1956, came complete with its own drama. Henry Kaiser wanted to see it go up, hopped a plane from San Francisco when workmen started assembling it, arrived in Honolulu to find the dome already built. As a finishing fillip, the Hawaiian Symphony Orchestra that evening started playing to an audience of 1,832 just twenty-two hours after the construction of the dome had begun. Domes are now beginning to be used throughout the United States for banks, factories, civic centers, and very successfully, in Fort Worth, Texas, as a theater-in-the-round (Figure 25·2–3).

A landmark in dome construction is the Union Dome (Figure 25·4), erected in Baton Rouge by the Union Car Company as a roundhouse. Made of ⅛-inch steel sheet and pipe (the entire bill of materials included only eight items), it has an enclosed floor area of 115,558 square feet. Built, as are most domes, as a one-quarter circle, it was assembled with six-sided pieces that would be welded together, with one five-sided piece at the top and five around the bottom. In building it, Fuller had achieved a ratio of thickness to diameter of 2,000 to 1, some twenty times more efficient than the shell of an egg.

The question inevitably arises, what will Fuller turn to next? "The domes," he insists, "are now out of the way." Next he intends to exploit further the world of "tenegrity" structures, a word he has coined from "tensional integrity." These structures (Figure 25·12) bear a striking resemblance to the system the cosmos itself uses in its structuring, from the atom to the solar system. In essence it consists of "islands" of rods or tubes under compression held under continuous tension by light struts. Or, as Fuller would put it, by a system of continuous tension–discontinuous compression. The parallel in our solar system would make the earth the compression unit, gravity the source of continuous tension. These curious structures Fuller has already designed to fold up like umbrellas, be fired out into space where they will pop open to form space islands. "It's a cinch," Fuller declares, "I can make them look like a dragon or a cuckoo bird." Nor is Fuller's claim to be taken lightly. "If we ever build a base on the moon," one highly placed Washington, D.C., scientist has said, "You can bet it will be roofed over with a Fuller dome."

Fuller actually disclaims any intention of being an architect at all. He prefers to think of himself as "a research laboratory for architecture." But his geodesic dome in many ways is the direct descendant of Sir Joseph Paxton's Crystal Palace (1851), the first major prefabricated, demountable space covering which used the most modern materials of its time, iron and glass, much as Fuller uses plastics, aluminum, and high-tensile alloys.

Fuller's domes may also trend toward the future in another significant way. He has calculated a dome that would span 2 miles, vast enough to cover midtown Manhattan and all the skyscrapers in it, and yet would weigh no more than the steel used for the liner Queen Mary. "The really great program in our era is from the track to the trackless, from the wire to the wireless, from the visible to the invisible," Fuller maintains. And with such a structure as his Manhattan dome, he would nearly have achieved his ideal of invisible architecture. For the aluminum-and-plastic dome would soar to such heights that the structural members, when seen from within, would be no more noticeable than the fine wire mesh on a screen door. With such proposals, Buckminster Fuller points to the day when whole cities will no longer be seen as agglomerations of individual buildings, but as vast areas of controlled environment. It is a form of the new metropolis that may well appear on the moon before it is seen on earth.

CHAPTER 1

1. Conversation with Frank Lloyd Wright, 1958.
2. Conversation with author.
3. Frank Lloyd Wright, *Genius and Mobocracy*, Duell, Sloan & Pearce, Inc., New York, 1949.
4. Louis H. Sullivan, "The Tall Building Artistically Considered," in *Kindergarten Chats and Other Writings*, George Wittenborn, Inc., New York, 1947, pp. 202–213.
5. Louis H. Sullivan, "Ornament in Architecture," in *ibid.*, p. 187.
6. Louis H. Sullivan, *The Autobiography of an Idea*, Dover Publications, New York, 1956, p. 325.
7. Conversation with author.

CHAPTER 2

1. Conversation with author, February, 1959.
2. *Ibid.*, April, 1959.
3. Frank Lloyd Wright to Taliesin Fellowship, Taliesin West, February, 1959.
4. Frank Lloyd Wright, *An Autobiography*, Duell, Sloan & Pearce, Inc., New York, 1943, p. 49. (Copyright 1943, the Frank Lloyd Wright Foundation.)
5. Frank Lloyd Wright, *Architectural Forum*, May, 1930.
6. Wright, *An Autobiography*, p. 14.
7. Grant Carpenter Manson, *Frank Lloyd Wright to 1910: The First Golden Age*, Reinhold Publishing Corporation, New York, 1958, pp. 7–9.
8. Conversation with author, July, 1958.
9. *Ibid.*
10. Wright, *An Autobiography*, p. 446.
11. Frank Lloyd Wright, *The Future of Architecture*, Horizon Press, New York, 1953, p. 112.
12. Frank Lloyd Wright, *An Organic Architecture, the Architecture of Democracy*, Lund-Humphries Company, London, 1939.
13. Wright, *The Future of Architecture*, p. 189.
14. *Ibid.*, p. 136.
15. Wright, *An Autobiography*, p. 141.
16. Wright, *The Future of Architecture*, p. 137.
17. Wright, *An Autobiography*, p. 147.
18. Wright, *The Future of Architecture*, p. 144.
19. *Ibid.*, pp. 191–192.
20. Manson, *op. cit.*, p. 154.
21. Kaufmann, Edgar, Jr., ed.: *An American Architecture: Frank Lloyd Wright*, Horizon Press, New York, 1955, p. 140.
22. Conversation with author, February, 1959.
23. Manson, *op. cit.*, p. 39.
24. Wright, *An Autobiography*, p. 196.
25. *Ibid.*, p. 222.
26. Conversation with author, July, 1958.
27. Wright, *An Autobiography*, p. 309.
28. *Ibid.*, p. 314.
29. *Ibid.*, p. 452.
30. Conversation with author, May, 1958.
31. *Ibid.*
32. Kaufmann, *op. cit.*, p. 245.
33. Communication from Eero Saarinen, March, 1956.

CHAPTER 3

1. Auguste Perret, *La Construction moderne*, Apr. 19, 1936.
2. Auguste Perret, *Techniques et architecture*, vol. 9, nos. 11–12, p. 87.
3. Charles Edouard Jeanneret-Gris [Le Corbusier], *Oeuvre complète de 1910–1929*, 6th ed., ed. W. Boesiger and O. Stonorov, Editions Girsberger, Zurich, 1956, p. 11.
4. Felix Candela, "The Shell as a Space Enclosure," *Arts & Architecture*, January, 1955, p. 15.
5. Conversation with Frank Lloyd Wright, 1958.
6. Le Corbusier: *L'Architecture d'aujourd'hui*, October, 1932.
7. Perret, *La Construction moderne*. Apr. 19, 1936, p. 6.
8. Peter Collins, *Concrete: The Vision of a New Architecture*, Horizon Press, New York, 1959, p. 157.

CHAPTER 4

1. Siegfried Giedion, *Le Corbusier Catalogue*, Whitefriars Press, Ltd., London, 1959, p. 10.
2. Maxwell E. Fry, "Chandigarh," *Architectural Record*, June, 1959.
3. Conversation with Costantino Nivola.
4. Le Corbusier, *Towards a New Architecture (Vers une architecture)*, The Architectural Press, London, 1927, p. 31.
5. Le Corbusier and Pierre Jeanneret, *Oeuvre complète de 1910–1929*, 6th ed., Editions Girsberger, Zurich, 1956, p. 11.
6. *Ibid.*
7. Amédée Ozenfant, *Foundations of Modern Art*, Dover Publications, New York, 1952, p. 87.
8. R. H. Wilenski, *Modern French Painting*, Faber & Faber, Ltd., London, 1940.
9. Ozenfant, *op. cit.*, p. 325.
10. Le Corbusier, *Towards a New Architecture*, p. 27.
11. *Ibid.*, p. 12.
12. Conversations with Jacques Lipchitz.
13. "Stompin' on the Savoye," *Time*, Mar. 23, 1959, p. 66.

14. Charles Edouard Jeanneret-Gris [Le Corbusier] *Oeuvre complète, 1946–1952,* ed. W. Boesiger, Editions Girsberger, Zurich, 1953, p. 119.

CHAPTER 5

1. Unless otherwise identified, quotations in this chapter are from conversations with author.
2. Herbert Bayer, Walter Gropius, and Ise Gropius, *Bauhaus 1919–1928,* Charles T. Branford Company, Boston, 1952, p. 12.
3. Paul Rudolph, "The School of Gropius," *L'Architecture d'aujourd'hui,* Paris, February, 1950.
4. Siegfried Giedion, *Walter Gropius: Work and Teamwork,* Reinhold Publishing Corporation, New York, 1954, p. 11.
5. Walter Gropius, "Address to the Harvard Club of Boston," May 24, 1958.
6. Walter Gropius, "Address to the American Institute of Architects," June 25, 1959. (On occasion of receiving its gold medal.)
7. Siegfried Giedion, *op. cit.,* p. 17.

CHAPTER 6

1. Ludwig Mies van der Rohe, "1950: Address to Illinois Institute of Technology," in Philip C. Johnson, *Mies van der Rohe,* 2d ed., Museum of Modern Art, New York, 1953, pp. 203-204.
2. Conversation with author.
3. *Ibid.*
4. Ludwig Mies van der Rohe, "1940: Frank Lloyd Wright, Introduction to Catalogue for Museum of Modern Art Exhibition," in Johnson, *op. cit.,* pp. 200–201.
5. Siegfried Giedion, *Space, Time and Architecture,* 3d ed., Harvard University Press, Cambridge, Mass., 1956, p. 311.
6. Mies van der Rohe, "1940: Frank Lloyd Wright, Introduction to Catalogue for Museum of Modern Art Exhibition," pp. 200–201.
7. Johnson, *op. cit.,* p. 34.
8. Conversation with author.
9. Henry-Russell Hitchcock, Jr., *Architecture: Nineteenth and Twentieth Centuries,* Penguin Books, Inc., Baltimore, 1958, p. 376.
10. Conversation with author.
11. Johnson, *op. cit.,* p. 60.
12. Conversation with author.
13. Report to *Time.*
14. Conversation with Frank Lloyd Wright, 1958.
15. *Ibid.,* 1959.
16. Mies van der Rohe, "1950: Address to Illinois Institute of Technology," p. 203.
17. Conversation with author.
18. Report to *Time.*
19. Ludwig Mies van der Rohe, "Address at Dedication of Illinois Institute of Technology Chapel," 1952. (News release.)
20. Conversation with author.
21. Johnson, *op. cit.,* p. 167.
22. Conversation with author.
23. Conversation with Philip C. Johnson.

CHAPTER 7

1. Alvar Aalto, "Instead of an Article," *Arkitekti-Arkitekten,* January-February, 1958 (English summary, p. IV).
2. Report to *Time,* 1959.
3. *Ibid.*
4. Conversation with Eero Saarinen.
5. Aalto, *op. cit.*
6. Communication to *Time,* 1959.
7. *Ibid.*

CHAPTER 8

1. In this chapter communications to author are not individually identified.

CHAPTER 9

1. Marcel Breuer, *Sun and Shadow,* ed. Peter Blake, Dodd, Mead & Company, Inc., New York, 1955, p. 32.
2. In this chapter communications to author are not individually identified.
3. Herbert Bayer, Walter Gropius, and Ise Gropius, *Bauhaus 1919–1928,* Charles T. Branford Company, Boston, 1952, p. 172.
4. *Ibid.,* p. 126.
5. Conversation with Frank Lloyd Wright, 1958.
6. Breuer, *op. cit.,* p. 71.

CHAPTER 10

1. "Cheops' Architect," *Time,* Sept. 22, 1952, p. 87.
2. In this chapter communications to author are not individually identified.

CHAPTER 11

1. In this chapter communications to author are not individually identified.

CHAPTER 12

1. "The Architects from 'Skid's Row,' " *Fortune,* January, 1958, p. 140.
2. In this chapter communications to author are not individually identified.
3. "Building with a Future," *Time,* Sept. 16, 1957, pp. 86–91.

CHAPTER 13

1. In this chapter communications to author are not individually identified.

CHAPTER 14

1. In this chapter communications to author are not individually identified.
2. Russell Bourne: "American Architect Yamasaki," *Architectural Forum,* August, 1958.
3. Minoru Yamasaki, "Address to the Architectural League of New York," May 21, 1959.
4. Minoru Yamasaki, "Case Study Seminar at School of Architecture, Tulane University, January, 1957," *Progressive Architecture,* August, 1957.
5. Yamasaki, "Address to the Architectural League of New York," 1959.
6. *Ibid.*

CHAPTER 15

1. Henry-Russell Hitchcock, Jr., and Philip C. Johnson, *The International Style: Architecture since 1922,* Museum of Modern Art, New York, 1932, pp. 17–39.

2. *Ibid.*

3. *Ibid.*

4. Philip C. Johnson, *Mies van der Rohe,* 1st ed., Museum of Modern Art, New York, 1947.

5. In this chapter communications to author are not individually identified.

6. Henry-Russell Hitchcock, Jr., "Philip Johnson," *Architectural Review,* London, April, 1955, pp. 241–242.

7. *Ibid.,* p. 246.

8. Philip C. Johnson, "Lecture on Non-Miesian Direction." (Manuscript in possession of architect.)

9. *Ibid.*

CHAPTER 17

1. In this chapter communications to author are not individually identified.

2. Paul Rudolph, "Address to the American Institute of Architects, Boston, 1954," *Architectural Forum,* July, 1954.

3. "The Bold Roofs," *Time,* April 4, 1960, p. 64.

CHAPTER 18

1. Sigmund Freud, *Civilization and Its Discontents,* Hogarth Press, Ltd., London, 1958, p. 25.

2. In this chapter communications to author are not individually identified.

3. Walter McQuade, "Louis Kahn," *Architectural Forum,* October, 1957.

4. *Ibid.*

CHAPTER 19

1. Kenzo Tange: "An Approach to Tradition," *The Japanese Architect,* January-February, 1959, p. 55.

2. In this chapter communications to author are not individually identified.

3. Shinji Koike: *Japan's New Architecture,* Shokokusha Publishers, Tokyo, 1956, p. 26.

CHAPTER 20

1. In this chapter communications to author are not individually identified.

2. Oscar Niemeyer, *Works in Progress,* Reinhold Publishing Corporation, New York, 1956.

CHAPTER 21

1. Robert Maillart, "The Development of the Beamless Floor-slab in Switzerland and USA," in Max Bill, *Robert Maillart,* 2d ed., Editions Girsberger, Zurich, 1955, p. 165.

2. Robert Maillart, "Design in Reinforced Concrete," in *ibid.,* p. 17.

3. Bill, *op. cit.,* p. 17.

CHAPTER 22

1. In this chapter communications to author are not individually identified.

2. Eduardo Torroja, *The Structures of Eduardo Torroja,* © 1958 by F. W. Dodge Corporation, New York, p. 8.

3. Eduardo Torroja, *Philosophy of Structures,* University of California Press, Berkeley, Calif., 1958, p. 80.

4. "The Art of Structures," *Time,* June 1, 1959, p. 70.

5. Torroja, *Philosophy of Structures,* p. 312.

CHAPTER 23

1. Esther McCoy, "Concrete Shell Forms: Felix Candela," *Arts & Architecture,* May, 1957, p. 19.

2. *Ibid.,* p. 32.

3. In this chapter communications to author are not individually identified.

4. "Work of Felix Candela," *Progressive Architecture,* July, 1955, p. 107.

5. Felix Candela, "Understanding the Hyperbolic Paraboloid," *Architectural Record,* July, 1958, p. 191.

6. Felix Candela, "Structural Digressions around Style in Architecture," North Carolina State College School of Design Student Publications, vol. 5, no. 1, 1955, p. 19.

7. Felix Candela, "The Shell as a Space Encloser," *Arts & Architecture,* January, 1955, p. 15.

8. Candela, "Structural Digressions around Style in Architecture," p. 18.

9. Felix Candela, "Stereo-structures," *Progressive Architecture,* June, 1954, p. 93.

CHAPTER 24

1. G. E. Kidder Smith, *Italy Builds,* Reinhold Publishing Corporation, New York, 1955, p. 222.

2. Pier Luigi Nervi, *The Works of Pier Luigi Nervi,* Frederick A. Praeger, New York, 1957, p. VIII.

3. "Poetry in Concrete," *Time,* Nov. 11, 1957, p. 102.

4. Pier Luigi Nervi, *Structures of Pier Luigi Nervi,* © 1956 by F. W. Dodge Corporation, New York, p. 101.

5. Pier Luigi Nervi, "Nervi's View on Architecture, Education and Structure," *Architectural Record,* December, 1958, p. 118.

6. *Ibid.*

7. Pier Luigi Nervi, "On Relation between Construction Processes and Architecture," North Carolina State College School of Design Student Publications, vol. 6, no. 2, p. 5.

CHAPTER 25

1. R. Buckminster Fuller, *Nine Chains to the Moon,* J. B. Lippincott Company, Philadelphia, 1938.

2. Robert W. Marks, *The Dymaxion World of Buckminster Fuller,* Reinhold Publishing Corporation, New York, 1960, p. 20.

3. In this chapter communications to author are not individually identified.

4. Marks, *op. cit.,* p. 35.

5. *Ibid.,* p. 55.

6. Henry C. Lane, *Final Report: A Study of Shelter Logistics for Marine Corps Aviation,* U.S. Marine Corps, Aviation Logistics and Materiel Branch, Washington, D.C., p. 1.

Bibliography

GENERAL

Andrews, Wayne: *Architecture, Ambition and Americans,* Harper & Brothers, New York, 1955.

Drexler, Arthur: *The Architecture of Japan,* Museum of Modern Art, New York, 1955.

Giedion, Siegfried: *Space, Time and Architecture,* 3d ed., Harvard University Press, Cambridge, Mass., 1956.

Greenough, Horatio: *Form and Function: Remarks on Art,* ed. Harold A. Small, University of California Press, Berkeley, Calif., 1957.

Gutheim, Frederick: *One Hundred Years of Architecture in America,* Reinhold Publishing Corporation, New York, 1957. (Catalogue for an exhibition commemorating the 100th anniversary of the American Institute of Architects.)

Hamlin, T. F.: *Form and Function of Twentieth-century Architecture,* Columbia University Press, New York, 1952, 4 vols.

Hitchcock, Henry-Russell: *Architecture: Nineteenth and Twentieth Centuries,* Penguin Books, Inc., Baltimore, 1958.

Hudnut, Joseph: *Architecture and the Spirit of Man,* Harvard University Press, Cambridge, Mass., 1949.

Madsen, Stephan Tschudi: *Sources of Art Nouveau,* George Wittenborn, Inc., New York, 1958.

McCallum, Ian: *Architecture USA,* Reinhold Publishing Corporation, New York, 1959.

Moholy-Nagy, Sibyl: *Native Genius in Anonymous Architecture,* Horizon Press, Inc., New York, 1957.

Mumford, Lewis: *Roots of Contemporary American Architecture,* Reinhold Publishing Corporation, New York, 1952, Grove Press, Inc., 1959.

———: *Sticks and Stones: A Study of American Architecture and Civilization,* 2d ed., Dover Publications, New York, 1955.

———: *The Brown Decades: A Study of the Arts in America,* Dover Publications, New York, 1955.

———: *From the Ground Up: A Collection of Essays from the New Yorker,* Harcourt, Brace and Company, Inc., New York, 1956.

Peter, John: *Masters of Modern Architecture,* George Braziller, Inc., New York, 1958.

——— and Paul Weidlinger: *Aluminum in Modern Architecture,* Reynolds Metals Company, Louisville, Ky., Reinhold Publishing Corporation, New York, 1956–1958, 2 vols.

Pevsner, Nikolaus: *Pioneers of Modern Design,* Museum of Modern Art, New York, 1949.

Richards, J. M.: *The Functional Tradition in Early Industrial Buildings,* The Architectural Press, London, 1958.

——— and Elizabeth B. Mock: *An Introduction to Modern Architecture,* Penguin Books, Inc., Baltimore, 1947.

Scott, Geoffrey: *The Architecture of Humanism,* Doubleday & Company, Inc., New York, 1954.

Tunnard, Christopher, and Henry Hope Reed: *American Skyline,* New American Library, New York, 1956.

Zevi, Bruno: *Architecture as Space,* Horizon Press, Inc., New York, 1957.

PART I

Bayer, Herbert, Walter Gropius, and Ise Gropius: *Bauhaus 1919–1928,* Charles T. Branford Company, Boston, 1952.

Collins, Peter: *Concrete, the Vision of a New Architecture,* Horizon Press, Inc., New York, 1959.

Connely, Willard: *Louis Sullivan as He Lived: The Shaping of American Architecture,* Horizon Press, Inc., New York, 1960.

Drexler, Arthur: *Mies van der Rohe,* George Braziller, Inc., New York, 1960.

Giedion, Siegfried: *Walter Gropius: Work and Teamwork,* Reinhold Publishing Corporation, New York, 1954.

Gropius, Walter: *The New Architecture and the Bauhaus,* Charles T. Branford Company, Boston, 1936.

———: *Scope of Total Architecture: A New Way of Life,* Harper & Brothers, New York, 1954.

Gutheim, Frederick: *Alvar Aalto,* George Braziller, Inc., New York, 1960.

Hilberseimer, L.: *Mies van der Rohe,* Paul Theobald and Company, Chicago, 1956.

Hitchcock, Henry-Russell: *The Architecture of H. H. Richardson and His Times,* Museum of Modern Art, New York, 1936.

———: *In the Nature of Materials: The Buildings of Frank Lloyd Wright (1887–1941),* Duell, Sloan & Pearce, Inc., New York, 1942.

——— and Philip C. Johnson: *The International Style, Architecture since 1922,* Museum of Modern Art, New York, 1932.

Johnson, Philip C.: *Mies van der Rohe,* 2d ed., Museum of Modern Art, New York, 1953.

242 Jones, Cranston (ed.): *Form Givers at Mid-century: A Survey of the Work of Thirteen Architects*, Time, Inc., New York, 1959.

Kaufmann, Edgar, Jr. (ed.): *An American Architect: Frank Lloyd Wright*, Horizon Press, Inc., New York, 1955.

———: *Louis Sullivan and the Architecture of Free Enterprise*, Art Institute of Chicago, 1956.

———: *Frank Lloyd Wright: Drawings for a Living Architecture*, Horizon Press, Inc., New York, 1959.

Le Corbusier [Jeanneret-Gris, C. A.]: *Oeuvre complète de 1910–1929*, 4th ed., ed. W. Boesiger and O. Stonorov, Editions d'Architecture, Erlenbach, Switzerland, 1946.

———: *Towards a New Architecture*, 2d ed., The Architectural Press, London, 1946.

———: *When the Cathedrals Were White: A Journey to the Country of Timid People*, Reynal & Hitchcock, Inc., New York, 1947.

———: *Le Corbusier et P. Jeanneret: Oeuvre complète 1934–1938*, ed. Max Bill, Editions Girsberger, Zurich, 1953.

———: *The Modulor: A Harmonious Measure to the Human Scale Universally Applicable to Architecture and Mechanics*, Harvard University Press, Cambridge, Mass., 1954.

———: *Le Corbusier: Oeuvre complète 1938–1946*, 3d ed., ed. W. Boesiger, Editions Girsberger, Zurich, 1955.

———: *Oeuvre complète, 1946–1952*, 2d ed. augmented, ed. W. Boesiger, Editions Girsberger, Zurich, 1955.

———: *The Chapel at Ronchamp*, Frederick A. Praeger, Inc., New York, 1957.

———: *Le Corbusier et Pierre Jeanneret: Oeuvre complète 1929–1934*, 6th ed., ed. W. Boesiger and O. Stonorov, Editions Girsberger, Zurich, 1957.

———: *Le Corbusier et son atelier rue de Sèvres 34: Oeuvre complète 1952–1957*, ed. W. Boesiger, Editions Girsberger, Zurich, 1957.

Manson, Grant Carpenter: *Frank Lloyd Wright to 1910: The First Golden Age*, Reinhold Publishing Corporation, New York, 1958.

McAndrew, John (ed.): *Aalto, Architecture and Furniture*, Museum of Modern Art, New York, 1938.

Morrison, Hugh: *Louis Sullivan: Prophet of Modern Architecture*, Peter Smith, Inc., New York, 1952.

Neuenschwander, E., and C. Neuenschwander: *Finnish Architecture and Alvar Aalto*, Frederick A. Praeger, Inc., New York, 1954.

Scully, Vincent, Jr.: *The Shingle Style*, Yale University Press, New Haven, Conn., 1955.

———: *Frank Lloyd Wright*, George Braziller, Inc., New York, 1960.

Sullivan, Louis H.: *The Autobiography of an Idea*, Dover Publications, New York, 1947.

———: *Kindergarten Chats and Other Writings*, George Wittenborn, Inc., New York, 1947.

Szarkowski, J.: *The Idea of Louis Sullivan*, University of Minnesota Press, Minneapolis, 1956.

Werfel, Alma Mahler: *And the Bridge Is Love*, Harcourt, Brace and Company, Inc., New York, 1958.

Whittick, Arnold: *Eric Mendelsohn*, 2d ed., F. W. Dodge Corporation, New York, 1956.

Wright, Frank Lloyd: *Frank Lloyd Wright on Architecture: Selected Writings, 1894–1940*, ed. Frederick Gutheim, Duell, Sloan & Pearce, Inc., New York, 1941.

———: *An Autobiography*, Duell, Sloan & Pearce, Inc., New York, 1943.

———: *When Democracy Builds*, University of Chicago Press, Chicago, 1945.

———: *Genius and Mobocracy*, Duell, Sloan & Pearce, Inc., New York, 1949.

———: *The Future of Architecture*, Horizon Press, Inc., New York, 1953.

———: *The Story of the Tower*, Horizon Press, Inc., New York, 1956.

———: *A Testament*, Horizon Press, Inc., New York, 1957.

Wright, John Lloyd: *My Father Who Is on Earth*, G. P. Putnam's Sons, New York, 1946.

Wright, Olgivanna Lloyd: *Our House*, Horizon Press, Inc., New York, 1959.

PART II

"The Architects from 'Skid's Row,' " *Fortune Magazine*, January, 1958.

Breuer, Marcel: *Sun and Shadow*, ed. Peter Blake, Dodd, Mead & Company, Inc., New York, 1955.

Goodwin, P.: *Brazil Builds*, Museum of Modern Art, New York, 1943.

Hitchcock, Henry-Russell: *Latin American Architecture since 1945*, Museum of Modern Art, New York, 1955.

———: *Built in U.S.A.: Postwar Architecture*, Museum of Modern Art, Simon and Schuster, Inc., New York, 1952.

Koike, Shinji: *Contemporary Architecture in Japan*, Shokokusha Publishers, Tokyo, 1953.

———: *Japan's New Architecture*, Shokokusha Publishers, Tokyo, 1956.

Mills, Edward David: *New Architecture in Great Britain, 1946–1953*, Reinhold Publishing Corporation, New York, 1954.

Mindlin, Henrique E.: *Modern Architecture in Brazil*, Reinhold Publishing Corporation, New York, 1956.

Mock, Elizabeth B.: *Built in USA 1932–1944*, Museum of Modern Art, New York, 1944.

Nelson, George: *The Industrial Architecture of*

Albert Kahn, Architectural Book Publishing Company, Inc., New York, 1939.

Neutra, Richard: *Richard Neutra: Buildings and Projects 1927–1950*, ed. W. Boesiger, Editions Girsberger, Zurich, 1949.

———: *Survival through Design*, Oxford University Press, New York, 1954.

———: *Life and Human Habitat*, Verlagsanstalt Alexander Koch, Stuttgart, Germany, 1956.

———: *Richard Neutra: Is Planning Possible; Can Destiny Be Designed?* ed. Frederick S. Wight, University of California in Los Angeles Art Gallery, Los Angeles, 1959.

———: *Richard Neutra: Buildings and Projects 1950–60*, ed. W. Boesiger, Editions Girsberger, Zurich, 1959.

North, A. T. (ed.): *Raymond M. Hood*, McGraw-Hill Book Company, Inc., New York, 1931.

Papadaki, Stamo: *The Work of Oscar Niemeyer*, 2d ed., Reinhold Publishing Corporation, New York, 1950.

———: *Oscar Niemeyer: Works in Progress*, Reinhold Publishing Corporation, New York, 1956.

Smith, G. E. Kidder: *Switzerland Builds*, Bonniers, Inc., New York, 1950.

———: *Sweden Builds*, 2d ed., Reinhold Publishing Corporation, New York, 1957.

——— and George Everard: *Italy Builds*, Reinhold Publishing Corporation, New York, 1954.

Stoddard, Whitney S.: *Adventure in Architecture: Building of the New St. John's*, Longmans, Green & Co., Inc., New York, 1958. (Drawings by Marcel Breuer.)

Stubblebine, Jo: *The Northwest Architecture of Pietro Belluschi*, F. W. Dodge Corporation, New York, 1953.

Time: "Frank Lloyd Wright," Jan. 17, 1938.

———: "Richard J. Neutra," Aug. 15, 1949.

———: "Wallace K. Harrison," Sept. 22, 1952.

———: "Eero Saarinen," July 2, 1956.

———: "Edward D. Stone," March 31, 1958.

Whittick, Arnold: *European Architecture in the Twentieth Century*, Crosby Lockwood, London, 1952, 2 vols.

PART III

Candela, Felix: "Stereo-structures," *Progressive Architecture*, June, 1954.

———: "The Shell as a Space Encloser," *Arts & Architecture*, January, 1955.

———: "Structural Digressions around Style in Architecture," North Carolina State College School of Design Student Publications, vol. 5, no. 1, 1955.

———: "Toward a New Philosophy of Structures," North Carolina State College School of Design Student Publications, vol. .5, no. 3, 1956.

———: "Understanding the Hyperbolic Paraboloid," *Progressive Architecture*, July-August, 1958.

Fuller, R. Buckminster: *Dymaxion Index 1927–1953*, Fuller Research Foundation, New York, 1953.

Huxtable, Ada Louise: *Pier Luigi Nervi*, George Braziller, Inc., New York, 1960.

Maillart, Robert: *Design in Reinforced Concrete*, ed. Max Bill, Editions Girsberger, Zurich, 1955.

Marks, Robert W.: *The Dymaxion World of Buckminster Fuller*, Reinhold Publishing Corporation, New York, 1960.

McHale, John: "Buckminster Fuller and Total Design," *Architectural Review*, London, July, 1958.

Mock, Elizabeth B.: *The Architecture of Bridges*, Museum of Modern Art, New York, 1949.

Nervi, Pier Luigi: *Structures of Pier Luigi Nervi (Costruire Correttamente)*, F. W. Dodge Corporation, New York, 1956.

———: *The Works of Pier Luigi Nervi*, Frederick A. Praeger, Inc., New York, 1957.

Raafat, Aly Ahmed: *Reinforced Concrete in Architecture*, Reinhold Publishing Corporation, New York, 1958.

Torroja, Eduardo: *Philosophy of Structures*, University of California Press, Berkeley, Calif., 1958.

———: *The Structures of Eduardo Torroja*, F. W. Dodge Corporation, New York, 1958.

Addenda:

Blake, Peter: *The Master Builders*, Alfred A. Knopf, New York, 1960.

Breuer, Marcel: *Marcel Breuer: Works & Projects 1921-1961*, ed. Cranston Jones, Frederick A. Praeger, Inc., New York, 1961.

Burchard, John, and Bush-Brown, Albert: *The Architecture of America: A Social and Cultural History*, Little, Brown and Company, Boston, 1961.

Le Corbusier: *Le Corbusier 1910-60*, Editions Girsberger, Zurich, 1960.

: *Creation is a Patient Search*, Frederick A. Praeger, Inc., New York, 1960.

Smith, G. E. Kidder: *New Architecture of Europe*, Meridian, New York, 1961.

Index